*A Donation Has been made to the
Clay County Public Library
in Memory of:*

LEON HOLT

This donation has been made by:

Frank and Avos Haisall
Fred and Frankie Scott
2000

CLAY CO. LIBRARY
CELINA, TENN.

John W. Carpenter's
K·E·N·T·U·C·K·Y
COURTHOUSES

John W. Carpenter, Photographer
William B. Scott, Jr., Text and Historic Photographs

© Copyright 1988. John W. Carpenter and William B. Scott, Jr. All Rights Reserved.

Library of Congress Number: 88-72161

ISBN: 0-9621337-0-1

Printed in the United States of America

John W. Carpenter, Publisher
P. O. Box 804
London, Kentucky 40741

Produced by

JM Productions

P.O. BOX 1911 • BRENTWOOD, TN 37024-1911

DEDICATION

To

My Father and Mother,

W. S. Carpenter and Bess Carpenter

and

My Wife's Father and Mother

Lee Bisset and Pearl S. Bisset

Introduction

As you look at these photographs — the one of your courthouse as well as those of others — it will be apparent that I am an amateur photographer, but a true professional photographer could not have enjoyed this project more than my wife and I as we toured our marvelous state. Actually "finding" the towns in some cases, and then locating the courthouse was a lot of fun. We would say almost simultaneously, "beautiful" — "nice"" — or "good grief." We had originally planned to take about two years for the actual photographing; as we progressed getting them all became an obsession. We were complete in about four months. Lighting is of prime importance to any photographer. The ideal way to photograph a project like this is to go into a town, check the time of day at which the best lighting occurs, and then wait for a sky filled with beautiful clouds. This, of course, could have taken weeks at one location. Since the time required to do it this way was prohibitive, your courthouse may have been photographed in very poor or flat lighting with a "chalk"" sky as a result. For this, I apologize. If you are a serious camera buff, you will notice that all the courthouse photographs have been perspective corrected (walls vertical), using a view camera with full movements, front and rear.

After something over 6,000 miles of driving, it became apparent why we could not find a book picturing all the Kentucky courthouses. It is a big undertaking! Why would anyone other than a candidate for a state-wide political office visit all the 122 county seats? (Even though our state has only 120 counties. Kenton and Campbell Counties each have two county seats). We have a big, beautiful, highly diversified state. Between Pikeville and Hickman the panorama of terrain, agriculture, architecture, industry, plant life, people, and politics are mind-boggling. I think that those who constantly harp about our state being 49th or 50th in everything should get in a car and take a look. It is magnificent.

After several locations had been photographed, we gave up trying to eliminate or hide antennae, wires, traffic signs, traffic lights, telephone booths, and trash cans from the camera. If the fiscal court and the "locals" did not object, why should we? Taking this into account, we tried to locate an optimum angle for the available lighting with complete disregard for any man-made clutter. It is doubtful that anyone actually notices this since its accumulation has been so gradual. I am sure that at the turn of the century all were untrammelled; and as the state of the art of communication and electronics developed, each bureaucracy wanted their own antenna, etc....

In reviewing all the 122 courthouses, it becomes obvious that the older ones of classical design are more handsome and elegant than some of the more modern structures, post-1930, - no offense intended to the architectural community. I think that it behooves all fiscal courts, officials, and the voting public to take a long, hard look before razing old buildings for something modern, just for the sake of being modern. Several counties have met the need for expansion by retaining the classic and taking the overflow of bureaucracy to a new annex. Good examples of this are Elkton, Springfield, and Greensburg. Elkton made a county library out of their classic Greek Revival building and Greensburg installed a museum in the 1799 stone structure. London shows an attempt at a "modern classic," with most of the usual man-made clutter removed. It was built in 1961.

Some unique architecture is displayed in the courthouses: turrets at all four corners in Fulton County, the combination of diverse architectural features in Bardstown and Newport, or the octagonal corners at West Liberty and Grayson are good examples. Courthouse clocks were an interesting feature. Fifty-four courthouses have "public" clocks, and thirty were either not working or had the wrong time. Several had different times on the four faces.

There is some interesting trivia about the county-county seat relationship. Only three county seats take their county names directly; Harlan, Greenup, and Henderson. Twenty county seats use the county names of counties other than their own county. Six county seats use their county names with a "burg" or a "ville" added. In the county seat names there are 29 "villes", 12 "burgs", 12 "tons", six "towns", four "sons", three "fields", and two "fords". Fulton is not the seat of Fulton County; its seat is Hickman, which is also the name of the neighboring county whose seat is Clinton. The county of Clinton is half-way across the state in Central Kentucky. Madisonville is not in Madison County, but in Hopkins, and Hopkinsville in in Christian County. Neither Morgantown nor Morganfield is in Morgan County of which West Liberty is the county seat — and, paradoxically is located about 100 miles east of Liberty... and the list goes on and on.

There have been 401 structures built to house the county seats of government; included are 251 brick, 67 log, 32 stone, 11 frame, and five concrete or glass. The balance were not identifiable from our research but were probably of log construction. Ninety-three of these buildings have met with violent end; 89 to fire, three to floods, and one to bombing. The rest were either abandoned or razed. Forty have been listed in the National Register of Historic Places and will probably be preserved, thanks to the foresight and interest of local groups. To those who have tried but failed to preserve your old building, thanks for trying.

There are 17 county seats with a population of less than 1,000, and there is one listed under 300 in the latest atlas. These county seats and courthouses carry out the same bureaucratic functions as the ones with over a million population; the only difference is the volume of work being handled. In the beginning, most counties were sized so that a resident could get to the seat of government and home again in the same day on horseback. Repetition of services in some of the smaller counties could eventually lead to the need for consolidation. The furor that would be caused by such suggestion, if made seriously, is beyond comprehension. If economics force such in the future, this book will be a record of "the way it was" in the 1980's. If any of the written material or photographs offend anyone, please accept this as my formal apology.

— John W. Carpenter

ACKNOWLEDGEMENTS

I would like to express my sincere thanks to the following:

Wallace G. Wilkinson, Kentucky's Governer, for his interest in this book and his most welcomed support.

Martha Layne Collins, Kentucky's lovely and first lady governor, 1984-87, governor during all our photographing.

William B. Scott, Jr., co-author and architectural historian for his splendid work and research for the text of this book.

Betty Garr Lawrence, author of *History of Kentucky Courthouses*. Betty's sincere support and assistance were invaluable. I'll bet that our copy of her book is the only one that has been read in front of 122 courthouses!

Stanley Baker, Sue Bennett College, for his technical skills and moral support.

Bennett H. Wall, University of Georgia, for suggestions and sharing from his vast knowledge of book publishing.

Glenn "Buddy" Westbrook, Cumberland Valley Area Development District, for his liaison with the Governor's office.

C. K. Green, *Sentinel-Echo,* for a biographical sketch of the author.

To the many police officers who "looked the other way" when I parked illegally to get a picture.

Last but not least, my very patient wife, who went with me on all our travels and tolerated my many hours of absence in the darkrooom.

— John W. Carpenter

Contents — Alphabetical by County Seats

Item #	County Seat	County	Page	Item #	County Seat	County	Page	Item #	County Seat	County	Page
1	Albany	Clinton	2	42	Greenup	Greenup	84	83	Mt. Vernon	Rockcastle	166
2	Alexandria	Campbell	4	43	Greenville	Muhlenburg	86	84	Munfordville	Hart	168
3	Barbourville	Knox	6	44	Hardinsburg	Breckinridge	88	85	Murray	Calloway	170
4	Bardstown	Nelson	8	45	Harlan	Harlan	90	86	New Castle	Henry	172
5	Bardwell	Carlisle	10	46	Harrodsburg	Mercer	92	87	Newport	Campbell	174
6	Beattyville	Lee	12	47	Hartford	Ohio	94	88	Nicholasville	Jessamine	176
7	Bedford	Trimble	14	48	Hawesville	Hancock	96	89	Owensboro	Davies	178
8	Benton	Marshall	16	49	Hazard	Perry	98	90	Owenton	Owen	180
9	Booneville	Owsley	18	50	Henderson	Henderson	100	91	Owingsville	Bath	182
10	Bowling Green	Warren	20	51	Hickman	Fulton	102	92	Paducah	McCracken	184
11	Brandenburg	Meade	22	52	Hindman	Knott	104	93	Paintsville	Johnson	186
12	Brooksville	Bracken	24	53	Hodgenville	Larue	106	94	Paris	Bourbon	188
13	Brownsville	Edmonson	26	54	Hopkinsville	Christian	108	95	Pikeville	Pike	190
14	Burkesville	Cumberland	28	55	Hyden	Leslie	110	96	Pineville	Bell	192
15	Burlington	Boone	30	56	Independence	Kenton	112	97	Prestonsburg	Floyd	194
16	Cadiz	Trigg	32	57	Inez	Martin	114	98	Princeton	Caldwell	196
17	Calhoun	McLean	34	58	Irvine	Estill	116	99	Richmond	Madison	198
18	Campbelllsville	Taylor	36	59	Jackson	Breathitt	118	100	Russellville	Logan	200
19	Campton	Wolfe	38	60	Jamestown	Russell	120	101	Salyersville	Magoffin	202
20	Carlisle	Nicholas	40	61	LaGrange	Oldham	122	102	Sandy Hook	Elliot	204
21	Carrollton	Carroll	42	62	Lancaster	Garrard	124	103	Scottsville	Allen	206
22	Catlettsburg	Boyd	44	63	Lawrenceburg	Anderson	126	104	Shelbyville	Shelby	208
23	Clinton	Hickman	46	64	Lebanon	Marion	128	105	Shepherdsville	Bullitt	210
24	Columbia	Adair	48	65	Leitchfield	Grayson	130	106	Smithland	Livingston	212
25	Covington	Kenton	50	66	Lexington	Fayette	132	107	Somerset	Pulaski	214
26	Cynthiana	Harrison	52	67	Liberty	Casey	134	108	Springfield	Washington	216
27	Danville	Boyle	54	68	London	Laurel	136	109	Stanford	Lincoln	218
28	Dixon	Webster	56	69	Louisa	Lawrence	138	110	Stanton	Powell	220
29	Eddyville	Lyon	58	70	Louisville	Jefferson	140	111	Taylorsville	Spencer	222
30	Edmonton	Metcalfe	60	71	Madisonville	Hopkins	142	112	Thompkinsville	Monroe	224
31	Elizabethtown	Hardin	62	72	Manchester	Clay	144	113	Vanceburg	Lewis	226
32	Elkton	Todd	64	73	Marion	Crittenden	146	114	Versailles	Woodford	228
33	Falmouth	Pendleton	66	74	Mayfield	Graves	148	115	Warsaw	Gallatin	230
34	Flemingsburg	Fleming	68	75	Maysville	Mason	150	116	West Liberty	Morgan	232
35	Frankfort	Franklin	70	76	McKee	Jackson	152	117	Whitesburg	Letcher	234
36	Franklin	Simpson	72	77	Monticello	Wayne	154	118	Whitley City	McCreary	236
37	Frenchburg	Menifee	74	78	Morehead	Rowan	156	119	Wickliffe	Ballard	238
38	Georgetown	Scott	76	79	Morganfield	Union	158	120	Williamsburg	Whitley	240
39	Glasgow	Barren	78	80	Morgantown	Butler	160	121	Williamstown	Grant	242
40	Grayson	Carter	80	81	Mt. Olivet	Robertson	162	122	Winchester	Clark	244
41	Greenburg	Green	82	82	Mt. Sterling	Montgomery	164	Bibliography			246

Contents — Alphabetical by Counties

Item #	County	County Seat	Page	Item #	County	County Seat	Page	Item #	County	County Seat	Page
24	Adair	Columbia	48	121	Grant	Williamstown	242	17	McLean	Calhoun	34
103	Allen	Scottsville	206	74	Graves	Mayfield	148	11	Meade	Brandenburg	22
63	Anderson	Lawrenceburg	126	65	Grayson	Leitchfield	130	37	Menifee	Frenchburg	24
119	Ballard	Wickliffe	238	41	Green	Greensburg	82	46	Mercer	Harrodsburg	94
39	Barren	Glasgow	78	42	Greenup	Greenup	84	30	Metcalfe	Edmonton	60
91	Bath	Owingsville	182	48	Hancock	Hawesville	96	112	Monroe	Thompkinsville	224
96	Bell	Pineville	192	31	Hardin	Elizabethtown	62	82	Montgomery	Mount Sterling	164
15	Boone	Burlington	30	45	Harlan	Harlan	90	116	Morgan	West Liberty	232
94	Bourbon	Paris	188	26	Harrison	Cynthiana	52	43	Muhlenburg	Greenville	86
22	Boyd	Catlettsburg	44	84	Hart	Munfordsville	168	4	Nelson	Bardstown	8
27	Boyle	Danville	54	50	Henderson	Henderson	100	20	Nicholas	Carlisle	40
12	Bracken	Brooksville	24	86	Henry	New Castle	172	47	Ohio	Hartford	94
59	Breathitt	Jackson	118	23	Hickman	Clinton	46	61	Oldham	La Grange	122
44	Breckinridge	Hardinsburg	88	71	Hopkins	Madisonville	142	90	Owen	Owenton	180
105	Bullitt	Shepherdsville	210	76	Jackson	McKee	152	9	Owsley	Booneville	18
80	Butler	Morgantown	160	70	Jefferson	Louisville	140	33	Pendleton	Falmouth	66
98	Caldwell	Princeton	196	88	Jessamine	Nicholasville	176	49	Perry	Hazard	98
85	Calloway	Murray	170	93	Johnson	Paintsville	186	95	Pike	Pikeville	190
2	Campbell	Alexandria	4	56	Kenton	Independence	112	110	Powell	Stanton	220
87	Campbell	Newport	174	25	Kenton	Covington	50	107	Pulaski	Somerset	214
5	Carlisle	Bardwell	10	52	Knott	Hindman	104	81	Robertson	Mount Olivet	162
21	Carroll	Carrollton	42	3	Knox	Barbourville	6	83	Rockcastle	Mount Vernon	166
40	Carter	Grayson	80	53	Larue	Hodgenville	106	78	Rowan	Morehead	156
67	Casey	Liberty	134	68	Laurel	London	136	60	Russell	Jamestown	120
54	Christian	Hopkinsville	108	69	Lawrence	Louisa	138	38	Scott	Georgetown	76
122	Clark	Winchester	244	6	Lee	Beattyville	12	104	Shelby	Shelbyville	208
72	Clay	Manchester	144	55	Leslie	Hyden	110	36	Simpson	Franklin	72
1	Clinton	Albany	2	117	Letcher	Whitesburg	234	111	Spencer	Taylorsville	222
73	Crittenden	Marion	146	113	Lewis	Vanceburg	226	18	Taylor	Campbellsville	36
14	Cumberland	Burkesville	28	109	Lincoln	Stanford	218	32	Todd	Elkton	64
89	Davies	Owensboro	178	106	Livingston	Smithland	212	16	Trigg	Cadiz	32
13	Edmonson	Brownsville	26	100	Logan	Russellville	200	7	Trimble	Bedford	14
102	Elliott	Sandy Hook	204	29	Lyon	Eddyville	58	79	Union	Morganfield	158
58	Estill	Irvine	116	99	Madison	Richmond	198	10	Warren	Bowling Green	20
66	Fayette	Lexington	132	101	Magoffin	Salyersville	202	108	Washington	Springfield	216
34	Fleming	Flemingsburg	68	64	Marion	Lebanon	128	77	Wayne	Monticello	154
97	Floyd	Prestonsburg	194	8	Marshall	Benton	16	28	Webster	Dixon	56
35	Franklin	Frankfort	70	57	Martin	Inez	114	120	Whitley	Williamsburg	240
51	Fulton	Hickman	102	75	Mason	Maysville	150	19	Wolfe	Campton	38
115	Gallatin	Warsaw	230	92	McCracken	Paducah	184	114	Woodford	Versailles	228
62	Garrard	Lancaster	124	118	McCreary	Whitley City	236	Bibliography			246

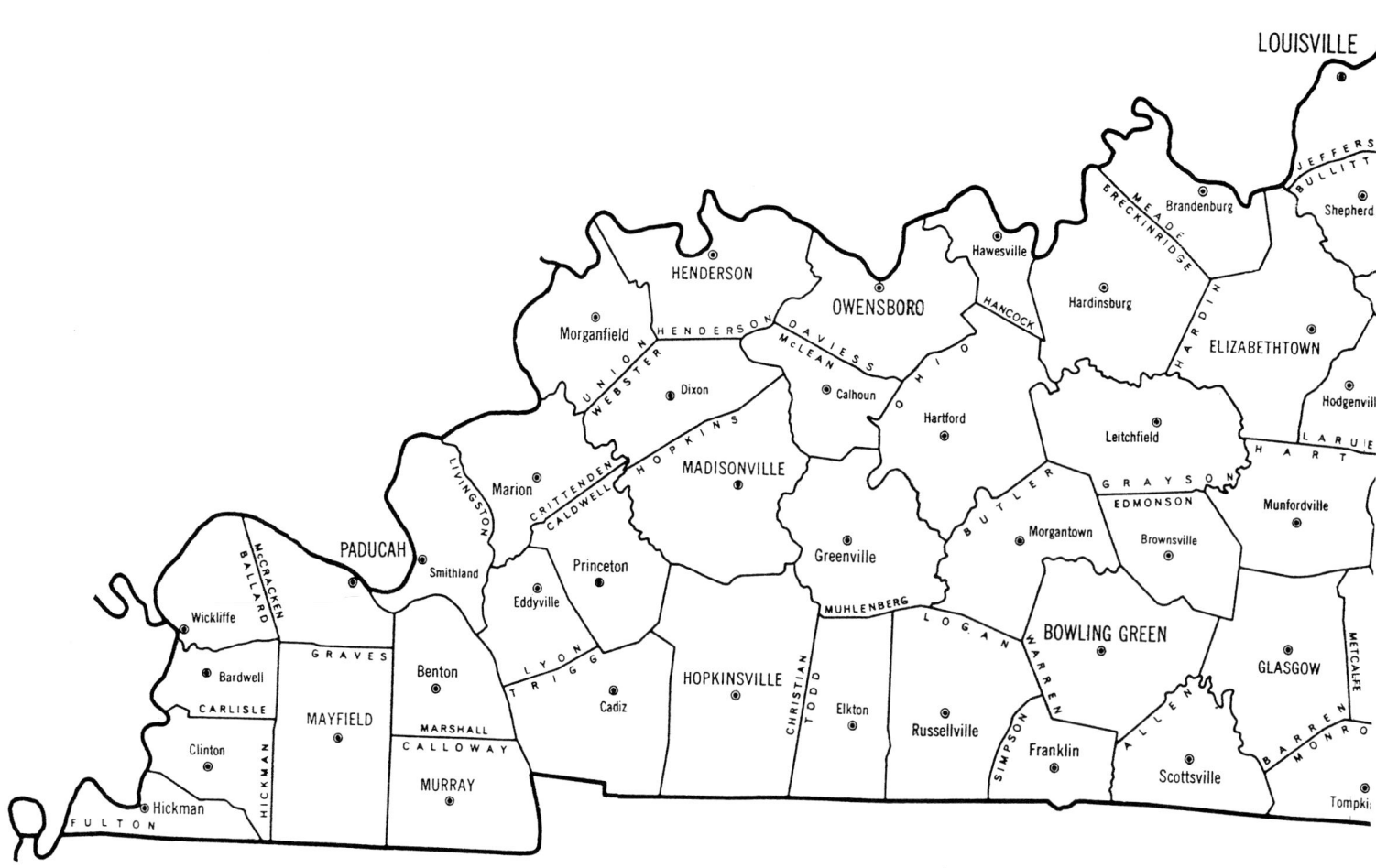

GOVERNOR WALLACE G. WILKINSON
CAPITOL
FRANKFORT, KENTUCKY 40601

July 15, 1988

Mr. John Carpenter
West Fifth Street
London, Kentucky   40741

Dear Mr. Carpenter,

    As I have travelled across Kentucky, I've had the opportunity to visit every courthouse in this beautiful Commonwealth. Only when you have seen them all, can you get a true appreciation for the history represented by these unique and individual landmarks.

    In most of our counties, the courthouse is the heart of the community. Each is different from the other; distinctive in its architecture and its history.

    Congratulations on compiling a magnificent tribute to Kentucky's courthouses. For the vast majority of Kentuckians, who will never have the opportunity to visit each of these magnificent structures, your book is the next best thing to being there.

Sincerely,

Wallace G. Wilkinson

One of the focal points of any community is the courthouse — the place where so much of Kentucky's rich and fascinating history has been written. We Kentuckians have a natural interest in our past, and John Carpenter's *Kentucky Courthouses* takes you on an unusual and fascinating trip, stopping at every courthouse in existence in the Commonwealth.

As a Kentuckian, a student of history, or a lover of photography, you will enjoy this journey. I also proudly commend John Carpenter for contributing his work to enhancing future generations' understanding and appreciation for this special place called home.

Martha Layne Collins
Governor
Commonwealth of Kentucky
1983-87

Preface

The purpose of this work is to provide information regarding the architectural style, date of construction, names of architects and builders, approximate cost, and illustrations, wherever possible, for every courthouse known to have been built in Kentucky. This work is not intended to be a complete history of each courthouse and does not deal with the county courts or politics. These areas have been given partial attention in *History of Kentucky Courthouses* by Elizabeth Garr Lawrence. Mrs. Lawrence's excellent 1972 book was published by the National Society of the Colonial Dames of America's Kentucky Chapter. It is still available, and though overlapping in some aspects, complements this work.

A thorough search has been made of county histories, articles, essays, newspapers, public documents, unpublished studies, manuscript collections, maps, atlases, and gazetteers to compile this work. An inclusive bibliography to these references is included. Another source has been the local survey records of the Kentucky Heritage Council, the state historic preservation office.

A number of individuals have been of particular assistance in this work. First, I am grateful to Mrs. Elizabeth Lawrence, who allowed me access to her materials and photographs. Numerous historians assisted me including Clay Lancaster, Walter Langsam, Dr. Patrick Snadon, Dr. Stuart Sprague, Dr. Samuel W. Thomas, and William Turner. Space would not permit acknowledging all the helpful people I talked with in researching and collecting photos. Photo contributors are noted in parenthesis below each photograph. Numerous institutions loaned photos for the book including *The Courier-Journal*, Pat Chapman, librarian; Transylvania University, Kathleen Bryson, director; University of Louisville Photographic Archives, David Horvath, director; and the University of Kentucky Special Collections, Tom House, audio-visual archivist.

A special thanks to my wife, Holly, for her support and her devotion to this project.

— William B. Scott, Jr.

Architectural History of Kentucky's Courthouses

The Kentucky courthouse has traditionally been the focal point of each county. The symbol of the community, the courthouse, is designed to reflect an image of security, prosperity, and stability. These temples of justice normally contain county offices. Each courthouse is, therefore, the only structure in most counties paid for by collective taxation. As a result, the courthouse is usually the best, or one of the best, buildings in that county. This is supported by 49 of the Kentucky's 80 eligible courthouses having been listed on the National Register of Historic Places. A building must be at least 50 years old to be listed on the National Register. A number of New Deal Era courthouses built by the Public Works Administration are recently eligible and will no doubt be listed in the near future.

KENTUCKY'S STATEHOOD

After the establishment of the original thirteen American colonies, western expansion dominated the thoughts of the ambitious young leaders of the United States. The principal geographic obstacle was the Alleghany Mountain range, beyond which Virginia extended to the Mississippi River, The intervening region was known as Kentucky County. After Daniel Boone and others blazed the trail through the Cumberland Gap, over 100,000 settlers from Pennsylvania, Maryland, Virginia, and the Carolinas followed them into Kentucky between 1775 and 1800.

Kentucky's fertile lands became a primary target of speculation for those seeking opportunity and fortune. Among these were powerful and wealthy figures desiring autonomy such as General James Wilkinson, Thomas Todd, and George Rogers Clark. Kentucky applied for statehood and separation from Virginia as early as 1786. However, the slow wheels of bureaucracy delayed this action until 1792 when Kentucky became the 15th state of the Union.

Between 1780 and today, Kentucky's 120 counties built just over 400 courthouses. Fayette, Lincoln, and Jefferson Counties were Kentucky's first three divided counties, created by an act of the Virginia legislature on November 1, 1780. McCreary County, the last formed, was established in 1912, bringing the total of Kentucky's counties to 120. Only Georgia and Texas surpass Kentucky in the total number of counties.

THE EIGHTEENTH AND EARLY NINETEENTH CENTURY

Courthouses built during the eighteenth and early nineteenth centuries in Kentucky differed little in appearance from houses of the period. Traditional building methods were used, employing three common construction materials — log, stone, and brick. A courthouse's principal distinction during this period was it's location in a central public square.

Log Construction

Log structures commonly served as the earliest courthouse of most Kentucky counties. The log construction method used in Kentucky was introduced in the United States by Swedes settling in Delaware in 1638. This simple system of construction was popular for several reasons including easily accessible materials, rapid construction and limited cost. Most log and other early courthouses contained only a courtroom and occasionally one or two auxiliary rooms, usually for the county clerk or Judge's office.

Between 1780 and 1826, just over fifty log courthouses were built in Kentucky, the first in Fayette County. Nine later examples were built primarily in the eastern section of the state, the last in Knott County in 1884. One log courthouse survives, the Calloway County courthouse, built in 1823. It is located on the campus of Murray State University.

Log construction soon evolved into heavy timber frame construction. Five courthouses of this type were built prior to 1824. The earliest timber frame courthouse was built for Bourbon County in 1787 and measured 32 X 20 feet. Scott County's courthouse, built in 1792-93, was a unique structure with a timber frame second story over a first story of stone construction.

Stone Construction

Stone soon became the building material of preference by those counties that could afford such construction. Eleven stone courthouses were built between 1785 and 1816, including the Scott County structure. These early courthouses still differed little in form from residences of the period — normally taking the form of a two-story, gable-ended structure. Occasionally, as in the case of the Mason County courthouse, the building was distinguished by an elaborate cupola. With the possible exception of heavy timber construction, stone masonry was the first building method requiring a skilled craftsman — the mason. The only surviving stone courthouse in the state, located in Green County, was built in 1802-04.

Captain John Cape, a Philadelphia native, is the first individual associated with the construction of stone courthouses in Kentucky. He built the first in Nelson County in 1785-86, as well as Fayette County in 1787, and Jefferson County in 1788. Cape may have been responsible for the design of the first Kentucky state house built in 1793-94, a well-designed stone building completed the year of his death.

Nelson County courthouse, 1787 — possibly earliest foursquare form in the United States (*The Filson Club*).

Thomas "Old Stone Hammer" Metcalfe, Kentucky's 10th governor, is the best known of the stone masons. He is popularly credited with a number of central Kentucky buildings including courthouses. In fact, Metcalfe is only documented to have worked on the Bourbon County courthouse and the Adams County courthouse at Union, Ohio. He laid only the foundation of the Bourbon structure, while his uncle John Metcalfe built the main structure.

Brick Construction

By the mid-1780s, brick was an optional building material in Kentucky. As with stone construction, early brick courthouses continued

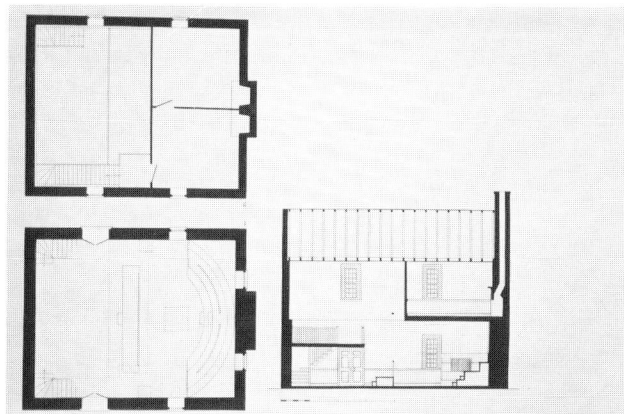

Mercer County courthouse, 1787-88 — first and second floor plans and cross section of side-gabled courthouse (*Reconstructed floor plan by Clay Lancaster*).

to differ little from residences — assuming the two-story, gable-ended vernacular form. Between 1796 and 1840, about fifty brick courthouses of this simple vernacular form were built. Clark and Shelby Counties were the first to start construction.

KENTUCKY COURTHOUSE DESIGN COMES OF AGE

Foursquare Courthouses

About 1800, Kentucky courthouses first became clearly distinguishable from residential architecture. The principal differing characteristic was the building's square form. Properly known as the four-square form, these courthouses are commonly referred to as the "coffee-mill" type. They ranged from 26 to 60 feet, two-storied and covered by a hipped roof with a central cupola. Typically these buildings contained a courtroom on one floor, while the other contained four offices of equal size.

Thirty-four known four-square form courthouses were built in Kentucky primarily from 1800 until 1844. However, isolated examples were built as late as 1858. The 1787 Nelson County courthouse of stone construction is believed to be the earliest four-square in Kentucky. If originally built square, it would be the earliest courthouse of this building type in the United States. Earliest drawings and photographs, show a square building; however, it was not originally specified as square.

The Franklin County courthouse of 1803-1806 is the earliest documented structure of the four-square type. Occasionally these buildings were made more elaborate by the addition of architectural details on entrances, windows, and cupolas. One such example, the Fayette County courthouse of 1806, was stylized with Georgian features as

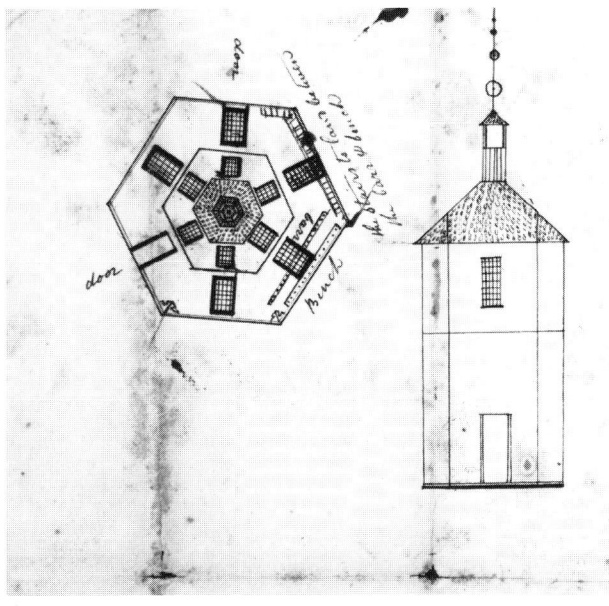

Hexagonal plan for proposed 1807 Warren County courthouse *(The Kentucky Museum — Western Kentucky University)*.

was the Nicholas County courthouse of 1816-18. Later examples, after 1830, had subtle decorative details of the Greek Revival style. Most, however, were plain vernacular buildings with no ornamentation. This type included the courthouses of Warren County, 1805 & 1809-11; Ohio County, 1813-15; Shelby, 1814; Campbell County, 1814-16; Harrison County, 1816; Scott County, 1816; Floyd County, 1818-21 and Letcher County, 1843-44.

Polyagonal Courthouses

Of the early brick courthouses, the most unique is the Allen County courthouse of 1816. Octagonal in form, this two-story building is the only known of this style in the state. Warren County planned to build a hexagonal structure as early as 1807, but instead built a four-square form courthouse. The Warren County planners stated the hexagonal design "has been considered by the best artists to be the most convenient as well as spacious form for public buildings." An octagonal form actually contains 20% more floorspace for the same length of wall as a square building.

Monumental Classicism

Thomas Jefferson promoted Roman and Renaissance classical forms to reflect the ideal, utopian image of the early republic. His favorite public building type was the classical Roman temple. He introduced this form to the United States through his design of the Virginia State Capitol in 1786. Jefferson County's fourth courthouse, built from 1810 to 1812, vaguely resembles the Virginia statehouse. The Jefferson County structure was designed by John Gwathmey of Louisville, the earliest known gentleman-architect in Kentucky. A temple-form structure, fronted by a portico of four Roman Doric columns, this building is the only known Kentucky courthouse utilizing the style known as Monumental Classicism.

The Greek Revival Style

The Greek Revival style evolved from Monumental Classicism, being a reference to Greek monuments as opposed to the loose mixing of Roman and Renaissance forms of the earlier style. The three primary motivating factors for the popularity of the Greek Revival were the anti-English sentiments following the War of 1812, the sympathy with the Greek War of Independence (1821-30), and the equating in American's minds of modern American democracy with ancient Greek democracy. The Greek Revival, an academic style, necessitated the introduction of trained architects.

About thirty Kentucky courthouses are known to have been designed in the Greek Revival style between 1832 and the beginning of the Civil War in 1861. A number of buildings were updated by adding details of the

Second Montgomery County Courthouse, 1851 (*Massachusetts Commandery Military Order of the Loyal Legion and the US Military History Institute*).

style, such as porticos. Seven Greek Revival courthouses have survived, including Franklin County, 1832-35; Jefferson County, 1835-59; Mason County, 1844-48; Madison County, 1848-50; Harrison County, 1851-53; Clark County, 1852-55 and Owen County, 1857.

Gideon Shryock is credited with the introduction of the Greek Revival style to Kentucky. In 1827, the 25-year-old Shryock created a design that was chosen for Kentucky's third state house, the first Greek Revival capitol building in the United States. Shryock designed the Franklin County Courthouse in 1832 and in 1835 the Jefferson County Courthouse. Other principal architects to design in this style include Hugh Roland, Christain County - 1837; Major Thomas Lewinski, Madison County - 1848; John McMurtry, Montgomery County - 1851 and Clark County - 1852; and Nathanial Center Cook, Owen County - 1857.

The Civil War - 1861-1865

Five counties were added to the state in 1860, bringing the total to 110 at the beginning of the Civil War. The war took a major toll on Kentucky's courthouses, twenty-four being destroyed.

Since Kentucky was part of the Union, Federal troops were stationed in many counties and they used courthouses as barracks and occasionally as jails. Ironically, Federal troops were the first to destroy a courthouse when one night in October 1862, a fire accidentally consumed the Morgan County courthouse and half the town. Accidental fires caused by Federal troops also destroyed the courthouses at Bath County on March 21, 1864, and Graves County later that year. Union troop occupation through the war left the courthouses at Garrard and Meade Counties in such bad condition that they were dismantled and replaced immediately following the end of hostilities. Thus, a total of five courthouses were destroyed by Union troops.

In addition, Federal troops garrisoned in Kentucky's courthouses made them legitimate military targets for Confederate aggression. From April, 1863 until March, 1865, less than one month before Lee surrendered at Appomattox, Confederates destroyed twenty courthouses. Usually courthouse burnings were isolated incidents in retaliation for Union hostility and were executed by Confederates mainly in the form of guerilla raids. These incidents included the destruction of the courthouses at Monroe County on April 22, 1863, Powell County in the Summer of 1863; Harlan County in October, 1863; Montgomery County on December 2, 1863; Rowan County, March 21, 1864; Clinton County in late 1864; Daviess County on January 4, 1865, Spencer County and Crittenden County later in the month; Larue County on February 21, 1865 and finally Metcalfe County in March, 1865.

The only organized Confederate campaign took the form of a difficult winter march through western Kentucky which lasted from December 11, 1864 until January 3, 1865. General Hylan B. Lyon commanded the approximately 800 men who were divided into two regiments. This force was to have captured Clarksville, Tennessee, but finding it too heavily fortified, decided to divert north and attack garrisoned fortifications in Kentucky, usually county courthouses. Lyon first advanced his troops to Hopkinsville, driving the Federal troops there in retreat to Russellville. Lyon left one regiment in Hopkinsville, then proceeded with the remainder of his command to Cadiz, Princeton, and then Eddyville. Lyon burned the Trigg County courthouse at Cadiz on the December 12th, and the Caldwell County courthouse at Princeton three days later. Also on the 12th, his regiment at Hopkinsville burned the Christian County courthouse and were awaiting Lyon's return two days later when they were forced to retreat by a Federal Cavalry regiment. The same Federal troops forced Lyon, who was returning to Hopkinsville, to divert north. Lyon's two regiments regrouped and proceeded east through Charlestown and Madisonville, burning the Hopkins County courthouse on the 17th. Continuing east, they were crossing the Green River at Ashbysburg when they encountered Union troops, but avoided a contact by moving downstream two miles and crossed. The unit reached Hartford on December 20th and burned the Ohio County courthouse. When Lyon reached Leitchfield on the 24th, he split his command and sent a force to

Elizabethtown, where they destroyed the Hardin County courthouse, then quickly rejoined the main force. The main force had advanced to Nolin Station, where they learned of General Hood's loss on December 16th at the Battle of Nashville, and his subsequent retreat from Tennessee. A mass desertion of 500 men prompted an immediate southern move by Lyon. The remaining troops passed through Hodgenville to Campbellsville, burning the Taylor County courthouse on the 25th. They then proceeded through Columbia and Burkesville, burning the Cumberland County courthouse on January 3rd, just before crossing into Tennessee. In all, Lyon's command destroyed eight Kentucky courthouses. In all, 19 courthouses were destroyed by the Confederate States of America. Most of these were Greek Revival style courthouses.

The Italianate Style

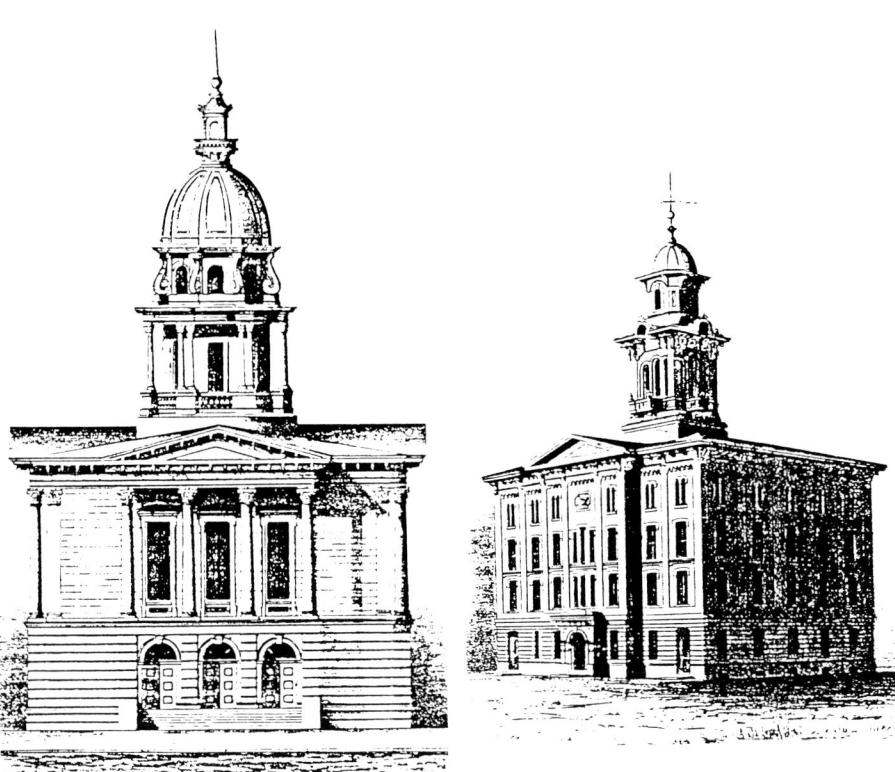

Left: Design VII — Courthouse Design.
Right: Design XXII — School Design.
Samuel Sloan's *City and Suburban Architecture, 1859).*

By the early 1850s, alternative architectural styles were becoming increasingly popular in Kentucky. Typical features of the Italian Revival style include a low-pitched roof with widely overhanging eaves supported by decorative brackets; and tall, narrow, semicircular topped windows sometimes with elaborate hoods. Roofs often sported a cupola. One specific architectural publication, Samuel Sloan's *City and Suburban Architecture* (1859), widely encouraged the style's popularity and was especially influential in Kentucky. Several Kentucky architects are known to have owned the Sloan book. Two plates from the publication - "Design VII - A Court-House" and "Design XXII - A Public School Edifice," both Italianate designs, were particularly influential.

The earliest Kentucky courthouses of this style were transitional and contained elements of the earlier Greek Revival style. Fifteen transitional, or "Greco-Italianate," courthouses are known to have been built between 1857 and 1874. The first was the McCracken County courthouse of 1857-59, designed by Stancliff & Vodges, architects of Louisville. A sophisticated design, the building combines a tetrastyle portico of the Greek Revival, with semi-circular topped windows and entrances plus quoins at the building's corners, typical of the Italianate style. Sloan's courthouse design is reflected in six Kentucky courthouses - Boyle County, 1860-62 (almost a literal copy); Garrard County, 1866-68; Warren County, 1867-68 (an enlarged version); Christain County, 1869; Crittenden County, 1871; and Pulaski County, 1873-74.

By the beginning of the Civil War in 1861, most courthouses were designed in a pure Italianate style. References to classical designs were now abstracted, such as pedimented porticos which were reduced to small flat pediments on fronts and occasionally on sides of courthouses. Thirty Kentucky courthouses are known to have been designed in the Italianate style, of which seven have survived. The bulk were built between 1860 and 1875. However, two courthouses, Monroe County, 1877-1889, and Harlan County, 1886-88, were built later.

Five courthouses were scaled down versions of Sloan's pure Italianate school design. These include the courthouses of Breckinridge County, 1868-69; McLean County, 1870; Hardin County, 1872-74; Knox County, 1874-75; and Harlan County, 1886-88.

Thomas T. Milburn, of Bowling Green, became known as a designer and builder of Italianate — style courthouses. Three courthouses of almost identical design are credited to him. These include Rockcastle County, 1871-73; Wayne County, 1875-78; and Russell County, 1877-78.

Milburn's son, Frank, would become a major courthouse designer during the 1890's.

MID-VICTORIAN PERIOD COURTHOUSES

This period is named for the reign of Britain's Queen Victoria (1837 - 1901). No dominant architectural style prevailed during the Victorian period from 1865 to 1885. Architecture was eclectic, the combining of styles. Elements of English Eastlake, "Queen Anne" and Jacobean, French Baroque and Rococo, Moorish, Flemish and Venetian styles were often incorporated in a single building design.. These styles were highly decorative and provided an impressive integration of art and sculpture for interiors and exteriors. Dark wall treatments were now used in courtrooms, creating a mysterious and impressive atmosphere.

The Mid-Victorian period saw the first major emphasis in design of specialized building types according to function. Consequently, courthouse and residential designs no longer resembled each other. In the Mid-Victorian period the number of Kentucky architects rose dramatically, as did the number of architect-designed courthouses.

"Balloon-Frame" Courthouses

The rapidly developing building technology of the 1840s and 1850s produced numerous changes in construction methods. The invention at the time of mass-produced machine sawed lumber and inexpensive machine-made wire nails resulted in the "balloon frame." Nine balloon-frame courthouses were built in Kentucky between 1860 and about 1890. Most were vernacular, front-gabled structures with limited ornamentation. With the exception of Menifee County, 1871-72, all were located in Eastern Kentucky, including Metcalfe County, 1860; Rowan County, c.1865; Perry County, 1866; Harlan County, 1870; Bell County, 1870-71; Jackson County, 1872; Martin County, 1882; and Knott County, c.1890.

Second Empire Style

The first major definable post-war style used in Kentucky courthouses was the Second Empire Style. Considered the classical style of the period, the primary influence was the 1852-57 additions to the Louvre in Paris for Napoleon III, based on French 17th century or Baroque sources. This style became popularly associated with public buildings as a result of the Supervising Architect of United States Treasury Department, Alfred B. Mullett, who designed numerous government buildings across the country. The most elaborate of these was his State, War and Navy Building of 1871-88, located immediately west of the White House in Washington, D.C. The style is known for horizontal layering, division into dominant pavilions flanked by end pavilions, separate mansard roofs (straight or curved, double sloped) atop each section, the whole with overlays of classical sculptural ornamentation.

The earliest Kentucky courthouse in the Second Empire style was built in Bourbon County during 1873-74, designed by Albert C. Nash of Cincinnati. Nash designed the later Campbell County courthouse of 1884, also Second Empire. Only Thomas Boyd, an architect of Pittsburg, Pennsylvania, designed more Kentucky courthouses in this style. Courthouses to his credit include those of Scott County, 1876-77; Jessamine County, 1878; and Fayette County, 1882-85. Phelix L. Lundin, a native of Sweden practicing in Lexington, designed the Woodford County courthouse of 1880-83 in the style. Later examples of Kentucky Second Empire courthouses include Hart County, 1893 and Allen County, 1903.

H.P. McDonald & Brothers

Harry P. McDonald, architect of Louisville, rose as one of the leading designers in the country of public buildings, including numerous court houses, asylums, jails, railway depots, churches, university buildings, and the 1887 Kansas state house. He was a Virginia native and a civil engineering graduate of Washington and Lee University. In 1873, he came to Louisville as superintendent of construction of the Crescent Hill Plant of the Louisville Water Works. After establishing his architectural office in 1876, he added his brothers to the firm, Kenneth (1852-1940) in 1878, and Donald (b.1858) in 1883, both also graduates of Washington and Lee University as well.

H. P. McDonald designed only one courthouse prior to the arrival of his brothers, the Henry County courthouse of 1875. This unique courthouse is one of the most elaborate Italianate style designs in the state, with a large cupola in the Second Empire style. After McDonald's brothers joined the firm, the company developed several standard designs for buildings, including courthouse designs. The design was eclectic and included details from the Second Empire, "Queen Anne," Eastlake and Romanesque styles. For a reasonable fee, it could be altered to fit any budget between $ 16,000 to $ 40,000. Eleven Kentucky courthouses were

Simpson County Courthouse, 1882 — H. P. McDonald & Brothers standard design. *(Collection of Mrs. Joan Butler).*

built on this plan by the McDonald brothers, including Simpson County, 1882; Trimble County, 1884; Carroll County, 1884; Laurel County, 1884; Adair County, 1884; Hickman County, 1884; Leslie County, c.1884; Pike County, 1888; Graves County, 1888; Bell County, 1889; Boone County, 1889. The same design was used in courthouses in Indiana, Illinois, Virginia, Minnesota, Kansas and other states. The Casey County courthouse of 1887 departs from this design, being of the Romanesque style.

THE LATE VICTORIAN PERIOD COURTHOUSES

The period from 1885 until the end of the century saw less eclecticism in architecture and a rise in the influence of Chicago architects, known as the "Chicago school" in American architecture. Three styles would dominate the period, Richardsonian Romanesque, High Victorian Gothic, and, after the 1893 Columbian Exposition - the Beaux-Arts and the Colonial Revival. The popularity of these styles was aided by the growing circulation of architectural periodicals such as the *American Architect and Building News* and the Chicago based *Inland Architect.* Most Kentucky architects aligned with the latter journal and illustrated their works in it.

Richardsonian Romanesque

The Romanesque Revival style in the United States was developed by Boston architect Henry Hobson Richardson and is commonly known as Richardsonian Romanesque. After studying at the Ecole des Beaux-Arts in Paris, the best architectural school in Europe, Richardson returned to the United States in 1865 and established an office in New York City. In 1872, he won the commission to design Trinity Church in Boston, propelling him to the center of architectural attention. The popularity of this style greatly increased after Richardson's death in 1886 and upon the publication of an 1888 monograph of his work. French Romanesque ornamental motifs and a strong geometric order established the basis of his buildings. Other characteristics include round-topped windows and entrances; rough masonry walls, occasionally broken by smooth surfaces; and large towers.

The Kentucky courthouses built in the Richardsonian Romanesque style did not occur until 1890. Two excellent designs were started in that time - the Montgomery County courthouse designed by B.J. Bartlett of Nashville and the Johnson County courthouse designed by Frank Pierce Milburn of Bowling Green, who will be discussed in detail later.

Numerous courthouses designed in other styles during this period would apply Romanesque details, making the design contemporary. One good example of such a treatment is the Nicholas County courthouse of 1893-94, which is basically a Second Empire design but has Romanesque details including round-topped windows and an entrance of rough stone.

The last Richardsonian Romanesque courthouse built in Kentucky was the Fayette County courthouse of 1898. Designed by the Cleveland, Ohio architectural firm of Lehman & Schmitt, it represents the most advanced Romanesque design of Kentucky's courthouses.

High Victorian Gothic

The High Victorian Gothic, or Venetian Gothic was developed in England and it was popularized in the United States shortly after the Civil War, as a counterpart of the Second Empire Style. The style found it's theoretical basis in books by English writer John Ruskin, *The Stones of Venice* and *The Seven Lamps of Architecture,* published at mid-century. London architect William Butterfield provided the major physical impetus for the High Victorian Gothic through his buildings which are noted for

United States Post Office & Customs House, Covington — William Appleton Potter *(The National Archives)*.

of Maury & Dodd, perhaps the most talented architects in the state during this period..

Mason Maury, a Louisville native, left in 1875 to train with a leading Boston architectural firm, returning and establishing his own firm in 1879. He is credited with the introduction of Richardsonian Romanesque to Louisville through his 1886 Judge Russell Houston residence.

William J. Dodd was trained under William Le Baron Jenney, the founder of the Chicago School and first to introduce skeletal building construction to the United States. He came to Louisville in 1885, and in 1891, formed a partnership with Maury. The same year, the firm won the competition for the Louisville Trust Company Building, the finest Richardsonian Romanesque structure at that time, and the first steel frame, fire-proof structure in Kentucky.

their rich exterior and interior surface polychromy. The first American architect to promote the style was Peter Bonnett Wight of New York. He also introduced the style to Kentucky in 1867 through his design for the Thomas P. Jacobs House in Louisville. The style's major introduction to Kentucky was through Federal Post Office and Customs House of 1875-76 at Covington, designed in the office of the Supervising Architect of United States Treasury Department. Construction began in the Second Empire style under A.B. Mullett, but was completed in the High Victorian Gothic style by the next Supervising Architect, William Appleton Potter.

The High Victorian Gothic was not used in Kentucky courthouses until the 1890s. While not as advanced a design as the Customs house, the Kenton County courthouse at Covington of 1899-02 represents the only major High Victorian Gothic courthouse in Kentucky. The designed was provided by Dittoe & Wisnall, architects of Cincinnati.

Maury & Dodd

Courthouses of Nelson County, 1891 and Hopkins County, 1892, are unique designs that combine the Richardsonian Romanesque and High Victorian Gothic styles, known as synthetic eclecticism.. The pair represent two of Kentucky's most elaborate county buildings of the Victorian period. Both were designed by the Louisville architectural firm

Frank Pierce Milburn

Frank P. Milburn was born in 1868 at Bowling Green, Kentucky where he grew up. He was the son of Thomas T. Milburn, architect and builder, who designed several Kentucky courthouses. In the 1880's he attended college in Fayetteville, Arkansas, afterward receiving architectural training in Louisville. In 1889, he collaborated with his father in the design and contruction of the Clay County courthouse. Starting his own practice, the next year he moved to Kenova, West Virginia. He again relocated in 1895 to Charlotte, North Carolina as architect of the Southern Railroad Company. He is said to have, in a few years, acquired the largest architectural business south of the Mason-Dixon line, with commissions from Virginia to Louisiana. According to Milburn's son, Thomas Yancey, his father traveled 30,000 miles a year on the railroads, usually overnight in sleepers, for 25 years, in order to personally oversee his numerous projects.

Just before leaving Kentucky in 1890, Milburn designed the Powell County and Johnson County courthouses. By 1893, in a practice similar to the McDonald Brothers, Milburn developed a standard courthouse design. Also similar to McDonald, Milburn could alter his design to fit budgets between $ 15,000 to $ 21,000. Typical of Victorian eclecticism, his design combines elements of several popular styles. Seven courthouses are known to have been executed on this plan including four Kentucky courthouses at Magoffin County, 1893; Trigg County, 1895; Wayne County, 1898-99; and Fulton County in 1901-03. Three built outside Kentucky

Standard Victorian design, c. 1891 — Frank P. Milburn, architect.

include the courthouses at Independence, Virginia and two in West Virginia at Hinton and Winfield.

Milburn designed two other Kentucky courthouses during the Victorian period not based on his standard design. The Clinton County courthouse of 1895 was a simple vernacular design. The Letcher County courthouse of 1899 was an eclectic design.

Perhaps the most interesting of Milburn's Kentucky commissions of this period was his c. 1896 enlargement of the Knox County courthouse. Milburn remodeled the 1874-75 Italianate courthouse, redesigning it as a Mission Revival style building.

The Colonial Revival

Neoclasscism again dominated the design of Kentucky courthouses from 1893 until the second World War. The World's Columbian Exposition of 1893 in Chicago was the main catalyst for this trend. Millions of Americans witnessed the fair in person, while millions more were fascinated by descriptions including the newly popular printed photograph. Major buildings of the Exposition were of the style of the Ecole des Beaux-Art located in France, but many smaller pavilions were of a harmonizing Colonial Revival.

Colonial Revival exteriors tended to be of smooth stone or brick, in contrast to the rough stone of the earlier Renaissance and Romanesque structures. Columns were placed along the front, and a symmetry prevailed, often to the detriment of the interior layout. The whole presented a unified model, utilizing all the components of classical construction, including monumental scale, balustrades, cupolas and raised foundations. The courtrooms became increasingly monumental with elaborate classical detailing. However, the courtroom was becoming increasingly subordinate to numerous county offices. This problem made many older courthouses, where the main focus was the courtroom, obsolete and in need of replacement.

Thirty-three Kentucky courthouses were built in the Colonial Revival style prior to 1935, and most of them still survive. Without exception, all Colonial Revival courthouse were designed by architects. The highest quality prevails, each courthouse being a unique expression of the individuality of its architect.

Not suprisingly, the earliest Beaux-Arts influenced courthouse in Kentucky was designed by Mason Maury. In 1893, Maury and Dodd had been selected to design the Kentucky building at the World's Columbian Exposition, an advanced Beaux-Arts influenced Colonial Revival design. In 1896, the partnership ended and Maury practiced alone. His first Beaux-Arts courthouse design was for Barren County in 1896. He also probably designed the similar Bullitt County courthouse of 1900. In 1907, Dodd formed a partnership with Kenneth McDonald, the younger brother of H.P. McDonald. The same year, McDonald & Dodd designed one of the largest Colonial Revival courthouses at Greenville in Muhlenburg County.

Frank P. Milburn relocated to Washington, D.C., in 1902, but retained a following in his native Kentucky. He formed a partnership with designer Michael Heister, calling the firm Milburn, Heister and Company. The same year, Milburn submitted a proposed Beaux-Arts influenced design for a new state capitol to be built in Frankfort. Another architect's design was finally built; however, Milburn's design was realized on a reduced scale in 1902-05 at Bourbon County. State-wide distribution of this design apparently served a major catalyst for Colonial style in county courthouses. Milburn, Heister and Company designed two other excellent Colonial style courthouses at Lincoln County in 1909 and Boyd County courthouse of 1910-12. Milburn died in Washington, D.C., in 1926.

Most of the Colonial style courthouses were designed by Kentucky architects. The bulk of courthouse designs originated with Louisville architects. Joseph & Joseph, one of the cities largest firms, designed the Shelby County courthouse of 1912, and Anderson County courthouse of

Proposed Beaux-Arts design for the Kentucky State House, 1902 — Frank P. Milburn, architect.

1915. Clarence Stinson designed the Hart County courthouse of 1928. Edgar W. Archer designed the Cumberland County courthouse of 1934. Thomas Nolan designed two later Beaux-Arts influenced courthouses in Hardin County in 1933-34, and Marion County in 1935.

One firm in Louisville during this period deserves special mention. The Falls City Construction Company was a unique entity in the state and offered a kind of package deal, which included all design and construction services in one contract. First, they would send one of their two architects, H.L. Lewman or Andrew J. Bryan, who would show the court numerous tantalizing perspectives of designs for courthouses at varying costs. After a design was chosen they would provide all construction services, including an on-site architect to supervise construction. The company is only identified with two courthouse designs in Kentucky, the Mercer County courthouse of 1912, and the Carlisle County courthouse alteration of 1913. They, no doubt, were involved in other Kentucky courthouses, as of yet have not been identified. When making a presentation to the Mercer County Court, it was stated that the firm had by that time built 125 courthouses in various parts of the country and had ten currently under construction, including a courthouse at Little Rock, Arkansas, which cost half a million dollars.

This type of national dissemination was brought about by improved transportation and communications of this period. In turn, it also facilitated the importation of a number of designs by architects from outside the state. As was the case with Falls City Construction, these individuals had national reputations as specializing in courthouse design. Included would be previously mentioned Frank P. Milburn of Washington, D.C., who is known to have designed over 50 courthouses, 12 in Kentucky. Jerome B. Legg, of St. Louis, who designed a number of similar Missouri courthouses, provided a typical design for the Ballard County courthouse of 1900-05. William Chamberlin of Atlanta, Georgia, won a competition for the Logan County courthouse of 1903-04. Robertson & Fahnstock, of Cincinnati, designed the courthouse for neighboring Kenton County at Independence of 1911. B.F. Smith, another Washington architect, provided the very advanced design for the Perry County courthouse of 1912. And finally, John W. Gaddis, of Vincennes, Indiana, designed the Bell County courthouse of 1919-20.

A number of Colonial style designs are of unidentified origin. These include McLean County, 1904-08; Carter County, 1907; Morgan County, 1907; Calloway County, 1913; Spencer County, 1914-15; Bracken County, 1915; Marshall County, 1915; Wolfe County, 1915-17; Harlan County, 1918-22; Trigg County, 1922; Menifee County, 1928; Owsley County, 1929-30; and Green County, 1930-31.

THE NEW DEAL-
WORKS PROGRESS ADMINISTRATION

During the depression, the administration of Franklin D. Roosevelt implemented a number of work programs known as the New Deal. One branch of the New Deal was the Public Works Administration, which was in charge of construction of buildings and engineering projects. P.W.A. projects commenced soon after passage of the National Recovery Act in 1933 and continued through the beginning of the second World War. The P.W.A. acted somewhat like a large building and loan association. They would underwrite 100% of a project, granting a county up to 45% of construction costs, and loaning them the balance.

Under the New Deal, thirteen courthouses were built in Kentucky, three were renovated, and eight had major additions. Many buildings of the New Deal were designed by the Public Buildings Branch of the Procurement Division of the Treasury Department. Due to the efforts of Kentucky's architects, however, most of our courthouses were designed by our own architects. Numerous and diverse styles were used for P.W.A. courthouses including the Colonial Revival, Art Deco, and Art Moderne.

The earliest and largest number of P.W.A. courthouses were built in the Colonial Revival style, which had been prominent prior to the depression. Five New Deal courthouses were built in this style, including

Hopkins County, 1937; Grant County, 1937-39; Grayson County, 1937-38; Lewis County, 1939-40; and McCracken County, 1939-40.

Poured concrete was a popular construction material as it maximized man-power dispersal, a main objective of New Deal projects. This technique advanced two new styles, Art Deco and Art Moderne.

Art Deco features smooth walls with chevrons, zig-zags and other geometric motifs as decorative elements. which often rise above the roof line. The only two examples are the Caldwell County courthouse of 1938-41, and larger Webster County courthouse of 1939-40. Similar to each other, both buildings are the design of Lawrence Casner, an architect of Madisonville.

Art Moderne featured smooth walls; curved corners; a flat roof, usually with a small ledge at the roof line; and horizontal bands contributing to a horizontal effect. The only Art Moderne style courthouse and last built under the New Deal is that of Ohio County of 1940-43. Walter Scott Roberts of Owensboro was the architect..

One of the most unique courthouses of the New Deal is the Knott County courthouse remodeled during 1935-36 in the Mission Style. Hispanic in inspiration, the Mission Style is primarily associated with California and is not common outside the southwestern states. A typical feature of this style is the curved parapet above the entrance.

The other five courthouses built during the New Deal were of relatively simple design. They all use stone as the primary building material. Again, the main reason was the diversion of work to use as many people as possible. Courthouses of stone construction include Martin County, 1936; Elliott County, 1937; Greenup County, 1937-39; Clay County, 1939; and Estill County, 1939-41.

THE MODERN KENTUCKY COURTHOUSE

With World War II consuming most of the Nation's resources, no courthouses were built in Kentucky from the end of the New Deal until 1950. Forty Kentucky courthouses have been built from 1950 to date.

The Jackson County and Wayne County courthouses were started in 1965, both of the Art Deco style. Bayless, Clotfelter, and Johnson designed the Jackson structure. These were the last Art Deco courthouses.

The next built was the Fleming County courthouse of 1951-52. It marks the continued appreciation of Kentuckians for courthouses of classical design. The Colonial style was again popularized and remains so. A total of 13 Colonial style courthouses have been built in Kentucky since 1950. One of the most recent courthouses built in Kentucky, the Clinton County courthouse of 1980-81, is of this style. Other modern courthouses built in the Colonial style include those in Montgomery County, 1958-59; Laurel County, 1961; Knox County, 1963-64; Larue County, 1964; Barren County, 1964-65; Perry County, 1964-65; Woodford County, 1968; Pulaski County, 1975; Butler County, 1975; Todd County, 1975-76; and Monroe County, 1976.

Several courthouses of good modern design have been built since 1950. Some of the better examples include the courthouses of Lyon County, 1961; Daviess County, 1963; Powell County, 1977-78; Meade County; and the most recent Kentucky courthouse in Carlisle County, 1981-82.

Kentucky's New State Capitol and Its Construction, 1910[1]

The first actual step toward the erection of the new Captiol was taken by the 1904 General Assembly. This body appropriated $ 1,000,000 for that purpose and constituted a State Capitol Building Commission.

At its meeting, April 7, 1904, C.M. Fleenor, of Bowling Green, Ky., was elected superintendent of construction for the State. On June 10, 1904 Frank M. Andrews, of Dayton, Ohio, was elected architect. The preliminary work of clearing and excavating for the site was begun on May 25, 1905. On August 10 the general contract for the construction of the building was let and the work on the excavation for the foundation was begun four days later. The building was offically dedicated June 1, 1910.

It will be seen from the foergoing that the total appropriation for the Capitol building proper was $ 1,250,000; for its furnishing and outfitting, $255,000; for the power plant and its equipment $ 90,000; for the architectural terrace and landscape work of the grounds, $ 115,000, and for the grounds themselves, $ 40,000; making a total of $ 1,750,000.

The building is of French renaissance architecture with the neo-classic feature of the dome, which characterizes the general designs of State Capitols. In size it is 402 feet and 10 inches east and west, and 180 feet through central pavillion north and south, these figures being exclusive of the terrace walls which add some thirty or forty feet each way.

The base of the exterior of the building is of Vermont granite; the rest of the face work, including the dome, is of Bedford limestone. By reason of the liberality of the 1906 Legislature which made possible the handsome pediment, money was also appropriated for an extra in the interior finish of the building, namely, the changing of the finish of the corridors, nave, etc., from Bedford stone to Georgia marble and Vermont granite. The difference is marked and it gives richness and tone to the general treatment. Charles H. Niehaus, sculptor of New York City, being selected for the work to be done on the pediment.

The nave deserves special mention on account of its generous length and breadth and the thirty-six great monolithic columns supporting massive cornices. The columns are of Vermont granite, the stairs, pilasters and cornices Georgia marble, and the floors of Tennessee and Italian marbles bordered with Verde antique.

— C.M. Fleenor,
State Superintendent of Construction

[1] Excerpts from reprint, William B. Scott, Jr., Publisher.

Kentucky's Oldest Courthouse

Specifications for the Original construction of the Courthouse as recorded in the Green County Records, November 29, 1803 — Deed Book 4

The house to be of stone three squares of the house to be laid in straight regular courses, and the other square to be good common work two stories high to be forty by thirty-four feet from outside to outside walls to be two feet thick, and to be sunk in the ground at least two feet in every part and to be 24 feet high above the surface at the front door, to have seventeen windows those in the lower story to be twenty-four lights 8 by 10 inches the upper windows to be of 18 lights of the same size, to be arranged in such as a majority of the Commissioners shall direct.

To have an inside chimney in one of the ends of the popular and one fireplace in each jury room two outside doors. The doors and window frames to be of single architrave made of solid timber, the doors and window shutters to be paneled and doors lined, made of walnut, arches over each of the doors and windows, the glass to be furnished and put in with putty, the doors to be hung with sufficient iron hinges, the windows also with sufficient hinges one of the outside doors to have a lock of the best quality the other a bolt, all the windows to have bolts a principal roof joint shingles of lasting wood, a good plain cornice, the roof to be put on with nails, of a sufficient size, the roof to be sheeted, the whole of the wood work exposed to the weather to be well painted, the roof Spanish brown, the cornice and frames white the second story to extend halfway the house, for the purpose of a lobby of six feet, and two jury rooms the partitions to be framed lathe and plastered, the jury rooms to have good seats with paneled doors well hung and good locks, a staircase from the bar with handrails and bannisters the front of the lobby to be wainscotted, the bar to be raised a proper height from the floor of the poplars, also to be wainscotted a clerks table and to be wainscotted around also, the justices seat in a circular form to be wainscotted in back and front of all walnut, twelve walnut framed chairs for the use of the court one large armed chair, the floor of the poplar to be laid with stone.

The floors of the lobby and jury rooms also the floor contained in the case clerks apartment and justices seat to be ash well tongued and grooved at least one and a half inch thick nailed down and the necessary steps to such as may be wanting, the whole house to be well plastered, also to be lathed and plastered under the upper story and under the jury room chair and wash boards in every part of the house where wanting sheriffs box at the opposite end of the bar from the stair case of the a convenient size, the length of the base to be under the direction of the Commissioners as to its length and size, a panel door at each end of the bar of walnut two fluted columns from the lower floor to support the upper floor the whole of the above work to be done in a complete and workman like manner, and the house to be furnished by the 25th day of December 1809 except the plastering and that by the first of June following under the penalty of Eighteen Hundred Pounds. In testimony whereof we have hereunto set our hands and seals the date and date above written.

Witnesses present:

Waller Bullock
Daniel White
Robert Ball
Robert Allen

Frederick Halk
James Blane
Robert Wickliff
Johnathan Cowherd

1. **ALBANY** in

   CLINTON COUNTY

   Year Formed: 1835

   Formed From: Cumberland and Wayne Counties

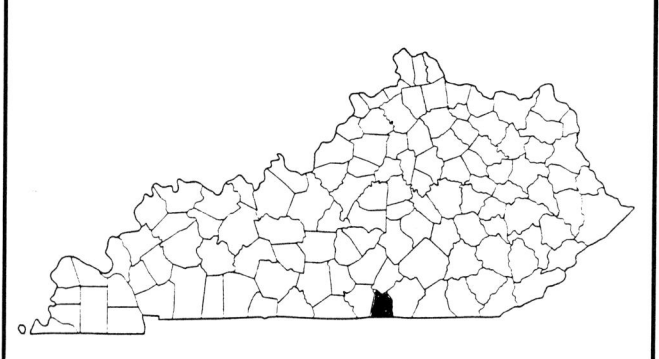

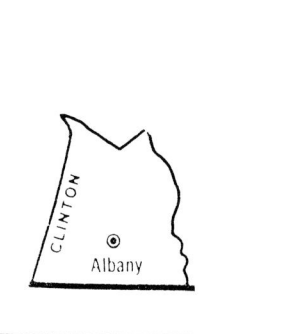

Clinton County, 85th in order of formation, was named for Governor DeWitt Clinton of New York — a popular politician of the period. Albany was established as the county seat in 1838 and named for the New York town.

The first Clinton County courthouse was built in 1835-36. It was burned in late 1864 by Confederate troops, and all the county records were destroyed.

Several years passed before the second Clinton County courthouse was started in 1870 and finished in 1873.

The third Clinton County courthouse was built in 1895 at a cost of $15,000. Kentucky native Frank P. Milburn was the architect. W. L. McDonald of Albany, the contractor, owned the local general store and is said to have paid many workers with merchandise. The courthouse burned on August 2, 1980.

The fourth and current Clinton County courthouse was built shortly after the fire in 1980. It is a two-story brick building of modern design. The entrance of the modern Colonial style, is delineated by two large, two-story arches.

Third Courthouse, 1895, *(Fackler Collection, University of Kentucky Collection)*.

2. ALEXANDRIA IN CAMPBELL COUNTY

Year Formed: 1794

Formed From: Harrison, Mason, and Scott Counties

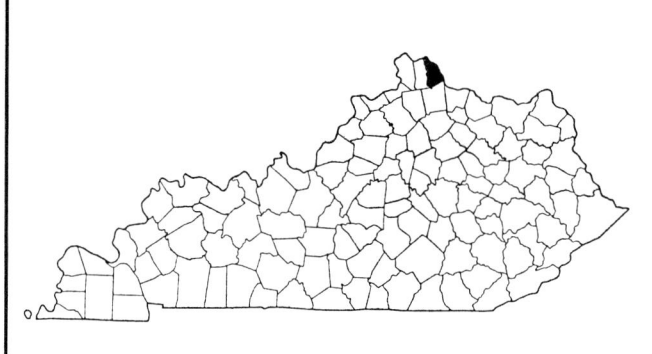

Campbell County, 19th in order of fromation, was named in honor of Colonel John Campbell — Jefferson County's representative at Kentucky's first Constitutional Convention. Campbell County has had several county seats, including Wilmington, Visilia, Newport, and Alexandria.

The first three courthouses were built at Newport (see p. 174).

During the year 1827, the town of Visilia was county seat due to its proximity to the proposed railroad. The county government later moved back to Newport and in 1840 moved again to Alexandria — deemed the center of the county.

Alexandria built the fourth Campbell County courthouse under commissioners James McCron, William Riley, and John Straube. On August 10, 1840, the court accepted the plan proposed by William Riley for a structure of the foursquare form measuring 40 feet square. James M. Jolly, a local Baptist minister, contracted for construction of the building, which he completed in 1842 at a cost of $5,885. During 1928, the building went through major remodeling, adding the front portico and a new clock tower.

Fourth Courthouse, Alexandria, 1840 *(University of Kentucky)*.

3. BARBOURVILLE in KNOX COUNTY

Year Formed: 1799

Formed From: Lincoln County

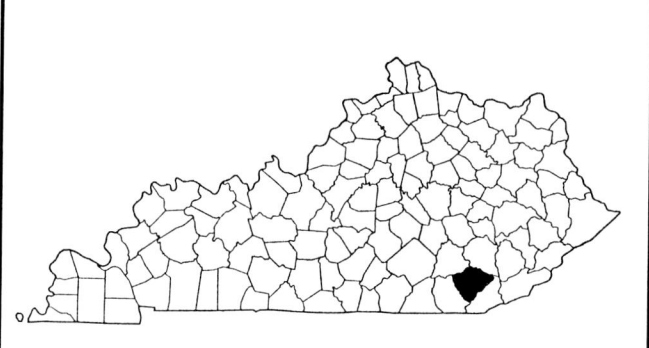

Knox County, 41st in order of formation, was named for Henry Knox — Revolutionary War hero, commandant of West Point. He was appointed Secretary of War in 1785. Barbourville was established as the county seat.

The first Knox County courthouse was built in 1802. The courthouse was built of log by Daniel Deweese for $240. The building was used until replaced in 1812.

The second Knox County courthouse was ordered by the court on November 4, 1811 and finished the next year. The courthouse was a brick structure not to cost more than $1,200.

The third Knox County courthouse was ordered by the court in 1829. John Click, Richard Adams, and Leighton Adams were appointed commissioners to let the building of the courthouse on the April 1, 1829. The building was to be modeled on the Laurel County courthouse. Jarvis Jackson was the contractor.

The fourth Knox County courthouse was built in 1874-75. The brick, two-story courthouse was of the Italianate style. About 1907-08, wings were added to the ends of the building in a similar style. Architect Frank P. Milburn remodeled the building in the Mission style. This courthouse served the county until 1963.

The fifth and present Knox County courthouse was built in 1963-64. The brick, two-story courthouse is of colonial styling with a classical portico supported by Corinthian columns.

Left: Fourth Courthouse, 1874 *(The Filson Club)*.

Right: Fourth Courthouse, 1874 — after wings added *(Monograph of F. P. Milburn, 1905)*.

4. BARDSTOWN in NELSON COUNTY

Year Formed: 1784

Formed From: Jefferson County

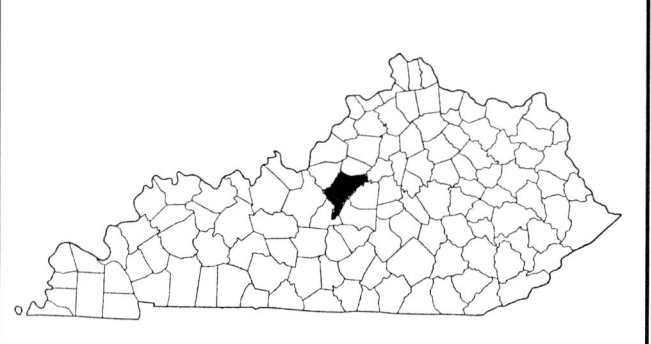

Nelson County, 4th in order of formation, was named for Governor Thomas Nelson of Virginia, who was a signer of the Declaration of Independence. Bardstown, originally Salem, was established as the county seat in 1785 and named for David Baird by his brother James, the original owner of the town site.

The first Nelson County courthouse was built in 1784 of hewn logs and measured 20 x 30 feet.

The second Nelson County courthouse was built in 1787. At the May 12, 1787, meeting of the Nelson County court, Issac Cox, James Rogers, James Baird, and Jesse Davis were appointed commissioners to supervise construction. John Cape designed and constructed this courthouse as well as those in Fayette and Jefferson Counties of the same period. The plans called for a two-story, stone courthouse measuring 40 x 23 feet, to cost 450 pounds. The building was completed by December of 1787 and stood until the building of the current courthouse.

The third Nelson County courthouse was built in 1891-92. Designed by the partnership of Mason Maury and William J. Dodd, architects of Louisville, the building is in the Richardsonian Romanesque style so popular during this period. The building is built of stone and brick with wood framing. The contractor, Edward Baker Smith, built the courthouse for $33,000. The building was remodeled in the 1960s. The Nelson County courthouse was listed on the National Register of Historic Places in 1983 as a contributing property of a historic district.

Second Courthouse, 1785 *(The Filson Club)*.

Third Courthouse, 1891 *(University of Louisville)*.

5. BARDWELL in CARLISLE COUNTY

Year Formed: 1886

Formed From: Ballard, Breckinridge, and Green Counties

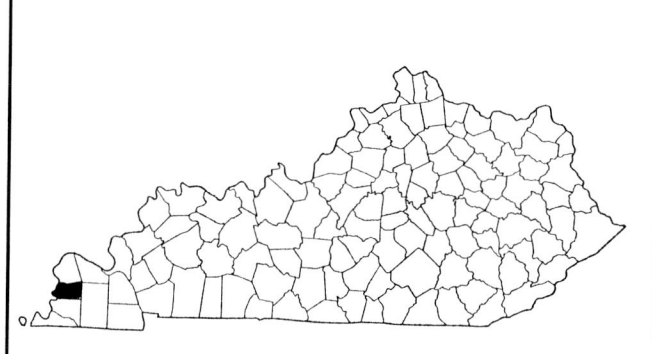
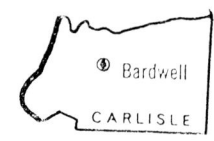

Carlisle County, 119th in order of formation, was named for John Griffin Carlisle. Bardwell was established as the county seat in 1886.

The first Carlisle County courthouse was build shortly after the formation of the county in 1886. The courthouse was a simple design of the Victorian period style, a two-story brick structure crowned by a square wooden cupola. In 1913 the Falls City Construction Company of Louisville heavily remodeled the building at a cost of $18,917. The cupola was removed and the portico added, giving the building a Colonial Revival style appearance popular around the turn-of-the-century. On October 22, 1980, an arsonist destroyed the original courthouse.

The second and current Carlisle County courthouse was started in September of 1981 and was completed in July 1982. The modern, single-story, brick building cost $440,000.

First Courthouse, 1886. *(Ran Grave's History of Carlisle County).*

First Courthouse, 1886, after 1913 remodeling *(Collection of William B. Scott).*

6. BEATTYVILLE in LEE COUNTY

Year Formed: 1870

Formed From: Breathitt, Estill, Owsley, and Wolfe Counties

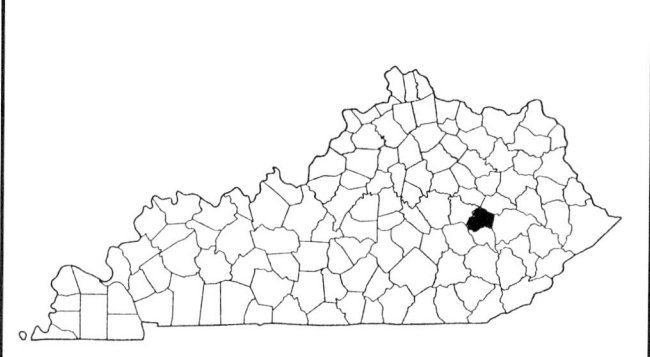

Lee County, 115th in order of formation, was named for General Robert E. Lee — hero of the Civil War. Proctor was the first county seat, but about 1872 Beattyville was established as the permanent county seat.

The first Lee County courthouse was built in 1871-73. The builders of the courthouse include the names Pryse, Brandenburg, and McGuire. The courthouse, a front gable two-story, brick structure of vernacular design stood until 1976 when it was replaced by the current structure.

The second and present Lee County courthouse was built in 1976-77. The courthouse is a brick, three-story structure of contemporary design. The original iron fence still remains.

First Courthouse, 1871 — from prospectus of the Three Forks Investment Company, its Beattyville town site, 1899 (*University of Kentucky Special Collection*).

7. BEDFORD in TRIMBLE COUNTY

Year Formed: 1837

Formed From: Gallatin, Henry, and Oldham Counties

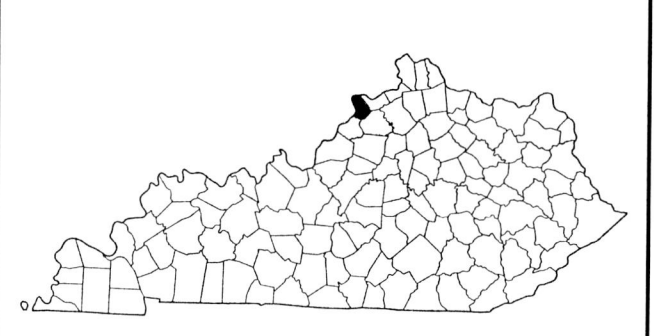

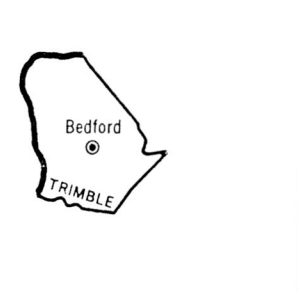

Trimble County, 86th in order of formation, was named for Judge Robert Trimble — Chief Justice of the Kentucky Court of Appeals and later a United States Supreme Court Judge. Bedford was established as the county seat.

The first Trimble County courthouse was built in 1837. The courthouse was a two-story, brick building of the foursquare form covered by a hip roof. A square cupola with Ionic columns at the corners tops the building.

The second Trimble County courthouse was built in 1884. H. P McDonald & Brothers, architects of Louisville, provided their standard courthouse design for the courthouse. B. F. Trester, Jr., an Indiana builder, contracted to build the courthouse for $13,000. On March 5, 1952, the courthouse suffered a severe fire which gutted the building and destroyed the second floor. Using the walls of the first floor, Louisville architect Carl D. Russell redesigned the structure. The Barnett Lumber Company, W.W. Burgess and J. D. Frost, were the contractors for rebuilding the structure, which retains much of its original style.

Second Courthouse, 1884 — about 1950, before the fire *(The Courier-Journal)*.

8. BENTON in MARSHALL COUNTY

Year Formed: 1842

Formed From: Calloway County

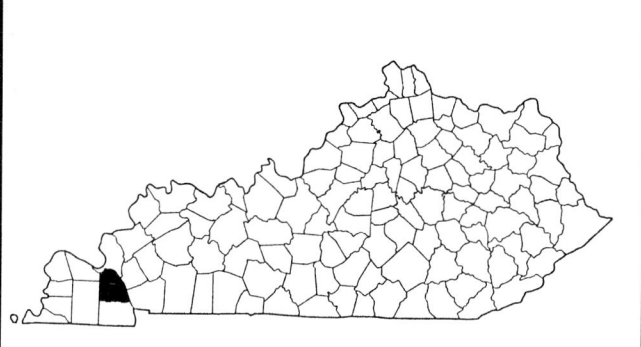
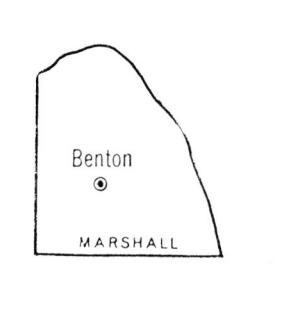

Marshall County, 92nd in order of formation, was named for John Marshall — Chief Justice of the Supreme Court. Benton was established as the county seat and named for Thomas Hart Benton — U.S. Senator from Missouri.

The first Marshall County courthouse was built in 1843-44. Francis Clayton built the log structure.

The second Marshall County courthouse was built in 1847. The courthouse was built by Thomas McElrath, principal contractor and Lewis Henderson, chief carpenter, for $6,000. Fire destroyed the courthouse in 1888.

The third Marshall County courthouse was built in 1888. The cost of the building was $14,000. Fire also destroyed this courthouse in December 1914.

The fourth and present Marshall County courthouse was built in 1915. The building is a brick, two-story structure of classical Beaux-Arts influenced design. The courthouse was built at a cost of $24,000. An addition was made to the north side of the building in 1961. It contained a new fiscal court room, jail and jailer's quarters, and other offices and cost $125,000.

Third Courthouse, 1888 *(History of Marshall County)*.

Fourth Courthouse, 1915 *(The Courier-Journal)*.

9. BOONEVILLE in OWSLEY COUNTY

Year Formed: 1843

Formed From: Breathitt, Clay, and Estill Counties

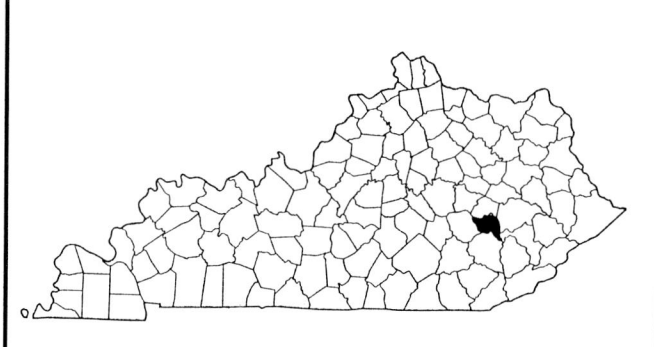
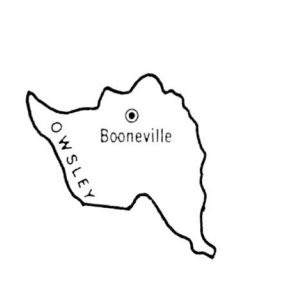

Owsley County, 96th in order of formation, was named for Governor William Owsley of Garrard County. Booneville, originally known as Owsley Courthouse, was established as the county seat and named for Daniel Boone.

The first Owsley County courthouse was built in 1844. From the date, it is likely this was a brick structure. Little, however, is known of the Owsley County courthouses due to the records being destroyed in January 1929, when this courthouse or a successor burned to the ground.

The next Owsley County courthouse was built in 1929-30. This courthouse was a brick, two-story structure of the Colonial Revival style being fronted by a portico of eight Doric columns. In May 1930 the first meeting of the court was held in the new courthouse. The building cost $42,987. Having been previously condemned, the courthouse burned on January 5, 1967.

The current Owsley County courthouse, built in the early 1970s, is of modern design — a two-story, brick building covered by a flat roof.

Second Courthouse, 1929-30 *(Cusick Photo, The Kentucky Historical Society)*

Second Courthouse, 1929-30 — on January 6, 1967 *(The Courier-Journal)*.

10. BOWLING GREEN in WARREN COUNTY

Year Formed: 1796

Formed From: Logan County

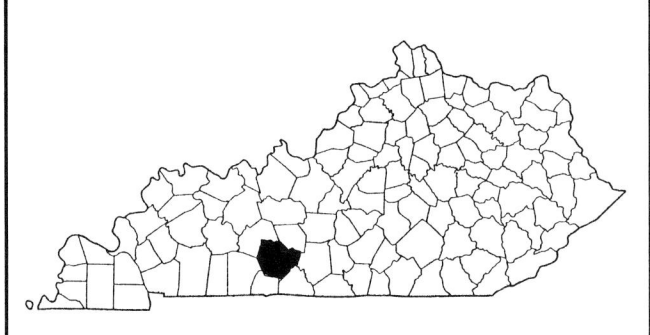
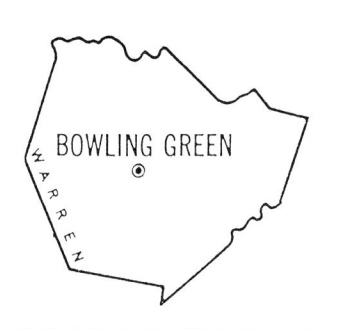

Warren County, 24th in order of formation, was named for General Joseph Warren, M.D. — veteran of the Revolutionary War, killed at Bunker Hill. Bowling Green was established as the county seat in 1796. In 1805, the center of Bowling Green shifted towards the river; there, a "new town" was established, and John McNeel received approval for another new town, Jeffersonville. Some Bowling Green residents started moving into the new sections, the majority to Jeffersonville. The county seat relocated to Jeffersonville in May 1808, where it remained until 1813 when it returned to Bowling Green.

The first Warren County courthouse was built in 1797-98. On July 4, 1797, the county ordered the courthouse built. The courthouse was a hewn log, one-and-a-half-story structure measuring 24 x 20 feet. The building was first used on March 6, 1798.

The second Warren County courthouse was built in 1805 at Jeffersonville. The plan for a new courthouse was presented in April, 1805 and in May a construction contract let to John McNeel for $2,597. The plan specifies a brick building of the foursquare form, 36 feet square, covered by a hip roof with a cupola. No record can be found of the building's construction.

The third Warren County courthouse was built in 1809-11. In 1807, officials of Bowling Green started planning a new courthouse to lure the county seat back. A first plan called for a two-story, hexagonal building, each side measuring 25 feet. In January 1809 the court adopted a plan for a brick courthouse of the foursquare form, 40 feet square. Thomas W. Frazier performed the brick work and James Riggins was the carpenter and joiner work. The courthouse was finished in December 1811 and underwent a major renovation in 1818.

The fourth and present Warren County courthouse was built in 1867-68. Warren County realized the need for a new courthouse prior to the Civil War, construction of which was approved by the state legislature in 1863. A new site was approved, the old building sold, and the court appointed County Judge Charles E. Blewett to head the committee to select a plan in June 1865. Plans by J. K. Frick of Evansville, Indiana, and H. P. Bradshaw and D. J. Williams of Louisville, Kentucky, were considered. The Frick plan was initially chosen, but by April, 1867 the Williams design prevailed. Williams supervised construction and Charles Ott was the stone contractor for the courthouse, completed in 1868 at a cost of $125,000. The Warren County courthouse was listed on the National Register of Historic Places in 1979.

Left: Third Courthouse, 1809-11 — During the Civil War.

Right: Fourth Courthouse, 1867 — c. 1887 (*History of Warren County*).

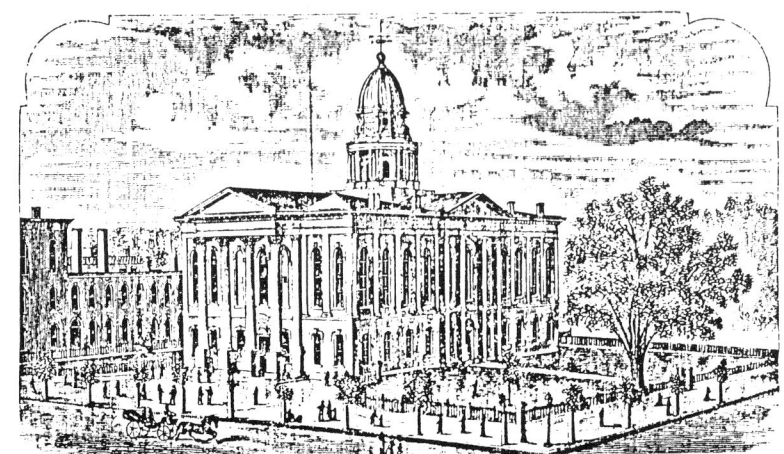

11. BRANDENBURG in MEADE COUNTY

Year Formed: 1823

Formed From: Breckinridge and Hardin Counties

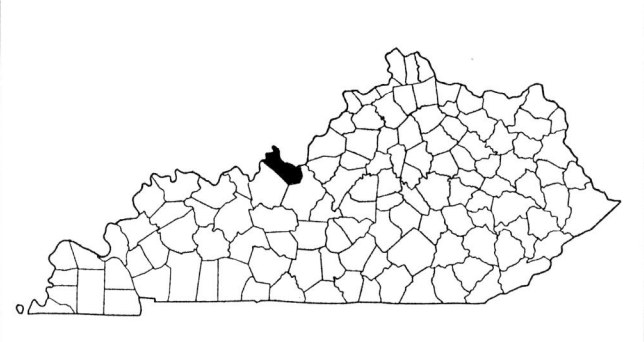
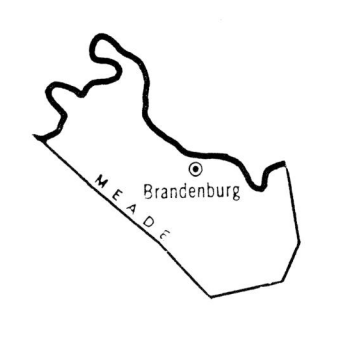

Meade County, 76th in order of formation, was named for Captain James Meade of Woodford County, a veteran of the War of 1812, who was killed at the Battle of River Raisin. Brandenburg was established as the county seat in 1825 and named for Solomon Brandenburg, its original proprietor.

The first Meade County courthouse was built in 1825. William L. McGehee, Samuel Simmons, Thomas B. Enlows, James B. Woolfolk, and William Fairleigh were appointed commissioners to "form a plan" and let construction "to the lowest bidder", not to exceed $6,000. The courthouse, described a brick structure of a single room, was built by Leonard B. Parker.

The second Meade County courthouse, also a brick structure, was built in 1850-51. During the Civil War, Federal troops occupied and damaged this building beyond repair, although the building remained in use until 1873. The county recouped $1,000 from the Federal Government in 1894.

Rather than being built on the previous site on the Ohio River, the third Meade County courthouse was built in 1872-73 on the original site of Brandenburg's own house. On July 8, 1872, the court authorized Franklin Ditto, Blant Shacklett, and T.P. Cundiff to let the bids for the courthouse. An addition was made to the building in 1959. A tornado destroyed the courthouse on April 3, 1974.

The fourth and present Meade County courthouse was dedicated on April 3, 1976. The courthouse is of tasteful modern design combining poured concrete, brick and steel.

Third Courthouse, 1872 *(The Courier-Journal)*.

12. BROOKSVILLE in BRACKEN COUNTY

Year Formed: 1796

Formed From: Campbell and Mason Counties

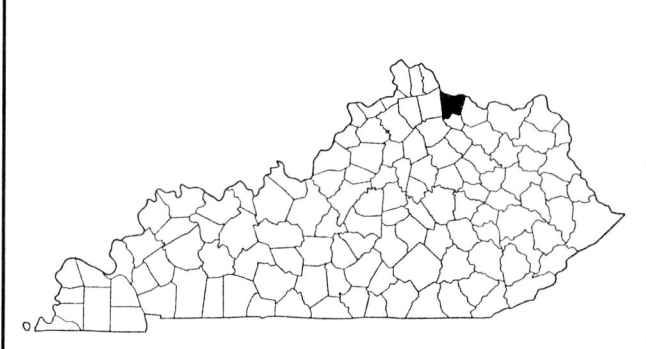
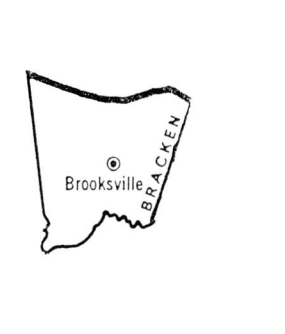

Bracken County, 23rd in order of formation, was named for William Bracken — an early settler of the region. Augusta, the largest town in the county, was established as the original county seat in 1797, but the county seat moved to Brooksville in 1839. Brooksville is named for Representative David Brooks who presented the bill establishing Brooksville as the county seat.

The first Bracken County courthouse was built in Augusta in 1802 on the public square. During the May, 1802 term of the court, Philip Buckner and Duke Morris were appointed commissioners to draft plans for the courthouse. This building served the court until 1839 when the county seat moved to Brooksville. Fire destroyed the building on April 20, 1848.

The second Bracken County courthouse, a brick structure at Brooksville, was constructed in 1838-39. The first session was held there in October, 1839. This building was replaced in 1862.

The third Bracken County courthouse was constructed in 1862-64. The one-and-a-half-story, brick building was designed in the popular Italianate style. Mr. Flora, a Brooksville builder, designed and built the courthouse. He also designed and built the Lewis County courthouse. The Bracken courthouse was condemned and ordered dismantled on July 22, 1913.

The present and fourth Bracken County courthouse was constructed in 1915. P. T. Cooke, Chairman; J. A. Thompson, A. H. Brooks, John Kearns, Valentine Bush, George Bradford, H. L. Corlis, Maurice Hook and Dr. W. B. Wallin were appointed as building commissioners. The courthouse is a brick, three-story, classical Beaux-Arts influenced building. The supervisor of construction was O. G. Wilson. The cornerstone was laid on June 14, 1915.

Third County Courthouse, 1862.

13. BROWNSVILLE in EDMONSON COUNTY

Year Formed: 1825

Formed From: Grayson, Hart, and Warren Counties

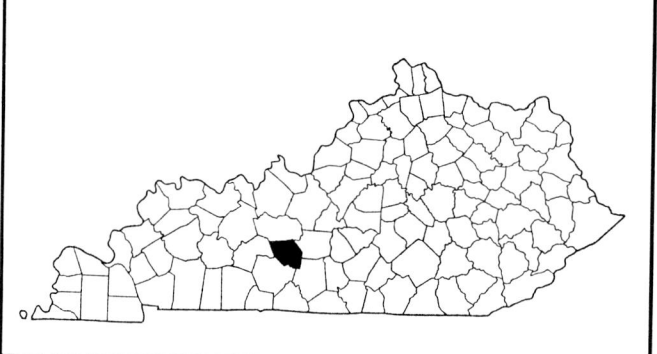
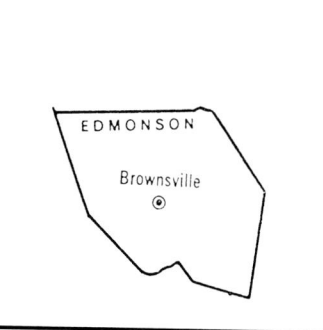

Edmonson County, 79th in order of formation, was named in honor of Captain John Edmonson of Fayette County — a member of Colonel John Allen's regiment in the War of 1812, killed at the Battle of River Raisin. The only town at that time, Brownsville was established as the county seat in 1825, and is named for General Jacob Brown.

The first Edmonson County courthouse was not constructed for that specific purpose but "an old dwelling" was converted for use. Fiscal Court members were indicted by a grand jury for failure to replace the deteriorated building, but the charges were not pressed to trial. When the first-story floor collapsed in 1872, action was finally taken.

The second and present Edmonson County courthouse was conceived at a meeting between court officials, Noah Morris and Major Woodford M. Houchin, on May 17, 1872. Both men were in their mid-thirties and together had organized the famous Company E of the Eleventh Kentucky Volunteer Infantry during the Civil War. Without waiting for the next court to convene the following order was entered,

"Ordered that the Clerk of this County issue summons for every justice of the peace in and for this County requiring them to convene or assemble at the courthouse in Brownsville on Monday, the 3rd day of June 1872, to take into consideration of the necessity of making an appropriation for the purpose of erecting a new courthouse at Brownsville, Edmonson County, and other things that they in their wisdoms may deem necessary." After this, Sheriff Willis C. Houchins notified the justices, who met on schedule. The only action taken was to raise the poll tax to $1.50 to raise funds for construction. On February 13, 1873, the necessary legislation was passed to accept bids for construction. The contractor for construction was James A. Shirley of Glasgow, who also built the Butler County courthouse of the same period. The brick, two-story structure is of the Italianate style and is topped by an hexagonal cupola.

14. BURKESVILLE in CUMBERLAND COUNTY

Year Formed: 1798

Formed From: Green County

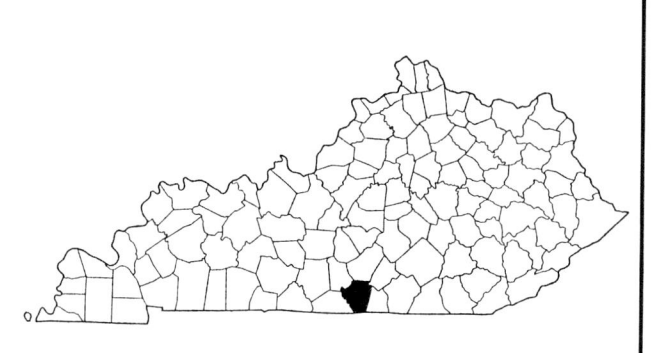
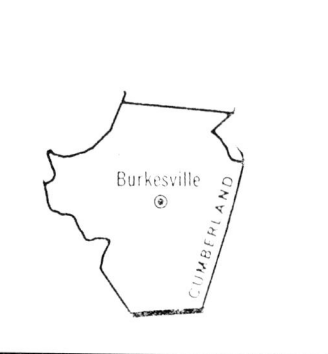

Cumberland County, 32nd in order of formation, was named for the Cumberland River, which runs through the county. Burkesville was established as the county seat and named for its original owner.

The first Cumberland County courthouse was the first order of business of the new court, although not contracted for until May of 1800. The building was described as a two-story, log building measuring 20 x 24 feet located on River Street. George Sexton, the builder, received about $600 for his effort. A flood in 1826 destroyed the courthouse.

The second Cumberland County courthouse was the first located of the current site of the courthouse. Built in 1858, the brick, two-story building of the foursquare form measured 60 feet square. M. G. Thompson, the contractor, built the structure for $7,103. The building commissioners were F. W. Alexander, D. R. Haggard, R. C. Logan, and A. G. Waggener. Four offices occupied the first floor and the courtroom on the second. In January 1864, during Confederate General Hylan B. Lyon's march through western Kentucky, his troops passed through Burkesville. On January 3, 1865, the Cumberland County courthouse became the last Kentucky courthouse burned by his troops.

The third Cumberland County courthouse was built in 1867-68. The Italianate style two-story brick building measured 50 feet square and like its predecessor had offices on the first floor and the courtroom on the second. The court appointed commissioners A. G. Waggener, W. J. Pace, Reubin Hicks, James Herriford, and Enoch Coop in charge of construction. James M. Boles contracted for the building for $18,000. Fire destroyed the building on December 30, 1933, along with most of the county records.

The fourth and present Cumberland County courthouse was built during 1934. The commissioners for construction were S. A. Cary, S. A. Smith, and J. W. Wells. The architect was Edgar W. Archer of Louisville and the contractor J. Fred Pace of Marrowbone. The Colonial Georgian style brick building is two-and-one-half-stories and measures 48 x 68 feet. The courthouse cost $37,080.

Third Courthouse, 1866 (*Glasgow Daily Times, January, 1966, "Favorite Photo"*).

15. BURLINGTON in BOONE COUNTY

Year Formed: 1798

Formed From: Campbell County

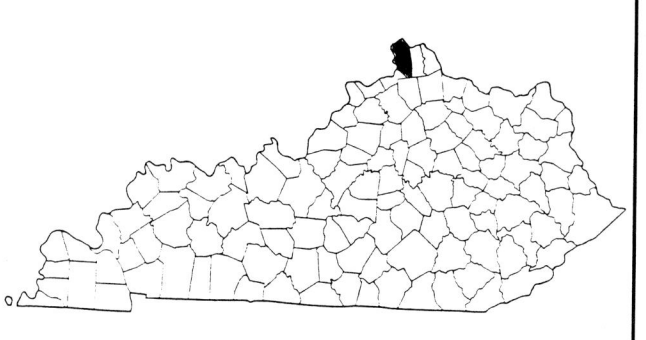

Boone County, 30th in order of formation, was named for Daniel Boone. Wilmington, the first county seat, was established in 1799. The town was laid from 740 acres owned by Robert Johnson and John H. Craig which included a courthouse square.

The first Boone County courthouse was ordered in June, 1799, at the same meeting of the court that established Wilmington as the county seat. The first specific reference to the completed courthouse is in January, 1801. The courthouse is believed to have been a log structure. In 1806, the town of Wilmington changed its name to Burlington.

The second Boone County courthouse was built in 1817. Abraham Depew and William Rogers were appointed commissioners to obtain plans for the building and see it through to completion. The courthouse was described as a brick building with brick floors and columns, measuring 36 x 40 feet. The building burned in the 1880s.

Construction of the third and present Boone County courthouse commenced in 1889. The courthouse was designed by the Louisville architectural firm of H.P. McDonald & Brothers and completed at a cost of $20,000. A modern wing has been added to the building in recent years. The Boone County courthouse was listed on the National Register of Historic Places in 1979 as a contributing property of a historic district.

Second Courthouse, 1817 (*Drawing by Earl R. Tayce, Erlanger*).

16. CADIZ in TRIGG COUNTY

Year Formed: 1820

Formed From: Caldwell and Christian Counties

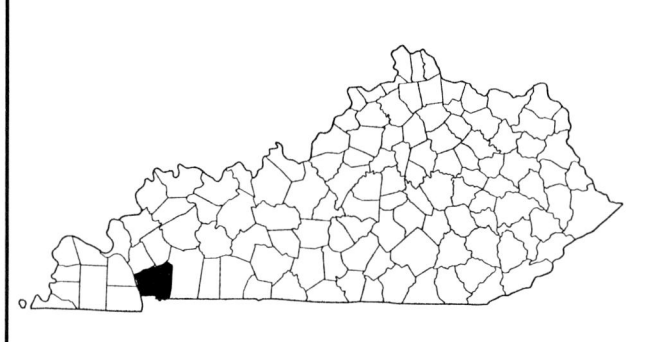
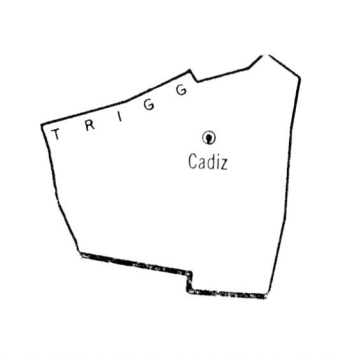

Trigg County, 66th in order of formation, was named for Colonel Stephen Trigg — who established Trigg Station in Mercer County and was killed at the Battle of Blue Licks. Cadiz was established as the county seat in 1822 by popular election.

The first Trigg County courthouse was built in 1821. The courthouse measured 22 x 24 feet. William Patterson was the builder, doing the work for $1,575. The court accepted the building on November 19, 1821. An addition was added several years later at a cost of $384 and bringing the size to 22 x 36 feet.

The second Trigg County courthouse was built in 1831. The courthouse was a brick structure costing $2,445. David Lipscomb was the contractor. The courthouse was demolished in 1842 for the next building.

The third Trigg County courthouse was built in 1843. Union troops used the courthouse as barracks during the Civil War, but fled on December 12, 1864, when Confederate General Hylan B. Lyon was reportedly approaching. They left behind a man with smallpox and Lyon burned the "contaminated" building on December 13, first allowing removal of the County records.

The fourth Trigg County courthouse was built in 1865. Pool and Boyd were the contractors, building the structure for $1,950. The courthouse was remodeled in January 1881 and destroyed by fire on January 13, 1892.

The fifth Trigg County courthouse was built in 1895. The courthouse was a large, two-and-a-half-story, brick structure of Victorian eclectic styling. Frank P. Milburn, a Bowling Green architect, designed the courthouse using a standard design. The Forbes Company built the courthouse for $12,800.

The courthouse and numerous downtown buildings burned on November 29, 1920.

The sixth and present Trigg County courthouse was built in 1922. The courthouse is of a classical Beaux-Arts influenced design, but has been remodeled in recent years and no longer maintains a cohesive design.

Upper left: Fourth Courthouse, 1865 *(History of Trigg County)*.

Upper Right: Fifth Courthouse, 1895 *(History of Trigg County)*.

17. CALHOUN in McLEAN COUNTY

Year Formed: 1854

Formed From: Daviess, Muhlenburg, and Ohio Counties

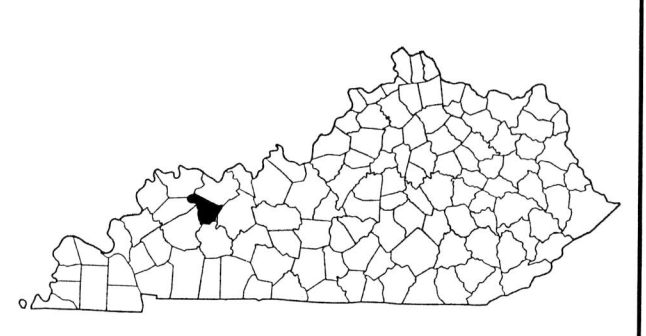

McLean County, 103rd in order of formation, was named for Judge Alney McLean of Muhlenburg County — veteran of the War of 1812 and member of the Kentucky legislature. Calhoun was established as the county seat in 1854 and named for Judge John Calhoun — circuit judge and Kentucky congressman (1835-39).

The first McLean County courthouse is believed to have been built shortly after 1854. No description exists of this courthouse.

The second McLean County courthouse was built in about 1870. The courthouse is a brick, two-story building designed in the Italianate style. The hexagonal cupola on the building appears to have been added in the late nineteenth century.

The third and present McLean County courthouse was built in 1904-08. The brick, two-story courthouse is of excellent Beaux-Arts influenced classical design with an inset Ionic portico. Luckett Brothers were the contractors of the courthouse.

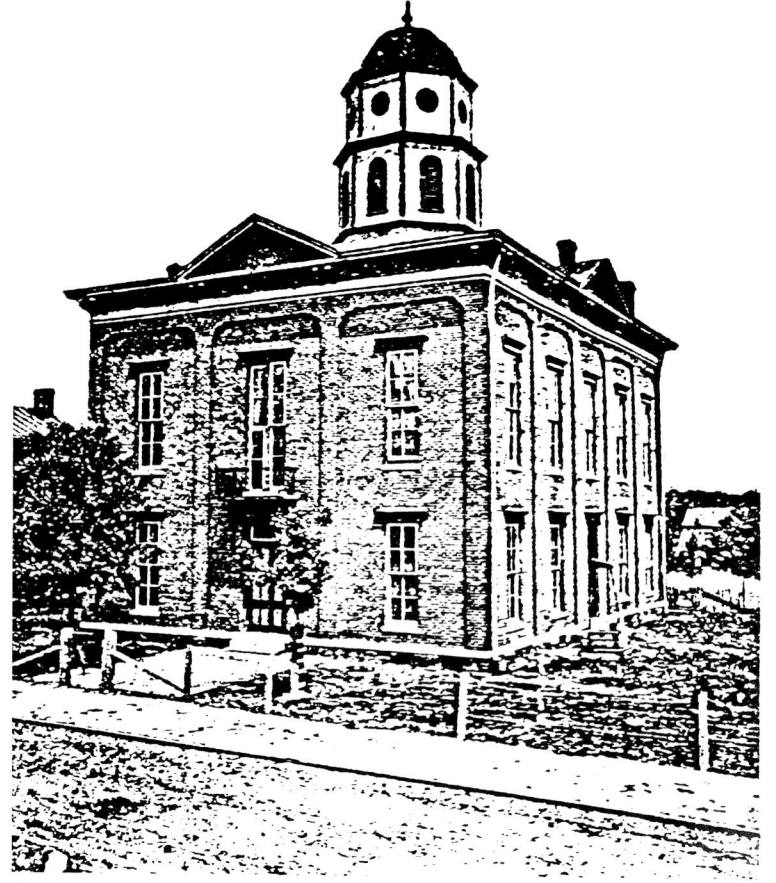

Second Courthouse, 1870

18. CAMPBELLSVILLE in TAYLOR COUNTY

Year Formed: 1848

Formed From: Green County

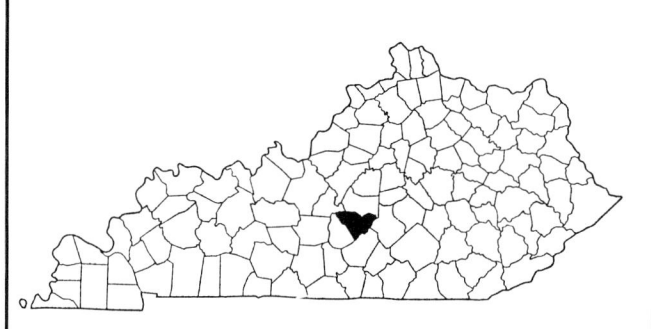

Taylor County, 100th in order of formation, as named in honor of General Zachary Taylor — hero of the Mexican War. Campbellsville was established as the county seat.

The building of the first Taylor County courthouse commenced prior to formation of the county in 1848 and was completed the summer of that year. The courthouse was a single-story, log structure. On December 25, 1864, during Confederate General Hylan B. Lyon's march through western Kentucky his troops passed through Campbellsville and burned the courthouse.

The second Taylor County courthouse was begun in 1865 and finished the next year. A. F. Gowdy, B. C. Hord, and R. S. Montague were appointed commissioners to let contracts for the building, which cost $6,000. The courthouse was a single-story structure of simple Greek Revival styling. By 1908 the county had outgrown the courthouse and instead of replacing the building as a number of counties did at the time, the building was remodeled. This remodeling included the addition of second and third floors and the four-story clock tower at the front of the building.

The third Taylor County courthouse was built in 1965-66. The courthouse is brick structure of modern design. The building is absent of any major stylistic reference and, with the exception of the front lobby, has practically no windows.

Top: Second Courthouse, 1867 (*Richard Allen Sanders*).

Left: Second Courthouse, 1867 — after 1908 remodeling, August, 1965 (*The Courier-Journal*).

19. CAMPTON in WOLFE COUNTY

Year Formed: 1860

Formed From: Breathitt, Morgan, Owsley, and Powell Counties

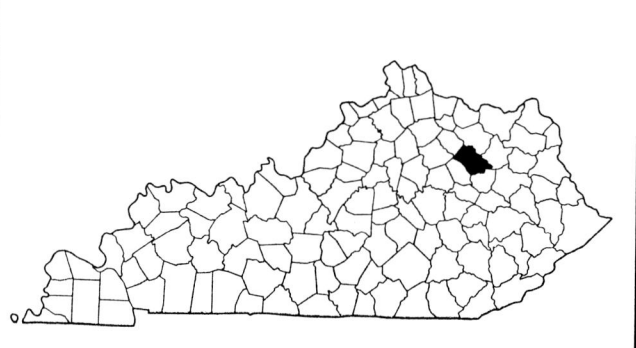

Wolfe County, 110th in order of formation, was named for Nathaniel Wolfe of Jefferson County — the first graduate of the University of Virginia, later a Kentucky State Senator. Campton, originally Camp Town, was established as the county seat and named for the original use of the town as a camping place for early travelers.

The first Wolfe County courthouse was built shortly after formation of the county in 1860. The courthouse was a log structure of unknown dimensions, which burned in 1884.

The second Wolfe County courthouse was built in 1884-85. The courthouse was a brick, two-story structure of the Victorian style. The building was finished in the summer of 1885. Fire also consumed this building in 1913.

The third and present Wolfe County courthouse was built in 1915-17. The courthouse is a yellow brick, two-story building of classical Beaux-Arts influenced design. The pediment of the portico contains a bas-relief of a wolf, in reference to the county name. The portico is of the Roman Doric order. Large, two-story wings were added to the sides of the courthouse in recent years.

20. CARLISLE in NICHOLAS COUNTY

Year Formed: 1799

Formed From: Bourbon and Mason Counties

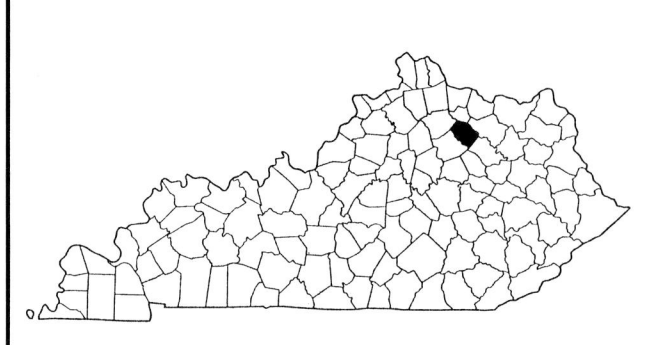
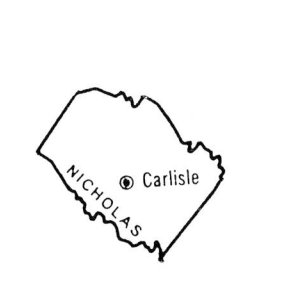

Nicholas County, 42nd in order of formation, was named for Colonel George Nicholas of Fayette County, a popular lawyer in early Kentucky. The first county seat was located at Bedinger's Mill in 1800 where it remained until 1804 when it moved to Ellisville. Carlisle became the permanent county seat in 1816.

The first Nicholas County courthouse, located at Ellisville, was built in 1805. The building is simply described as a log structure. This building was apparently moved to Carlisle in 1816, when the county seat was moved.

The second Nicholas County courthouse was built in 1816-18. The courthouse was a two-story building of the foursqaure form constructed of brick. Thomas Metcalfe, later Governor from 1828-32, Alexander Blair, Thomas West, and Samuel Fulton executed the stone and brick work for $1,700. Metcalfe also did the plastering, with Robert Dykes, for $840. The carpentry was performed by James P. Ashley and William McClannahan for $2,800. The building was dismantled in 1844 to make room for a new courthouse.

The third Nicholas County courthouse was built in 1844. The courthouse was a two-story, brick building of the foursquare form covered by a hip roof with a central cupola. William Secrist and Green Remington built the courthouse for $4,600.

The fourth and present Nicholas County courthouse was built in 1893-94. The courthouse's high style design is an eclectic combination of coarse stone work of the Romanesque style and other details of the Second Empire style, such as the mansard roofs topping the corner towers. Mox Metzger, a local stone artisan, performed the stone work on this building as well as a number of other Carlisle buildings. The new courthouse was dedicated on July 4, 1894. The building was remodeled in 1974.

Third Courthouse, 1844 *(Perrin's History of Nicholas County)*.

Fourth Courthouse, 1893 — aerial view *(The Courier Journal)*.

21. CARROLLTON in CARROLL COUNTY

Year Formed: 1838

Formed From: Gallatin, Henry, and Trimble Counties

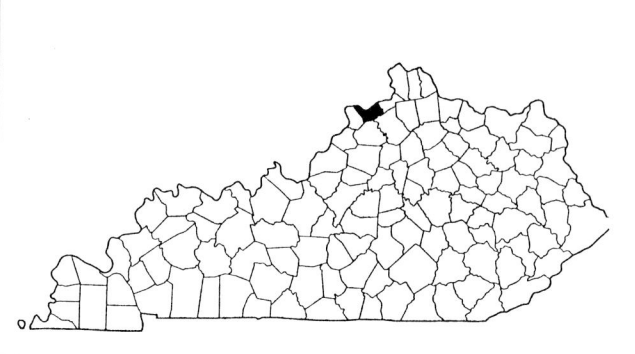

Carroll County, 87th in order of formation, was named for Charles Carroll of Carrollton, Maryland — patriot and signer of the Declaration of Independence. Port William, later Carrollton, was established as the county seat of Gallatin County in 1798. However in 1838, when Carroll County was formed it became that county's seat, and was renamed for Carroll's home. While the Gallatin County seat, two courthouses were located in the town. The latter was damaged in a storm during 1837.

The first Carroll County courthouse was ordered built at the first meeting of the court in 1839. Thomas Butler, Jacob Smith, Levi Abbott, Phillip Senours, and William Stringfellow were appointed commissioners to procure a plan and supervise construction. The courthouse was a brick two-story four-square form building topped by a square cupola. The courthouse was completed in two years at a cost of $10,800.

The second Carroll County courthouse was built in 1884 from a design by H. P. McDonald and Brothers of Louisville. The Victorian style, brick, two-story structure was constructed at a cost of $16,437. The building underwent a complete restoration in 1976 under the supervision of architects Howard and Thomas McClory. The renovation cost $570,000 and included the addition of a wing on each side. The Carroll County courthouse was listed on the National Register of Historic Places in 1982 as a contributing property of a historic district.

First Courthouse, 1839 *(The Courier-Journal)*.

Second Courthouse, 1884 *(Collection of John W. Carpenter)*.

22. CATLETTSBURG in BOYD COUNTY

Year Formed: 1860

Formed From: Carter, Greenup, and Lawrence Counties

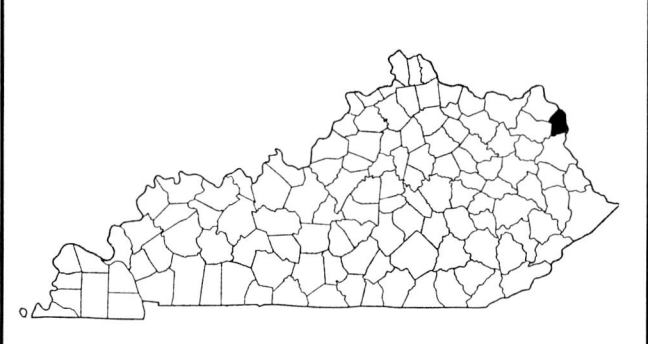
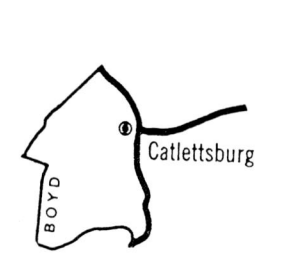

Boyd County, 107th in order of formation, was named for Linn Boyd — noted Kentucky legislator, elected Lt. Governor to serve with Beriah McGoffin but died before assuming office. Catlettsburg, established as the county seat in 1860, was named for Horatio Catlett, an early settler in that town.

The first Boyd County courthouse was built in 1860-61. At a meeting of the court on August 28, 1860, the front-gabled, slightly Greek Revival design of the courthouse was approved. The brick structure was built from funds collected by private subscription. The building stood until 1909.

The second Boyd County courthouse was begun in 1910 and finished in 1912. The Beaux-Arts influenced design was provided by Frank P. Milburn, architect of Columbia, South Carolina, who was the designer of several other Kentucky courthouses. Built of Indiana limestone, the building is noted as the first courthouse in the state with air conditioning.

First Courthouse, 1860 *(Collection of Mrs. Wallace Williamson)*.

Second Courthouse, 1910 *(University of Kentucky)*.

23. CLINTON in HICKMAN COUNTY

Year Formed: 1821

Formed From: Caldwell and Livingston Counties

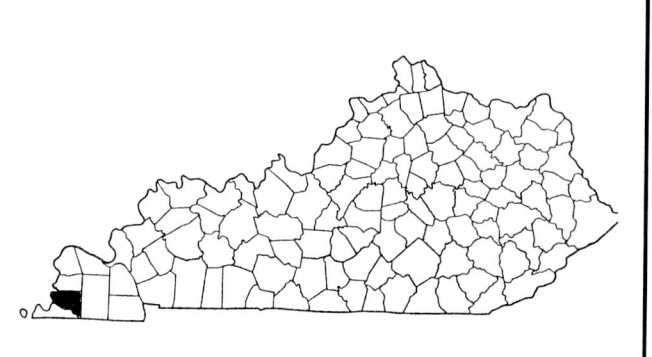
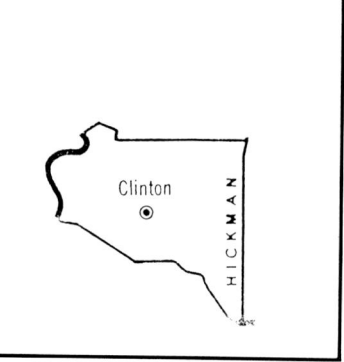

Hickman County, 71st in order of formation, was named for Pascal Hickman of Franklin County — a Captain during the War of 1812, killed at the Battle of River Raisin. The first county seat was Columbus, but in 1829 Clinton was established as the county seat.

The first Hickman County courthouse was built in 1823 and located at Columbus. Richard Taylor, Samuel Gibson, and William Edwards were appointed at the Spring 1823 term as commissioners to supervise construction. The courthouse was described as a one-and-a-half-story, log structure measuring 18 x 22 feet.

The second County courthouse was built in 1830, the year after the county seat was moved to Clinton. The courthouse was described as a "rude log structure."

The third Hickman County courthouse was built in 1832. Owen Glatz, Stephen Ray, H.L. Edrington, Thomas L. Owsley, and William Jordon were appointed commissioners to supervise construction. The brick, two-story building of the foursquare form measured 45 feet square, containing a courtroom on the first floor and three offices on the second. When built, this was the only brick courthouse in Kentucky west of the Tennessee River. In 1883, the court condemned the aged courthouse.

The fourth and present Hickman County courthouse was built in 1884-85. N. P. Moss, John T. Moore, and R. H. Dancy were appointed commissioners in August, 1883 to examine plans and let the contract for the courthouse. Plans by H. P. McDonald & Brothers of Louisville and Thomas Boyd of Pittsburg were presented, the former being approved by a 9 to 3 vote of the court. The Victorian two-story, brick courthouse is of the standard H. P. McDonald design used for numerous Kentucky courthouses. W. L. & T. J. Landrum of Mayfield were awarded the contract for $20,845. John A. Scott supervised construction of the courthouse, completed on May 11, 1885. The cupola was partially removed by the cyclone of May 27, 1917 and the rest removed in 1938. The Hickman County courthouse was listed on the National Register of Historic Places in 1975.

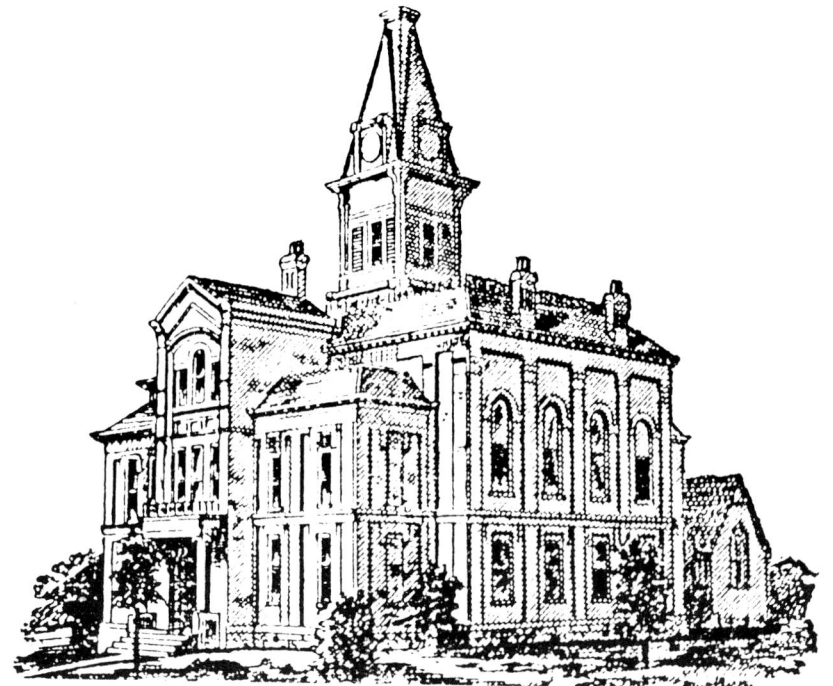

Fourth Courthouse, 1884 — from 1891 *Clinton Democrat* (Collection of Mrs. Virginia Jewell).

24. COLUMBIA in ADAIR COUNTY

Year Formed: 1801

Formed From: Green County

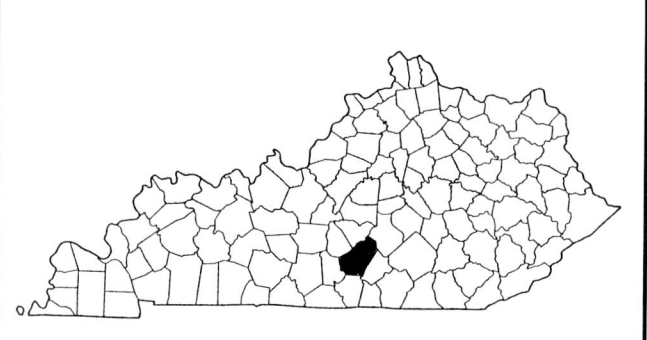

Adair County, 44th in order of formation, was named for General John Adair — an "Indian Fighter," who lived in Mercer County, led Kentucky troops at the Battle of New Orleans during the War of 1812, and became Governor of Kentucky in 1820. Columbia was established as the county seat in 1802.

The first Adair County courthouse, built on the public square, was purchased from Blackmore Hughes by order of the court at its meeting on June 28, 1802. Hugh Beard and James Walker were appointed commissioners to let a contract on September 28, 1802. William Sutton and Robert Ball, the lowest bidders, received the contract. Ball also worked on the Green County courthouse. The building was specified to be a one-and-a-half- or two-story building of brick or stone, measuring 20 x 37 feet. The first story was the courtroom, a "bair" separated a third of the space for use by the judge, jury, and lawyers. The second story was to be divided into two jury rooms. Constructed of brick, the building cost seven hundred pounds. Completed in 1806, the first session of court was held on December 9 of that year. In 1842 remodeling occurred, bringing it in style with the dominent architectural trend, the Greek Revival. Porticos were added to the long sides of the building, making the building square to accommodate the hip roof and new cupola.

In December 1864, during Confederate General Hylan B. Lyon's march through western Kentucky his troops passed through Columbia. Lyon normally burned any courthouse he encountered, but for unknown reasons he spared the Adair County courthouse.

The second and present Adair County courthouse was ordered by the court on May 5, 1884. The plans and specifications were prepared by H. P. McDonald & Brothers of Louisville. The general contractors were Hudson and Stone Company of Columbia. William Henry Hudson, a native of Green County, had relocated to Adair County by 1851. In recognition of dedicated service in building the courthouse, the faces of Major Conover and his sister were carved in the capitals of the columns on the portico of the building. The stone for the building was quarried at Sparksville in Adair County. Additions have been made to the sides. The Adair County courthouse was listed on the National Register of Historic Places in 1974.

First Courthouse, 1806, after 1842 remodeling *(Collection of Mrs. Betty deRossett)*.

Second Courthouse, 1884 *(Caufield & Shook Collection, University of Louisville)*.

25. COVINGTON in KENTON COUNTY

Year Formed: 1840

Formed From: Campbell County

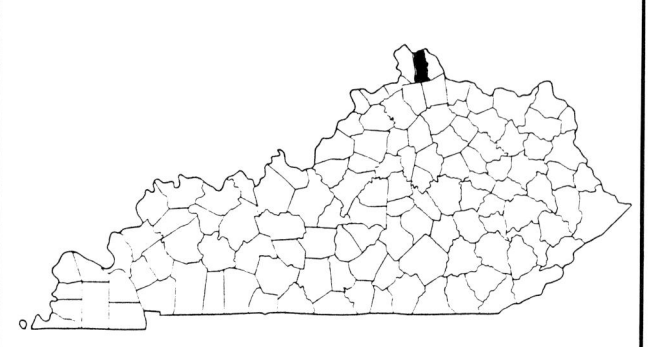
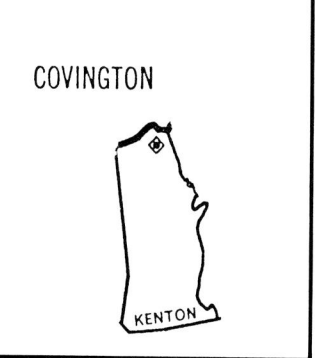

Kenton County, 90th in order of formation, was named for General Simon Kenton - a famous early Kentucky explorer. Independence was established as the first county seat in 1840 and named for Kenton County gaining its independence from Campbell County.

The first Kenton County courthouse in Covington was dedicated on June 24, 1843. Construction was authorized by the court on January 20, 1842. The elaborate Greek Revival style structure's most noted feature was the three tier cupola topped by a wooden statue of George Washington. In 1872-73 the building was extensively remodeled, the cupola removed, and Victorian features added.

The second Kenton County courthouse in Covington was built in 1899. The courthouse opened on January 15, 1902. The brick and stone, four-story, High Victorian period courthouse uses Richardsonian Romanesque and other styles in its details.

The third and present Covington-Kenton County Municipal Building replaced the courthouse in 1970. The modern building is a ten-story structure.

Lower left: First Courthouse, Covington, 1842 (*Ballou's Pictorial*).
Upper left: First Courthouse, Covington, 1842 — after 1872 remodeling (*Kenton County Public Library*).
Upper right: Second Courthouse, Covington, 1899 (*Kenton County Public Library*).

26. CYNTHIANA in HARRISON COUNTY

Year Formed: 1793

Formed From: Bourbon and Scott Counties

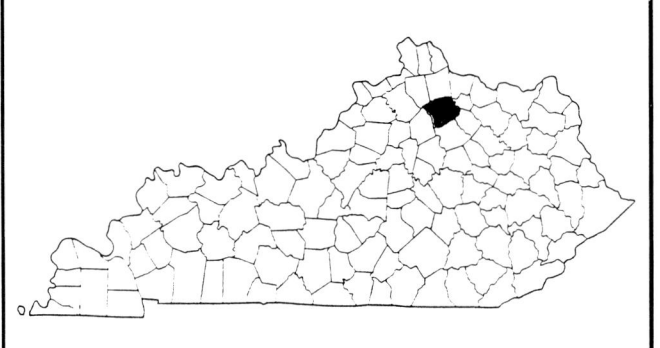

Harrison County, 18th in order of formation, was named after Colonel Benjamin Harrison of Bourbon County — a representative in the Kentucky Legislature and at the three Conventions which produced the first Kentucky Constitution in 1792. Cynthiana was established as the county seat in 1793 and named after Cynthia and Anna, the daughters of Robert Harrison, the original owner of the town site.

The first Harrison County courthouse was ordered built in June 1794. The courthouse was a two-story, log structure. The courthouse was sold in 1816 to help pay for its replacement.

The second Harrison County courthouse was built in 1816.

Gresham Forrest, William Brown, William Moore, James Kelley, and Thomas Holt were appointed commissioners to superintend construction. The courthouse was a brick, two-story building of the foursquare form measuring 50 feet square and covered by a hip roof with a cupola in the center. The courthouse cost approximately $12,000. This courthouse burned on January 24, 1851, destroying many records.

The third and present Harrison County courthouse was begun in 1851 and finished in 1853. The court approved the plan for the courthouse on July 14, 1851. John Huddleston was the original contractor hired on December 8, 1851, but failed to complete the courthouse. On November 8, 1852, the court made a new contract with R. M. and William B. Calhoon to finish the courthouse for $2,270. The building was completed in November of 1853. In 1856, the clock and bell were added to the cupola. John Hunt Morgan used the courthouse to jail several hundred Union soldiers after a battle in Cynthiana on July 17, 1862. The building was renovated in 1877 at a cost of $1,800. By 1915 the court had outgrown the facility and planned to replace the courthouse with a new structure. However, John T. Gillig, one of Kentucky's outstanding architects of the period and designer of several local buildings, convinced the court to add wings to the old building. The court approved Gillig's idea and hired him to execute the project, which was completed the next year. The Harrison County courthouse was listed on the National Register of Historic Places in 1974.

Third Courthouse, 1851 (Perrin's *History of Harrison County*).

Third Courthouse, 1851 — after wings added *(The Kentucky Historical Society)*.

27. DANVILLE IN BOYLE COUNTY

Year Formed: 1842

Formed From: Lincoln and Mercer Counties

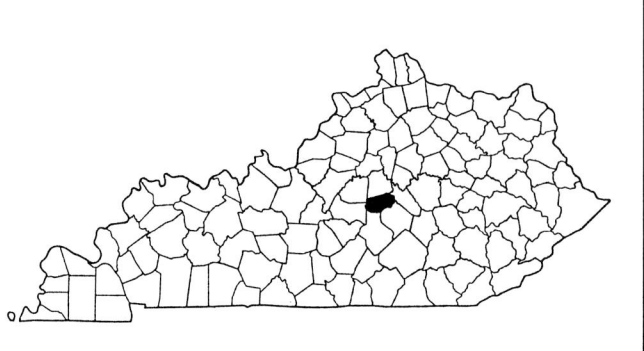
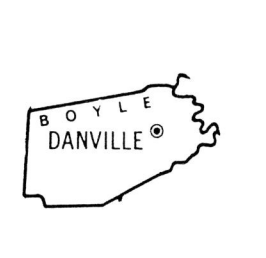

Boyle County, 94th in order of formation, was named for Judge John Boyle of Mercer County — Chief Justice of the Kentucky Supreme Court (1810-1826). Danville, established in 1785, held the first court of the state of Kentucky after separation from Virginia on March 14, 1785. Danville was selected as the county seat immediately upon the creation of Boyle County.

The first Boyle County courthouse was one of the first orders of business of the new county in 1842. The court specified that the new structure not cost over $8,000. Robert Montgomery was the general contractor, James Parr the carpenter, and John Cowan, a slave, laid the stone foundation. The building, although occupied in 1844, remained unfinished until April 1846. The courthouse burned in 1860.

The second Boyle County courthouse was built in 1860-62. James R. Carrigan, local builder and architect, adapted a design from Samuel Sloan's *City and Suburban Architecture,* a popular builder's guide published in 1859. Carrigan, also the contractor, completed the Italianate style courthouse in the summer of 1862 at a cost of $15,000. The court only held one session in the building before it was taken over as a hospital by the United States Army following the Battle of Perryville on October 8, 1862. Damage by the troops forced renovation of the courthouse during the years 1873 to 1875. Carrigan supervised this work as well, including the addition of fireplaces. The rear addition was added in 1899 and others alterations have been made this century. The Boyle County courthouse was listed on the National Register of Historic Places in 1973.

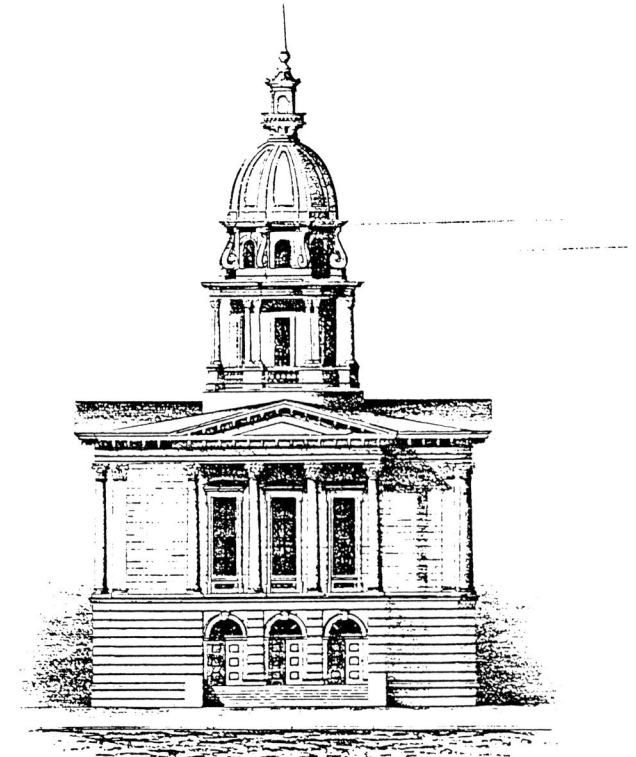

Second Courthouse, 1862 (*Design VII, Plate 42 — Samuel Sloan's City and Suburban Architecture, 1859*).

29. EDDYVILLE in LYON COUNTY

Year Formed: 1854

Formed From: Caldwell County

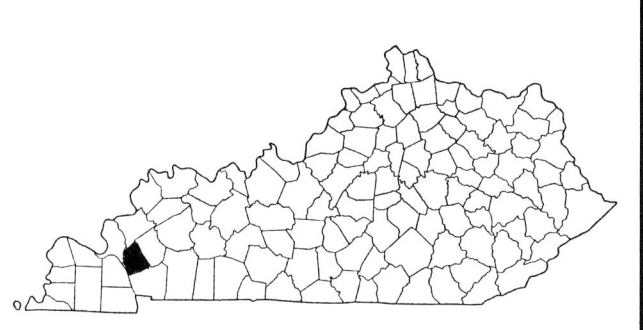

Lyon County, 102nd in order of formation, was named for Chittenden Lyon of Caldwell County — a Revolutionary War veteran and congressman, who was re-elected while imprisoned for remarks concerning the Alien & Sedition Acts. Eddyville was established as the county seat and is named for the eddies in the Cumberland River.

Little is known of Lyon County courthouses.

The first Lyon County courthouse was probably built shortly after 1854. In December 1864, during Confederate General Hylan B. Lyon's march through western Kentucky his troops passed through Eddyville. No reference is made to a courthouse located there. If so, Lyon likely would have burned it as was his normal practice. He did burn a "corral or a place of rendezvous of the negros."

The present Lyon County courthouse is a single story building of modern construction from 1961. James Allen Clark is the architect of the courthouse.

Left: First Courthouse, c. 1854 *(William Turner)*.

Right: First Courthouse, c. 1854 — after remodeling *(The Courier-Journal)*.

28. DIXON in
WEBSTER COUNTY

Year Formed: 1860

Formed From: Henderson, Hopkins, and Union Counties

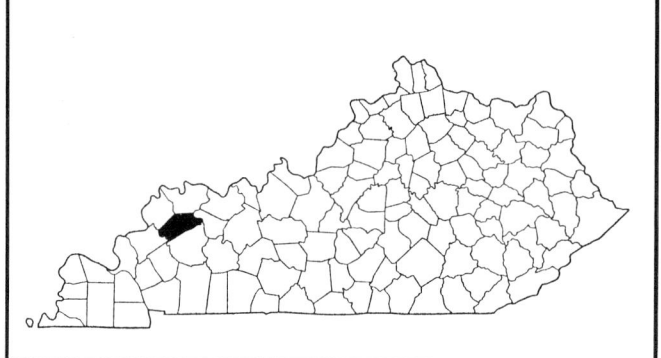

Webster County, 109th in order of formation, was named for Daniel Webster of Massachusetts — noted American statesman. Dixon was established as the county seat and named for Archibald Dixon.

The first Webster County courthouse was built shortly after formation of the county in 1860. No description is known of this courthouse.

The second Webster County courthouse was constructed with a grant provided by the Public Works Administration of the New Deal in 1939-40. C. W. Thomason, Assistant District Supervisor in charge of buildings; A. B. Cates, Area Engineer; Lawrence Casner, architect of Madisonville were employed by the P.W.A. and Russell Petrie, field engineer-Portland Cement Association. The structure was to cost about $143,000. The courthouse was constructed of poured concrete which utilized maximum manpower, a main objective of New Deal projects. Mrs. Lawrence Casner, wife of the architect, carved the ornaments, which were later converted to concrete.

29. EDDYVILLE in LYON COUNTY

Year Formed: 1854

Formed From: Caldwell County

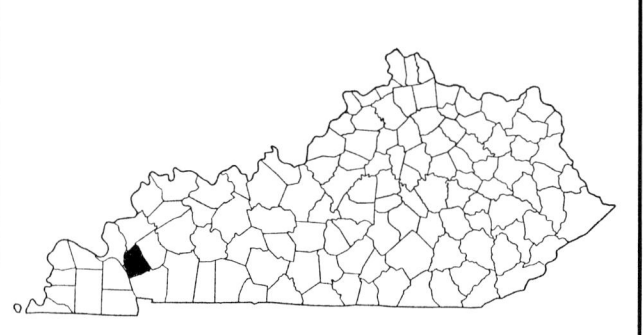

Lyon County, 102nd in order of formation, was named for Chittenden Lyon of Caldwell County — a Revolutionary War veteran and congressman, who was re-elected while imprisoned for remarks concerning the Alien & Sedition Acts. Eddyville was established as the county seat and is named for the eddies in the Cumberland River.

Little is known of Lyon County courthouses.

The first Lyon County courthouse was probably built shortly after 1854. In December 1864, during Confederate General Hylan B. Lyon's march through western Kentucky his troops passed through Eddyville. No reference is made to a courthouse located there. If so, Lyon likely would have burned it as was his normal practice. He did burn a "corral or a place of rendezvous of the negros."

The present Lyon County courthouse is a single story building of modern construction from 1961. James Allen Clark is the architect of the courthouse.

Left: First Courthouse, c. 1854 *(William Turner)*.

Right: First Courthouse, c. 1854 — after remodeling *(The Courier-Journal)*.

30. EDMONTON in METCALFE COUNTY

Year Formed: 1860

Formed From: Adair, Barren, Cumberland, Green, and Monroe Counties

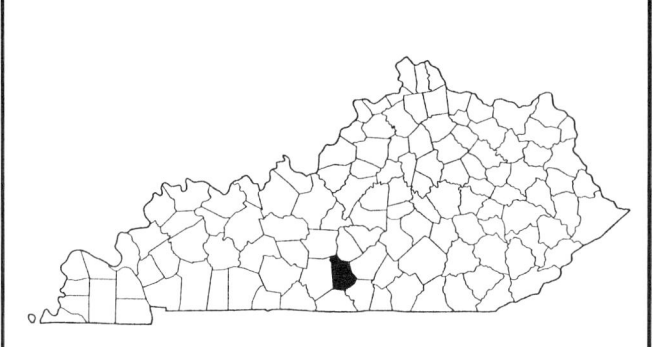

Metcalfe County, 106th in order of formation, was named for Governor Thomas Metcalfe of Nicholas County, who also served as congressman and senator. Edmonton was established as the county seat.

The first Metcalfe County courthouse was built in 1860. The only description of the building simply states it to be a "wooden building." Confederate guerillas burned the courthouse in March, 1865.

The second and present Metcalfe County courthouse was built in 1868-69. Thomas E. Young, W.R. Terry, William Evans, and R.R. Dohoney were appointed commissioners to supervise construction. They chose H. P. Bradshaw, architect of Louisville, to design the courthouse. Henry Perry was contracted to build the courthouse on September 29, 1868 for $9,550. The brick, two-story building of Italianate design has since lost the principal decorative feature, brackets supporting the roof overhang. The courthouse was renovated by 1967, including the addition of new front steps.

31. ELIZABETHTOWN in HARDIN COUNTY

Year Formed: 1792

Formed From: Nelson County

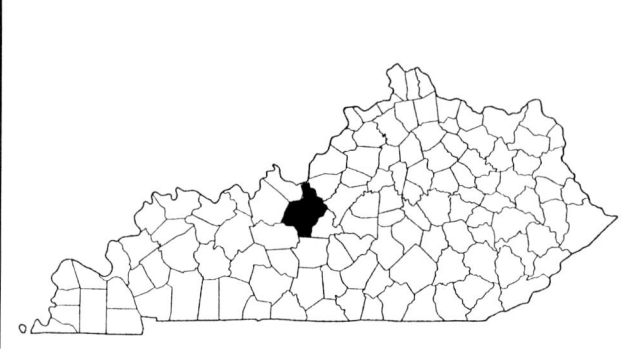

Hardin County, 15th in order of formation, was named in honor of Colonel John Hardin of Washington and Nelson Counties — a veteran of the Revolutionary War and early Kentucky explorer killed by Indians. Elizabethtown was established as the county seat and named after the wife of Mr. Hynes who laid out the town.

The first Hardin County courthouse was let in March 1795 and completed the next August. The courthouse was built of yellow poplar logs by John Crutcher for 66 pounds.

The second Hardin County courthouse was built in 1804-06. John Crutcher, Ben Helm, Robert Hudson, Samuel Haycraft, and John W. Holt were appointed commissioners for construction. The contract for construction was let to John Perceful on April 18, 1804. The courthouse, a two-story, brick structure, was completed on December 22, 1806. This building was burned during December, 1864 by troops under Gen. Hylan B. Lyons.

The third Hardin County courthouse was built in 1872-74. The brick, two-story courthouse was built in the Italianate style. In 1906 the cupola was added to the courthouse. The courthouse burned on December 6, 1932.

The fourth and current Hardin County courthouse was started in May 1933. Thomas Nolan of Louisville was the architect and H. G. Wittenburg the contractor. The courthouse is a brick, three-story structure of classical Beaux-Arts design. The new courthouse was dedicated on March 8, 1934, and cost $64,500.

Third Courthouse, 1872 (*Caufield & Shook Collection, University of Louisville Photographic Archives*).

32. ELKTON in TODD COUNTY

Year Formed: 1819

Formed From: Christian and Logan Counties

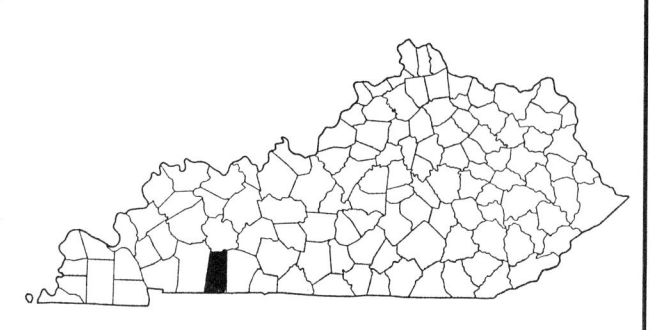
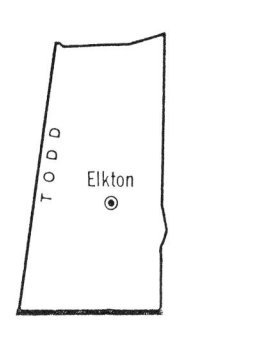

Todd County, 64th in order of formation, was named in honor of Colonel John Todd, an early resident of Boonsborough and an 1780 delegate to the Virginia Legislature from Kentucky County, later killed at the Battle of Blue Licks. Elkton was established as the county seat.

The first Todd County courthouse was built in 1821. Archibald Bristow, Roger Burns, Thomas Haddon, Elisha Edwards, and Gideon Thompson were appointed commissioners to plan the courthouse. The courthouse was described as "a two-story, 40 foot square brick building," a foursqaure form with a hip roof topped by a cupola. Major John Gray, the original owner of the land composing Elkton, donated the courthouse square and the labor to build this courthouse. Due to a lack of funds, completion of the building was delayed until September of 1822.

The second Todd County courthouse was built in 1835-36. At the meeting of November 11, 1834, the court determined a new courthouse was needed. The committee appointed by the court to secure a plan, choose the site, and let the contract contained numerous individuals at different times, too numerous to mention. The adopted plan was designed by R. Rowland, possibly Reuben E. Rowland who built the Calloway County courthouse of 1823. Jesse Russell was awarded the contract in April 1835. A legend involving the construction says that a different brick mason laid each of the four sides of the courthouse and the mason performing the best would receive a gold watch. Although this story can not be documented, a Mr. Shemwell is said to have received a new coat for the prize. The courthouse is a two-story, brick structure of the foursquare form, incorporating Greek Revival style details. During the Civil War the building was used as a Union headquarters. The wear on the building resulted in an 1871 refurbishing which included the addition of the cupola in the Second Empire style. The building has been renovated several other times including a $57,000 interior remodeling in 1961. This Todd County courthouse was listed on the National Register of Historic Places in 1975. The building has been retained even though a new courthouse has been built.

The third and current Todd County courthouse was built in 1975-76. The courthouse is a long, single-story, brick structure of colonial styling with a Doric order front portico and keystone arches over the windows. A dome crowns the building.

Second Courthouse, 1835 — in April, 1936
(The Courier-Journal).

33. FALMOUTH in PENDLETON COUNTY

Year Formed: 1798

Formed From: Bracken and Campbell Counties

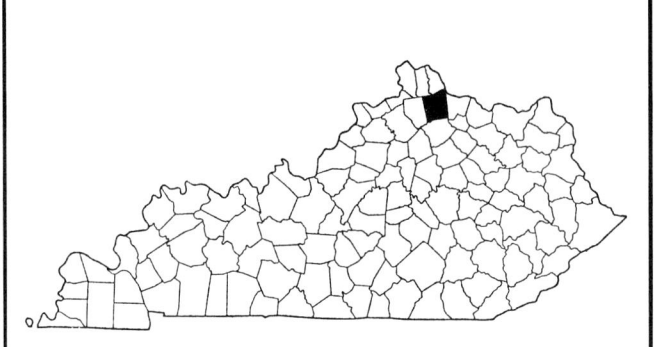
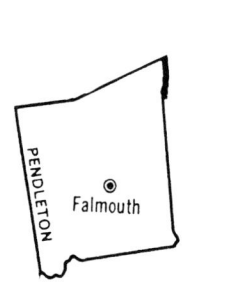

Pendleton County, 28th in order of formation, was named in honor of Edmund Pendleton of Virginia — president of the Virginia court of appeals, and the Virginia convention of 1775, he also served two terms in the United States Congress. Falmouth was established as the county seat and is named for Falmouth, Virginia, the birthplace of John Waller, who laid out the town and donated the courthouse square.

The building of the first Pendleton County courthouse commenced immediately upon formation of the county in 1798 and reached completion in 1800. The courthouse was a stone building of approximately square dimensions.

The second and current Pendleton County courthouse was built in 1848. The courthouse was a simple two-story, brick building of rectangular shape. The pilasters on the original facade indicate the building to have originally been in the Greek Revival style. In 1884, a remodeling took place to bring the building to Victorian standards. An addition was made to the south side of the building in front of which a clock tower connects the older structure. Other Victorian period trim was added as well, including the corbeled brick, brackets at the roof line, and the carved lintels over the windows. In 1975 the building underwent another renovation which included a new addition to the rear and sandblasting the exterior to reveal the original color. The Pendleton County courthouse was listed on the National Register of Historic Places in 1983 as a contributing property of a historic district.

Second Courthouse, 1848, after 1887 remodeling
(*Collection of Mr. Warren J. Shonert*).

34. FLEMINGSBURG in FLEMING COUNTY

Year Formed: 1798

Formed From: Mason County

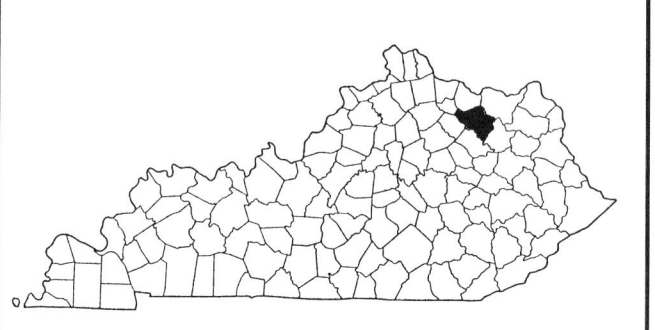

Fleming County, 28th in order of formation, was named for Colonel John Fleming — he came from Virginia in 1787 and soon established "Fleming Station," which became the nucleus of Fleming County. Flemingsburg was established as the county seat in 1798 and is also named for Colonel Fleming.

The first Fleming County courthouse was built in 1798 or 1799 and is believed to have been a log structure.

The second Fleming County courthouse was started in 1828 and completed in 1830. Samuel Stockwell was awarded the contract to build the courthouse, but subcontracted with James Eckels, who had a number of trained slaves with skills ranging from brick making to carving the fine interior and exterior woodwork. The building was of the foursquare form and was considered one of the finest examples of Federal architecture in Kentucky. The portico seen in photos of the building was added in 1869. This courthouse was demolished in September 1951, not due to bad condition, but because Nelson Fant bequeathed the county $105,000 towards construction of a new courthouse.

The third and current Fleming County courthouse was built in 1951-52. The courthouse was designed by Kenroy, Cormack and Scott, engineers and architects. The building unsuccessfully tries to emulate the style and details of the former building including a modern fan doorway. The Fleming County courthouse was listed on the National Register of Historic Places in 1985 as a contributing property of a historic district.

Second Courthouse, 1828 (*J. Winston Coleman Collection, Transylvania University*).

35. FRANKFORT in FRANKLIN COUNTY

Year Formed: 1794

Formed From: Mercer, Shelby, and Woodford Counties

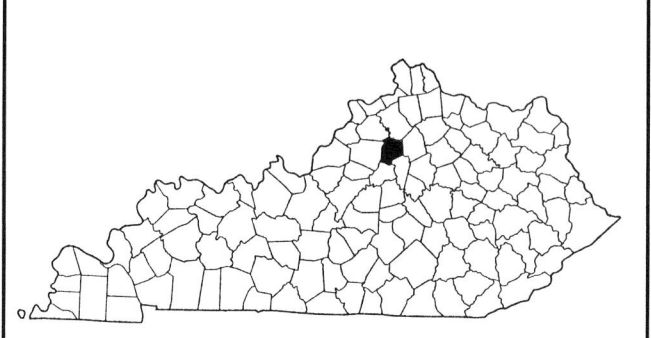

Franklin County, 18th in order of formation, was named for Benjamin Franklin. Frankfort was established as the county seat in 1795 and named for the German town.

The first Franklin County courthouse was first conceived in 1802 and in April, 1803, the court ordered bids for construction be accepted. Christopher Greenup, Daniel James, and Daniel Weisiger were appointed commissioners to superintend construction in May, 1803. Built on the southeast corner of the Capitol Square, the courthouse was completed on September 15, 1806. The building was a three-story, brick structure approximately 40 feet square with a front portico consisting of four brick columns. A third-story was added and paid for by the local Masonic lodge — Hiram No. 4.

The second and current Franklin County courthouse was needed by 1831. The first consideration, finding a new site, was accomplished when three leading citizens, John H. Hanna, J. Dudley, and J. J. Marshall conveyed the site on St. Clair Street. Commissioners James Shannon, Henry Wingate, Mason Brown and Phillip Swigert were appointed to procure a plan for the courthouse. In June, 1832, noted architect Gideon Shryock submitted the accepted design. The two-story, cut stone courthouse is a Greek Revival style, temple-front building. The building was completed, with Shryock as supervisor, in November, 1835, at a cost of $12,500.

The second courthouse went through its first major renovation in 1909, supervised by local architect, Leo L. Oberwarth. The major alteration was moving the courtroom from the first to the second floor, leaving more space for court offices on the first floor. The rear of the building extended back 30 feet and the roof line was raised three feet. The building went through renovations in 1927 and 1949 as well. The Franklin County courthouse was listed on the National Register of Historic Places in 1971 as a contributing property of a historic district.

Second Courthouse, 1832 — in 1910 *(The Kentucky Historical Society)*.

36. FRANKLIN in SIMPSON COUNTY

Year Formed: 1819

Formed From: Allen, Logan, and Warren Counties

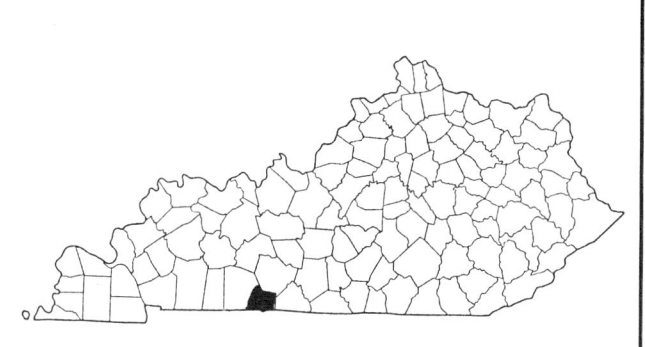
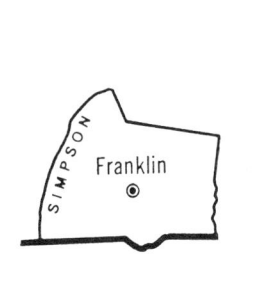

Simpson County, 63rd in order of formation, was named for Captain John Simpson, a veteran of the War of 1812, elected speaker of the Kentucky House of Representatives and later to the United States Congress. Franklin was established as the county seat and named for Benjamin Franklin.

The first Simpson County courthouse was built in 1822. The courthouse is only described as a log building.

The second Simpson County courthouse was built in 1860. The courthouse was two-story, brick building covered by a hip roof with a central cupola. In 1869, the suggestion was made that a fire pump and hoses be installed. This suggestion went unheeded and on May 16, 1882, the courthouse burned, destroying all the county records. Arson had been attempted twice, prior to this successful attempt.

The third and present Simpson County courthouse was built in 1882-83. I. J. Bogan, James N. LaRue, and W. W. Bush were appointed commissioners to supervise construction. On July 14, 1882, the committee selected a design provided by McDonald Brothers, architects of Louisville, the standard courthouse design of that firm. The building was finished in the spring of 1883. The McDonald Brothers later designed the First Franklin Presbyterian Church (1886), the Franklin Female College (1889), and the Goodnight House (1893). In 1962, wings were added to either side of the building, attempting to match the original style. The Simpson County courthouse was listed on the National Register of Historic Places in 1980.

Second Courthouse, 1860 *(The Kentucky Historical Society).*

Third Courthouse, 1882 *((University of Kentucky Special Collection)*

37. FRENCHBURG in MENIFEE COUNTY

Year Formed: 1869

Formed From: Bath, Montgomery, Morgan, Powell, and Wolfe Counties

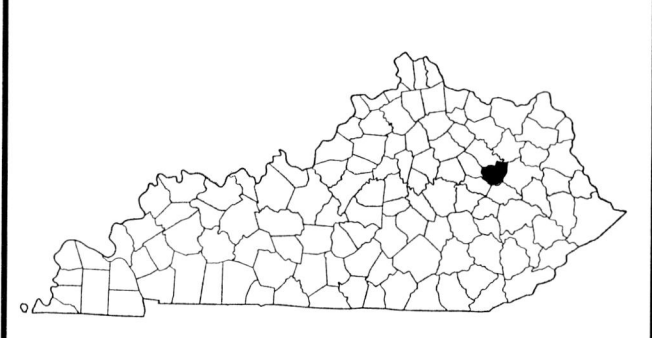

Menifee County, 113th in order of formation, was named for Richard A. Menifee — attorney and congressman. Frenchburg was established as the county seat and named for Judge Richard French who unsuccessfully opposed Menifee in the Congressional race of 1837.

The first Menifee County courthouse, a frame, two-story building with a large square cupola rising above the entrance was built in 1871-72. James M. Oliver designed and probably built the courthouse. This building was replaced in 1928.

The second and current Menifee County courthouse, built in 1928, is a stone, two-story structure. The courthouse entrance resembles a castellated Gothic tower which rises a story above the roof line and is topped by a colonial cupola.

First Courthouse, 1871 *(Collection of Mr. John Prewitt)*.

38. GEORGETOWN in SCOTT COUNTY

Year Formed: 1792

Formed From: Woodford County

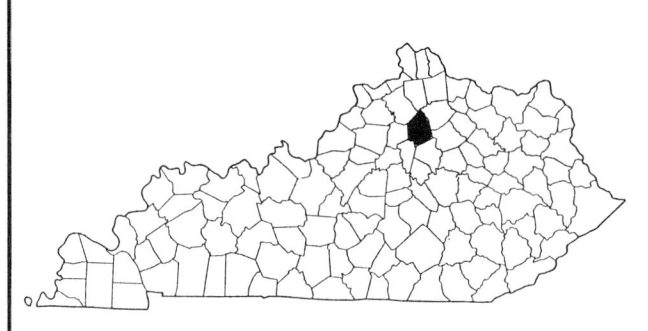

Scott County, 11th in order of formation, is named for Governor Charles Scott, a veteran of the Revolutionary War and an elected governor of Kentucky in 1808. McClelland's Station, settled in October 1775, was the original county settlement. In 1784 the named was changed to Lebanon and it became more of a town environment. The name was again changed in 1790 to Georgetown, in honor of George Washington, and became the county seat when the county was formed.

The first Scott County courthouse was built in 1792-93. Bartlett Collins, William Henry, and John Mosley were appointed commissioners to obtain a suitable plan. The courthouse is described as having a first story of stone and the second of frame construction. John Garnett built the first story of the courthouse for his low bid of 319 pounds and finished the building in February 1793. Later that year the court contracted with Barlett Collins to add the second floor at a cost of $1,800.

The second Scott County courthouse was built in 1816. Elijah Craig, Samuel Shepard, John Stevenson, and John Thompson were appointed commissioners to select a plan and let the contract for construction. They specified the building be a two-story, brick structure of the foursquare form measuring 50 feet square with a front door flanked by pillars. The building was to be similar to the Woodford County courthouse. Rhodes Smith contracted to build the courthouse for $5,800. On August 9, 1837, this courthouse burned, destroying the county records.

The third Scott County courthouse was built in 1845-46. A committee of twelve was appointed to select a plan and receive bids for construction at the May and July 1845 meetings of the court. The courthouse was a brick, two-story structure of the Greek Revival style. The court accepted the completed building at the October 1846 term of the court. This courthouse burned in 1876.

The fourth and present Scott County courthouse was built in 1877. Thomas Boyd, architect of Pittsburg, designed this courthouse, as well as the Jessamine County and Fayette County courthouses of the same period. Boyd received a premium of $150 in December 1876 and was retained to supervise construction. Bids were opened in February 1877, Isaac Graveson of Cincinnati being the lowest at $34,600. The building was restored in 1971 at a cost of $425,000 and the tower rebuilt in 1979-80 for $70,000. The Scott County courthouse was listed on the National Register of Historic Places in 1972.

Left: Third Courthouse, 1845 *(Sketch by Mr. Amos Lawrence from original picture by V. A. Bradley).*

Right: Fourth Courthouse, 1876 *(Perrin's History of Scott County).*

39. GLASGOW in BARREN COUNTY

Year Formed: 1798

Formed From: Green and Warren Counties

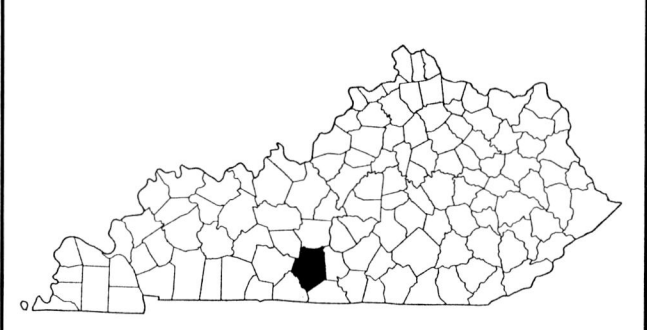

Barren County, 37th in order of formation, was named for the barrens or prairies which abound in this region of the state. Glasgow, established as the county seat in 1799, was named for the city in Scotland. The town's founder, John Gorin, donated fifty acres to establish the town, two acres of which were laid off for the public square.

The first Barren County courthouse was built in 1800. The courthouse was a rough-log, single room, which lacked chinking between the logs and had a roof made of pit-sawed clapboards. The building was located at the angle of Race and Washington Streets.

The second Barren County courthouse was built in 1802. The courthouse was of improved hewn-log construction measuring 20 feet square, and covered with wooden shingles. Colonel Simeon Buford was the contractor. The building was constructed on the northwest corner of the public square.

The third Barren County courthouse, centered on the public square, was a brick structure started in 1804 and completed in 1806. John H. Baker, John Adams, William Adams, and George Richardson were appointed by the court to supervise construction. They awarded the contract to Colonel Simeon Buford as contractor and Henry Miller as principal carpenter.

The fourth Barren County courthouse was planned in 1837 and finished in 1839. The building committee consisted of Franklin Gorin, S. M. Bagby, Henry Crutcher, George W. Trabue, and Richard Garnett. Bagby designed the building, a two-story, brick structure with a raised basement, topped by a hip roof supporting a cupola. The cupola, originally hexagonal with a small dome, later was made into a square cupola. The building is very conservative for the period, indicative of Federal styling. The building was topped by a ball and arrow weathervane/lightning rod made by J. V. J. Eubank, silversmith and tinner. This decorative addition was moved to the next building. In 1859 the courthouse was extensively repaired.

The fifth Barren County courthouse was built in 1896 during the administration of Judge G. M. Bohannan, who is greatly credited with its realization. Judge Bohannan, J. C. Hutcherson, and E. P. Chamberlain composed the building committee who selected Mason Maury of Louisville as architect. Four plans were submitted before a design was accepted. Walter Brashear of Henderson was the contractor. In 1962 Barren Countians voted to replace this structure which was considered unsafe and the building was dismantled in 1964.

The sixth and current Barren County courthouse, dedicated on May 8, 1965, was built under the administration of Judge James E. Gillenwater. Bayless, Clotfelter, and Johnson, a Lexington architectural firm, designed the courthouse and the Ernest Simpson Construction Company built the structure at a cost of $470,000. The Barren County courthouse was listed on the National Register of Historic Places in 1980.

Left: Fourth Courthouse, 1838 *(Dixon Rapp)*. Right: Fifth Courthouse, 1896 *(University of Louisville Photographic Archives)*.

40. GRAYSON in CARTER COUNTY

Year Formed: 1838

Formed From: Greenup and Lawrence Counties

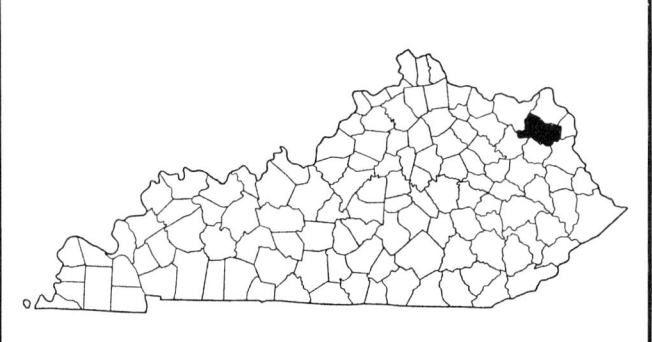

Carter County, 88th in order of formation, was named for Colonel William Grayson Carter — veteran of the Revolutionary War and an early settler of the region, who married a daughter of Isaac Shelby. Grayson, also named for Carter, was established as the county seat.

The first Carter County courthouse was a first order of business of the new court. A foursquare form brick courthouse was started in late 1838 and completed in 1840. An 1867 remodeling included raising the top of the building two feet, allowing for new brackets and the addition of a cupola, all giving the building an Italianate style updating. The court determined in 1906 that the dilapidated building had to be replaced.

The second and present Carter County courthouse was built in 1907. The courthouse is a yellow brick two-story building of classical Beaux-Arts influenced design. Unique hexagonal towers flank the corners of the building, providing usable space. In 1950 the west wing was added to the building and in 1964 the east wing was added.

First Courthouse, 1840, post-1867 *(George Wolford's Pictorial History of Carter County)*.

Second Courthouse, 1907 *(University of Kentuky Special Collections, Postcard Collection)*.

41. GREENSBURG in GREEN COUNTY

Year Formed: 1792

Formed From: Lincoln and Nelson Counties

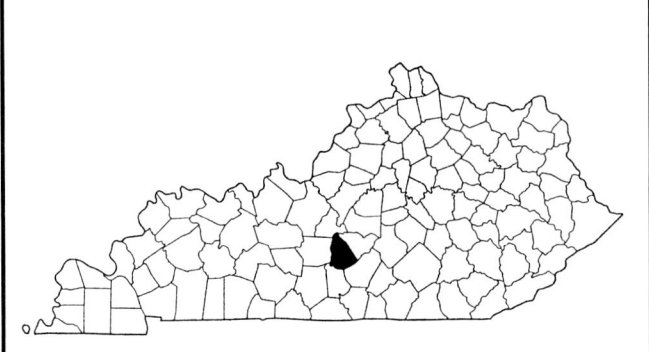

Green County, 16th in order of formation, was named for General Nathaniel Greene of Rhode Island — hero of the American Revolution. Greensburg, formerly Glover's Station, was established as the county seat in 1795 and also named for Greene.

The first Green County courthouse was built in 1796. The log courthouse was built by Isham Burke for 135 pounds.

The building of the second, one of two current, Green County courthouses commenced in 1802 and was accepted by the court on June 25, 1804. Jonathan Patterson, Daniel Brown, Elias Barbee, Jonathan Cowherd, and James Blain were appointed commissioners for construction on January 20, 1802. The contract for building the courthouse was given to Waller Bullock of Lexington. Robert Ball was in charge of the stone work, Edward J. Bullock and Daniel Lisle were the carpenters. The locally-quarried stone, two-story courthouse measures 34 x 40 feet with two-foot thick walls. The courthouse is topped by a small bell tower added in 1870. Many references have been made to tenth Kentucky Governor Thomas Metcalfe having designed and constructed the courthouse. However, no court documents substantiate this claim.

This building served as the courthouse until the third courthouse was built in 1931. The building was used until 1966 as the Green County Library. The Green County Historical Society took possession of the structure and restored it in 1972-73. The court has recently taken over parts of the building for use, supplying important funding for maintainence. This building is the oldest surviving Kentucky courthouse and is thought to be the oldest courthouse west of the Allegany Mountains, listed on the National Register of Historic Places in 1972.

The third and present Green County courthouse was built in 1930-31. The building's significance is greatly overshadowed by the second courthouse and little information is known. The courthouse is a brick, two-story building of classical Beaux-Arts style.

Second Courthouse, 1802-04 — about 1930 *(Caufield & Shook Collection, University of Louisville Photographic Archives).*

42. GREENUP in GREENUP COUNTY

Year Formed: 1803

Formed From: Mason County

Greenup County, 45th in order of formation, was named for Christopher Greenup — the third Governor of Kentucky. Greenup was established as the county seat and also named for Governor Greenup.

The first Greenup County courthouse was built in 1806. Thomas Waring, Seriah Stratton, Jesse Boone (son of Daniel Boone), Andrew Hook, and Thomas Hook were appointed commissioners for construction. The courthouse was of frame construction, using white pine. Benjamin Locke built the courthouse for $900.

The building of the second Greenup County courthouse commenced in 1811 and was finished in 1816. The courthouse was a two-story, brick structure of the foursquare form. Damaged during the 1937 flood, the courthouse was condemned and dismantled.

The third and current Greenup County courthouse was built in 1937-39 under a grant provided by the Public Works Administration of the New Deal. Stone for the building was quarried in neighboring Lewis County. Construction began January 4, 1938, and was completed on December 2, 1940, at a total cost of $107,631. The addition to the side of the courthouse was added in 1963.

Second Courthouse, 1811 *(The Kentucky Historical Society)*.

Third Courthouse, 1937-39 — just finished *(Goodman-Paxton Collection, University of Kentucky Special Collections)*.

43. GREENVILLE in MUHLENBURG COUNTY

Year Formed: 1798

Formed From: Christian and Logan Counties

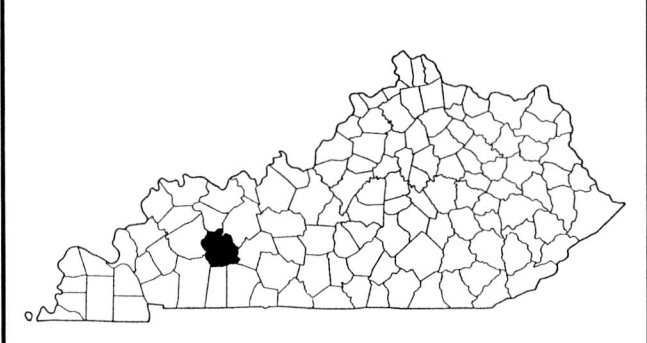

Muhlenburg County, 34th in order of formation, was named for General John Peter Gabriel Muhlenburg — hero of the Revolutionary War. Greenville, established as the county seat in 1799, was named for General Nathaniel Greene, another Revolutionary War hero.

The first Muhlenburg County courthouse was built in 1800. Henry Rhoads, Charles Lewis, and William Bell were appointed commissioners to prepare plans for the courthouse. They specified the two-story courthouse "to be built of hewn logs seven inches thick, . . . measure 26 feet by 18 feet" and covered by a shingle roof. Henry and Isaac Davis were the contractors. The court first met in the incomplete courthouse on February 25, 1800. The courthouse was finished in September.

The second Muhlenburg County courthouse was built in 1812-14. William Campbell, Henry Martin, Robert Glenn, John Dobyns, and Jeremiah Langley were appointed commissioners to draft a plan for a brick courthouse on November 11, 1811. Campbell, Glenn and John S. Eaves were appointed commissioners to supervise construction on August 9, 1813. Benjamin Coffman was chosen as the contractor and finished the courthouse in late 1814. Coffman did a poor job and by 1818 major repairs to the building commenced.

The third Muhlenburg County courthouse was built in 1834-36. In June, 1834, the court appointed James Taggart and Ephraim M. Brank, commissioners, to supervise construction of a new courthouse. The courthouse was of the foursquare form being 32 feet square, two-story building of brick. The contractor, William W. Hancock, finished the building in July of 1836. This courthouse was replaced by the current structure.

The fourth and present Muhlenburg County courthouse was built in 1907. The courthouse was designed by the Louisville architectural firm of Kenneth McDonald and William J. Dodd with Bailey and Koerner acting as the contractors. The building is a very elaborate example of the classical Beaux-Arts style. The courthouse is a two-story, brick structure fronted by a two-story, Corinthian order portico with an equally spectacular cupola. The courthouse underwent a major renovation in 1975. The Muhlenberg County courthouse was listed on the National Register of Historic Places in 1978.

Left: Third Courthouse, 1834 *(History of Muhlenburg County.)*
Right: Fourth Courthouse, 1907 *(History of Muhlenburg County).*

44. HARDINSBURG in BRECKINRIDGE COUNTY

Year Formed: 1799

Formed From: Hardin

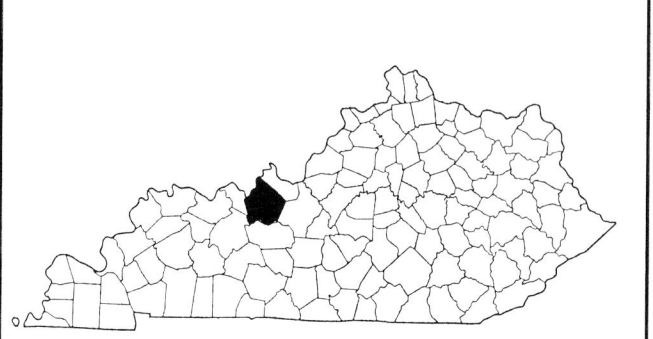

Breckinridge County, 39th in order of formation, was named for John Breckinridge of Fayette County — a leading Kentucky statesman and Attorney General of the United States under Thomas Jefferson. Hardinsburg was established as the county seat in 1800 and named for Captain William Hardin — the original settler of the area.

The first Breckinridge County courthouse was a "small log" structure built shortly after formation of the county.

The second Breckinridge County courthouse was started at the end of the Civil War, 1865, and completed four years later. The clay for bricks was dug from the location of the current Breckinridge County High School and the stone was quarried at Bennett's Quarry near Irvington. The Italianate style building cost about $37,000. Fire destroyed the building in February of 1958.

The third and present Breckinridge County courthouse was begun in May of 1958 from the designs of Roberts & Johnson, architects of Owensboro. The modern, three-story building, dedicated on July 30, 1960, cost $260,000.

Second Courthouse, 1865-69 (*R. C. Ballard Thruston Collection, The Filson Club*).

45. HARLAN in HARLAN COUNTY

Year Formed: 1819

Formed From: Floyd and Knox Counties

Harlan County, 60th in order of formation, was named for Major Silas Harlan — a veteran killed at the Battle of Blue Licks. Harlan, once known as Mount Pleasant, then Harlan Courthouse, was established as the county seat and is also named for Major Harlan.

The first Harlan County courthouse was built of log in 1820. Kentucky historian Lewis Collins described the site as follows: "The first courthouse in Harlan County was built upon a mound in Mount Pleasant upon which, in 1808, the largest forest trees were growing." The "mound" apparently refers to an Indian Mound.

The second Harlan County courthouse was built in 1838. "In August, 1838, a new court house was erected upon the same mound, requiring a deeper foundation and more digging, with these discoveries: Human bones, some small and other very large, indicating that the bodies had been buried in a sitting posture," describes Collins. The brick courthouse was supposedly burned in October 1863 by the Confederate marauders in reprisal for the burning of the Lee County Courthouse in Virginia.

The third Harlan County courthouse was built in 1870. The courthouse was a frame building built by Ben A. Rice of Tazewell, Tennessee, who supplied the wood from his local mill on the Cumberland River branch near Mill Street. The courtroom was of a unique design in the shape of a semi-circular amphitheatre rising towards the rear of the room. Its construction yielded more Indian remains. Collins reports "more human bones were dug from it, together with nicely polished weights, some pipes made of hard blue stone." This building was not torn down immediately upon construction of its successor, but used for years as the Masonic Hall and for other public meetings.

The fourth Harlan County courthouse, built in 1886-88, was the first on the present site, donated to the county by William Turner. Moses W. Howard was appointed to acquire an appropriate design. A Barbourville contractor was the low bidder and his work crew included the Gregory brothers, Alonzo, Alvay, and Walter, who relocated in Harlan. The two-story, brick courthouse was a plain Victorian period design highlighted by a large square cupola.

The fifth and present Harlan County courthouse was built in 1918-22. The courthouse is a two-story, stone structure indicative of the popular classical Beaux-Arts influence of the period. The courthouse is built of Indiana limestone, selected by then County Judge James Forrester. The jail is incorporated into the building which cost approximately $225,000. The courthouse was completed July 7, 1922.

Third Courthouse, 1870 — during Circuit Court in 1884 *(The Filson Club)*.

Fourth Courthouse, 1886 *(Harlan Daily Enterprise)*.

Fifth Courthouse, 1918 *(Caufield & Shook Collection, University of Louisville)*.

46. HARRODSBURG in MERCER COUNTY

Year Formed: 1785

Formed From: Lincoln County

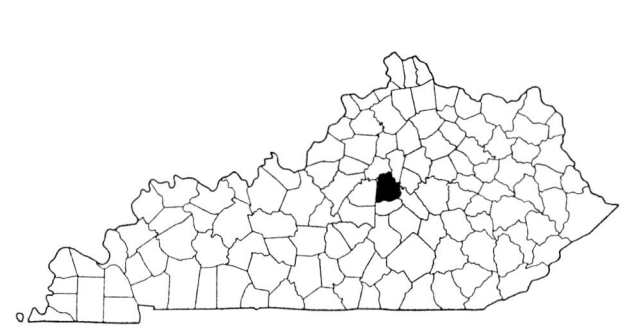

Mercer County, 6th in order of formation, was named in honor of General Hugh Mercer, a military leader and physician killed in the Revolutionary War. Harrodsburg was originally the county seat of Lincoln County. When Mercer County split, Harrodsburg was located in the new county and became the county seat. Harrodsburg was named for Captain James Harrod, an early explorer and settler who laid out the town.

The first Mercer County courthouse was built in 1787-89. On October 24, 1787, the court contracted with John Mosby and Jacob Froman to build the courthouse for 1200 pounds. The building was a stone two-story structure measuring approximately 39 x 31 feet. When completed on July 29, 1789, the completed building actually measured slightly larger.

The second Mercer County courthouse was built in 1817-20. At the October 7, 1817 meeting of the court, commissioners were appointed to provide a plan for a new courthouse. At the December 1st meeting, Dr. William Robertson, Samuel Daviess, Joseph Morgan, Edward Worthington, John Eccles and David Sutton were appointed commissioners to "perfect" the plan and let construction of the courthouse. Robert Neil was the contractor for the building and Joel P. Williams did the masonry and R. K. Fallis, the fine carving of the window frames and other woodwork. By 1910 the building was condemned and W. W. Stephenson started a movement to replace the aged building.

The third and present Mercer County courthouse was built in 1912-13. After considering plans by Leo Oberwarth of Frankfort, Weber Brothers of Cincinnati, T. Gaastra of Chicago and Andrew J. Bryan of the Falls City Construction Company, the latter was selected. Falls City Construction Company was awarded the construction contract, for $24,237, on June 11, 1912. Martin Geertz, architect of Lexington, supervised construction of the classical Beaux-Arts influenced structure. The old building was incorporated into the new structure which was finished in mid-1913. The courthouse suffered from a fire on May 15, 1928. Churchill & Gillig, architects of Lexington, were in charge of renovating the building and Peter Nolan Wilson of Harrodsburg was the contractor. The only visible difference is the replacement of the original dome shaped cupola. The Mercer County courthouse was listed on the National Register of Historic Places in 1980 as a contributing property of a historic district.

Left: Second Courthouse, 1820 *(Caufield & Shook Collection, University of Louisville Photographic Archives)*.

Right: Third Courthouse, 1912, *(J. Winston Coleman Collection, Transylvania University)*.

47. HARTFORD IN OHIO COUNTY

Year Formed: 1798

Formed From: Hardin County

Ohio County, 35th in order of formation, as named for the Ohio River, then the county's northern border. Hartford was established as the county seat in 1799.

The first Ohio County courthouse was built in 1800. The first county building was a one-story, log jail, built in 1799 by William L. Barnard for 53 pounds, 2 shillings. In 1800 the court ordered the courthouse be built as the second story of the jail to be of the same dimensions but to extend six feet in the front forming a overhang supported by three pillars. Charles Wallace was the builder at a cost of $1,800. In such poor condition, the building collapsed in 1813 and later that year was burned in celebration of one of Commodore Perry's naval victories.

The second Ohio County courthouse was built in 1813-15. The courthouse was a brick, two-story structure of the foursquare form supported by a stone foundation. Charles Wallace built this courthouse at a cost of $3,036. On December 20, 1864, during Confederate General Hylan B. Lyon's march through western Kentucky his troops passed through Hartford. They captured the local garrison and burned the courthouse. Through the efforts of Samuel Peyton, a local physician, the records were saved.

The third Ohio County courthouse was built in 1865-67. The courthouse was a brick, two-story structure. William H. Miller was the contractor, Henry Armendt the carpenter. I. H. Luce, A. D. White, William Kenney, David B. Ham, Louis Armendt, and a black man, Dennis Ross, were also associated with construction of the building. The building cost $18,500. The courthouse was demolished in November of 1940 to make way for the current structure.

The fourth and present Ohio County courthouse was built in 1940-43. The courthouse was built under a grant from the Public Works Administration of the New Deal, which provided 57% of the total cost of $135,000. The building, constructed of 3100 tons of poured concrete, measures 75 x 101 feet. Walter Scott Roberts was the architect and Wescott & Thornton, the engineers, all of Owensboro. Robert C. McLellan was the supervisor of construction with L. C. Riggins taking over towards completion. The courthouse was dedicated May of 1943.

First Courthouse, 1800 (*Mrs. Forrest P. Bell*).

Third Courthouse, 1865 (*Historic Hartford Sesquicentennial, June 1, 1958*).

Fourth Courthouse, 1940-43, original drawing by Walter Scott Roberts (*Goodman-Paxton Collection, University of Kentucky*).

48. HAWESVILLE in HANCOCK COUNTY

Year Formed: 1829

Formed From: Breckinridge, Daviess, and Ohio Counties

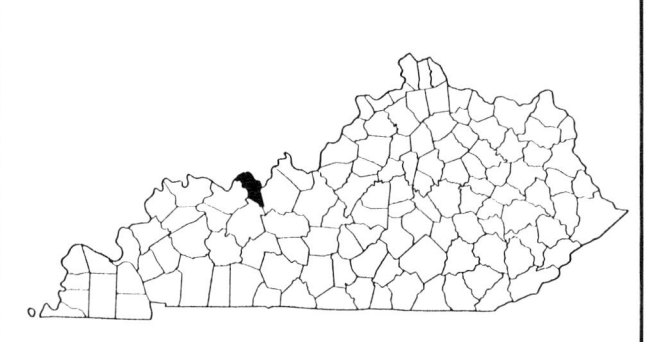

Hancock County, 83rd in order of formation, was named in honor of John Hancock — first signer of the Declaration of Independence. Hawesville was established as the county seat — named for Richard Hawes who originally owned the town site.

The first Hancock County courthouse was ordered built shortly after formation of the county in 1829. The order was given as follows: "The plan of said court house in Hawesville to be after the court house in Hardinsburg, except to be constructed so there shall be a chimney and fire place below and that the roof shall be so formed as to receive a cupola. The lower walls of said court house to be thirteen inches thick and the upper story nine inches thick." The courthouse described above is a brick, two-story building of the foursquare form with a hip roof supporting a cupola. The Breckinridge County courthouse at Hardinsburg of this period is reported to be log, but must have been very close to this description.

The second Hancock County courthouse was built from 1867-68. B. C. Davidson, Green Sterett, Stephen Powers, and R. Y. Bush were appointed commissioners for construction, but the latter two resigned and were replaced by Thomas H. Ayres and J. B. Ireland in March 1868. The Boston, Massachusetts architectural firm of Boyd, Mursina, and Boyd were contracted to design the courthouse in 1866. Partner Robert Boyd contracted to built the courthouse for $14,975. The courthouse was a brick, three-story structure of transitional styling combining Greek and Italianate styles. By the time the courthouse was finished on November 30, 1868, the final cost had risen to $21,353.17. The Hancock County courthouse was listed on the National Register of Historic Places in 1975. The courthouse was restored in 1978.

Second Courthouse, 1867 — from rear about 1935 (*Goodman-Paxton Collection, University of Kentucky Special Collections*).

49. HAZARD in PERRY COUNTY

Year Formed: 1820

Formed From: Clay and Floyd Counties

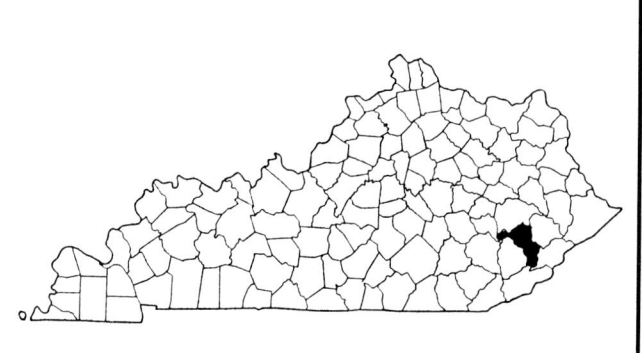

Perry County, 68th in order of formation, was named in honor of Commodore Oliver Hazard Perry — naval hero during the War of 1812. Hazard, referred to as Perry Courthouse until 1854, was established as the county seat.

The first Perry County courthouse may have been built as early as 1823. Most likely this courthouse was a log structure. In March 1836, the court appointed A. F. Caldwell and Elijah Combs to determine needed repairs to the building. They reported the county needed a new courthouse.

The second Perry County courthouse was built in 1836. Elijah Combs, Jesse Combs, and A. F. Caldwell presented the plan for the new courthouse at the November 1836 meeting of the court. The plans called for a single-story, brick building measuring 48 x 24 feet. George Martin was low bidder to construct the courthouse at a cost of $2,200.

The third Perry County courthouse was built in 1866. The courthouse was a two-story, frame structure. Harve Henly was the builder. He used the brick from the old courthouse for the chimneys of the new building. Fire consumed this building sometime between 1885 and 1890.

The court ordered a building similar to the Lee County courthouse of 1871 for the fourth Perry County courthouse. Accordingly this courthouse would have been a two-story, brick building. Colonel L. H. N. Salyers was the contractor. This courthouse burned in 1911.

An elaborate Colonial Revival style building designed in 1911-12 by B. F. Smith, architect of Washington, D.C., was the fifth Perry County courthouse. In 1934-38 an addition was added to the rear of the building under a grant provided by the Public Works Administration of the New Deal.

The sixth and present Perry County courthouse was built in 1964-65. The courthouse is a modern three-story building of classical design being fronted by a recessed Doric order portico. H. A. Spaulding was the architect of the building. The contract for construction was awarded to W. D. Johnson of Ashland on June 22, 1964. The cornerstone was laid on September 23, 1965 and dedicated on September 17, 1966. The courthouse cost $910,000, of which the Federal Government provided $575,267.

Fifth Courthouse, 1911 *(Library of Congress)*.

50. HENDERSON in HENDERSON COUNTY

Year Formed: 1798

Formed From: Christian County

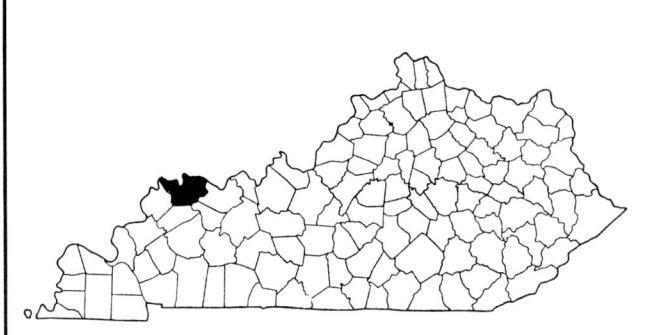
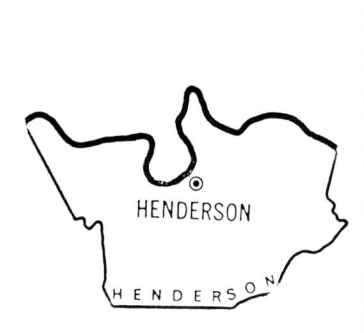

Henderson County, 38th in order of formation, was named for Colonel Richard Henderson — an early settler who purchased a large section of Kentucky from the Cherokee Indians, later settling at Boonesborough. Henderson was established as the county seat upon formation of the county and named for Henderson as well.

The first Henderson County courthouse was a log school house converted for use by the court for $50. The school house was used until 1814 when the first permanent courthouse was built.

The second Henderson County courthouse was built in 1813-14. At the January 1813 meeting of the court Daniel McBride, Samuel Hopkins, Jr., James M. Hamilton, and Ambrose were appointed commissioners to plan the new courthouse. Samuel Hopkins, Jr. drew the plan and wrote the specifications adopted by the court. Philip Barbour, on February 6, 1813, contracted to built the courthouse for $5140. The building was specified as a two-story, brick structure measuring 44 x 28 feet, covered by a gable roof. The courthouse was to be completed by October 1, 1814. James Alaves added an ell to the courthouse about 1830. This courthouse served until June, 1843, when it was dismantled.

The third County courthouse was built in 1842-43. By the April, 1840, meeting of the court it was determined a new courthouse was necessary. A plan was not approved until May ,1842, and in June construction began. A plan by Edmund H. Hopkins was approved and he was appointed a committee of one to supervise construction. Littleberry Weaver contracted for construction for $9,400. James Bacon was the sub-contractor for the woodwork, assisted by Philip Van Bussum. The brick, two-story courthouse measuring 48 x 70 feet was of the popular Greek Revival style of the period, fronted by a large, two-story, doric portico. The courthouse was completed in October 1843.

In 1858, the interior alterations were made from the plans of J. J. Kriss, architect. I. G. Livers was the contractor for the $1,000 job. During the Civil War the courthouse was badly abused by occupying forces and in the fall of 1865 was ordered renovated. In May, 1866, plans by Mursina and Boyd of Boston were adopted, Boyd also designed the Hancock County courthouse. Weaver and Digman did the brickwork and James H. Johnson, the carpenter's work. The changes were completed in December 1866. The wings of the courthouse were added in 1875 and 1881. The building was stuccoed in approximately 1912. After one of the monumental preservation efforts in Kentucky history, the courthouse was torn down in 1963.

The fourth and present Henderson County courthouse was built in 1964-65. The courthouse is a stone, two-story structure of modern design, fronted by a semi-circular portico with unusual columns of marble. Glover Brick Company of Henderson were the contractors for the building which cost just over $500,000.

Third Courthouse, 1842 — after 1875 & 1881 wings added
(Collection of John W. Carpenter).

51. HICKMAN in FULTON COUNTY

Year Formed: 1845

Formed From: Hickman County

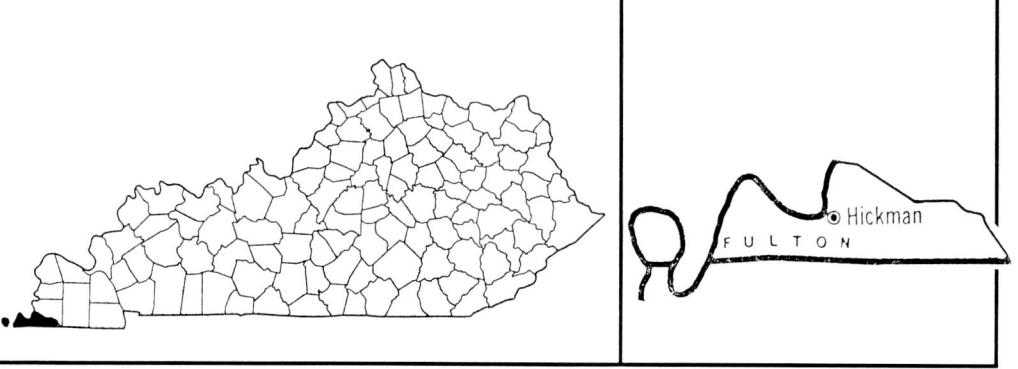

Fulton County, 99th in order of formation, was named for Robert Fulton — the engineer who greatly promoted use of steam engines in river boats. Hickman, originally Mill's Point, was established as the county seat and was the maiden name of the wife of G. W. L. Barr who laid out the town.

The first Fulton County courthouse was authorized by the court at the May 1845 session when the site was selected and $4,000 allocated for construction. The two-story, brick courthouse was completed in 1848. The most prominent feature of the courthouse was its setting on the Mississippi River.

The second and current Fulton County courthouse was authorized at a meeting of the Fulton County commissioners on May 29, 1899. In January 1901, Frank P. Milburn architect of Columbia, South Carolina, submitted the accepted plan. W. H. Spradlin, contractor of Fulton was the low bidder for construction on January 14, 1902. The original contract was for $20,250, but that was increased by $540 as the court requested the use of red mortar to match the brick. The eclectic building uses several historical styles such as the Flemish gables, creating harmony with its river site. The courthouse was completed in the summer of 1903. The Fulton County courthouse was listed on the National Register of Historic Places in 1976.

Second Courthouse, 1884 — from 1891 *Clinton Democrat (Collection of Mr. Virginia Jewell).*

COUNTY JUDGE, FULTON COUNTY, KENTUCKY.

HICKMAN, KY., January 28, 1904.

To Whom it May Concern:

The Fulton County Court appointed Frank P. Milburn as Architect for the new Court House recently completed. His plans were satisfactory and our people feel that he has done his duty as Superintendent of the work. We have the best arranged and constructed building in Western Kentucky. All our people are well pleased and there are no complaints from any source. I take pleasure in recommending Mr. Milburn to anyone in need of an Architect, as a first-class man—knowing that they will not be disappointed should they secure his services.

Yours very truly,

H. M. KEARBY.

Judge of Fulton County Court.

52. HINDMAN in KNOTT COUNTY

Year Formed: 1884

Formed From: Breathitt, Floyd, Letcher, and Perry Counties

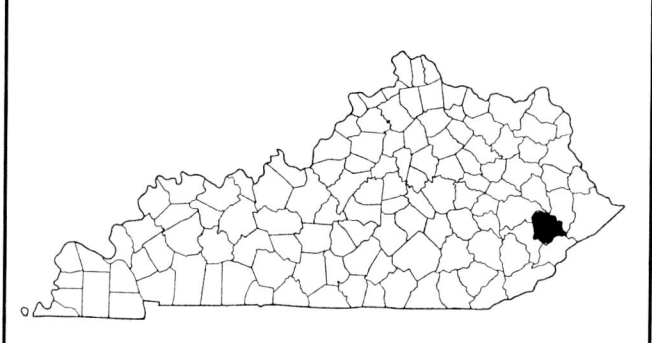
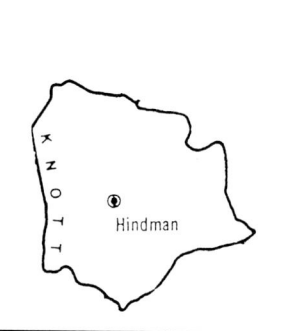

Knott County, 118th in order of formation, was named for J. Proctor Knott — the Governor of Kentucky when the County was formed. Hindman was established as the county seat.

The first Knott County courthouse, a log building, was built in 1884.

The second Knott County courthouse, built in the 1890s, burned in 1929.

The third and present Knott County courthouse was built in 1935-36. The courthouse was built under a grant provided by the Public Works Administration of the New Deal. Two men, Mr. Raymond and Mr. Pigman, supposedly supervised construction. The building was of Spanish Mission styling, highlighted by the two-story front balcony supported by four piers connected by semi-circular arches at the top. In 1980, this portico was enclosed and the exterior and interiors renovated.

Third Courthouse, 1935 — in December, 1957 *(The Courier-Journal)*.

53. HODGENVILLE in LARUE COUNTY

Year Formed: 1843

Formed From: Hardin

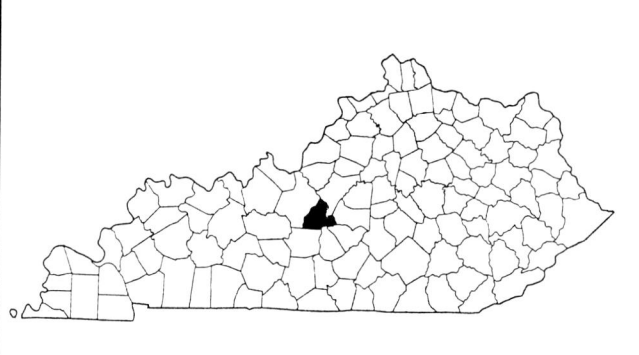

Larue County, 98th in order of formation, was named for John Larue — a Virginia immigrant who settled at Phillips' Fort, the county's first settlement. Hodgenville was established as the county seat and named for Robert Hodgen — Larue's brother-in-law and another resident of Phillips' Fort.

The first Larue County courthouse, a two-story, brick structure, was built in 1844. During the Civil War, the courthouse was used as barracks by Union troops and Confederate guerrillas burned the building on February 21, 1865. Fortunately, the records were saved.

The second Larue County courthouse was built in 1866. The courthouse was a two-story, brick building of Italianate styling, built on the same foundations of its predecessor. The courthouse underwent a renovation in 1892.

The third and present Larue County courthouse was built in 1964. The two-story, brick courthouse is of colonial styling and resembles the previous structure. R. H. Schoffner was the contractor of the building at a cost of approximately $300,000.

Second Courthouse, 1866 *(Caufield & Shook Collection, University of Louisville Photographic Archives)*.

54. HOPKINSVILLE in CHRISTIAN COUNTY

Year Formed: 1796

Formed From: Logan County

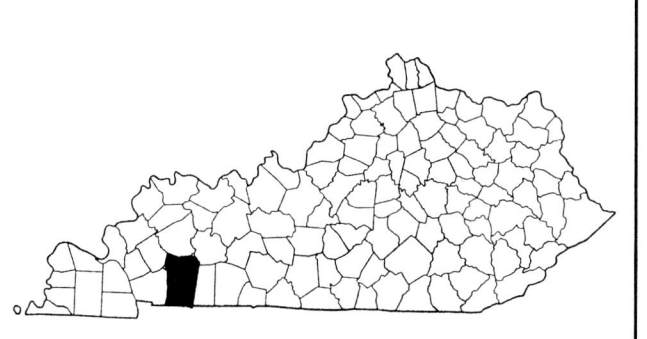

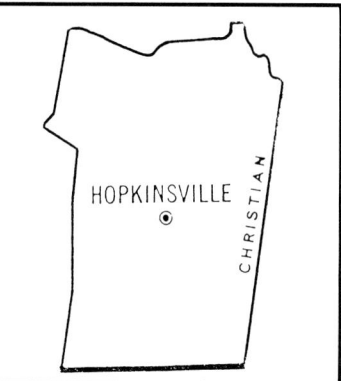

Christian County, 21st in order of formation, was named for Colonel William Christian — well known Indian fighter and Revolutionary War veteran. Hopkinsville, originally known as Elizabethtown, was established as the county seat in 1799 and named in honor of General Samuel Hopkins.

The first Christian County courthouse was built about 1800. William Blackburn, Bartholomew Wood and William Padfield were appointed commissioners "to let the court house." The building specified: "To be twenty feet square, a story and a half high, with a partition of logs above the loft 'skutched' inside and out, with a puncheon floor, two doors and one window, with a seat for the justices, a table for the Clerk and Barr for the attorneys and benches for the jury."

The second Christian County courthouse was ordered by the court in August 1802, but not started until May 1806 and completed September 1, 1810. John Clark, James H. McLaughlan, Revin Davidge, Edward Bradshaw, and Nehemiah Cravens were appointed commissioners to "let the building of the brick court house on the public square according to a model exhibited by Dr. Ramsey and others." The two-story brick courthouse of the foursquare form measured 26 feet square and cost $10,000.

The building of the third Christian County courthouse began in the summer of 1837 and reached completion in the fall of 1838. Hugh Roland, a Nashville architect, drew the plans for the courthouse. The two-story, brick courthouse measured 50 x 75 feet. Fronted by a recessed portico containing two Ionic columns flanking the entrance, the courthouse was typical of the Greek Revival style. In December 1864, during Confederate General Hylan B. Lyon's march through western Kentucky his troops passed through Hopkinsville. On December 12, 1864, Lyon's troops burned this courthouse.

The fourth and present Christian County courthouse replaced the burned courthouse. J. K. Frick, a Cairo, Illinois architect, designed the courthouse in 1869, the original drawing of which remains extant. The building was a transitional composition combining classical element of the Greek Revival style and Italianate details — such as the round arched windows. The building cost just under $100,000. In 1903, a brick cupola replaced the original hexagonal cupola. The brick cupola was removed in 1960 to its poor condition and the weight it created on the roof structure. The Christain County courthouse was listed on the National Register of Historic Places in 1979 as a contributing property of a historic district.

Third Courthouse.

Third Courthouse, 1869.

Fourth Courthouse, 1869 — c. 1870

Fourth Courthouse, post-1903.

(Photos from Collection of William Turner).

55. HYDEN in LESLIE COUNTY

Year Formed: 1878

Formed From: Clay, Harlan, and Perry Counties

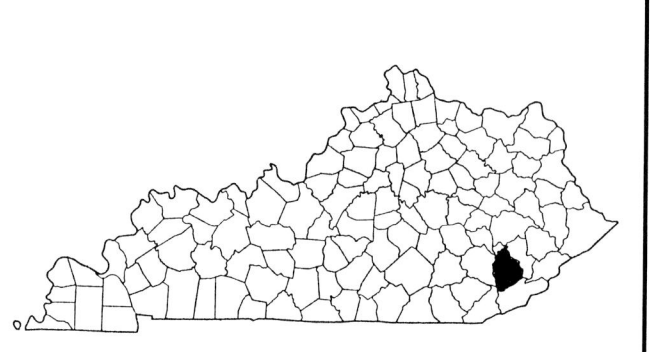
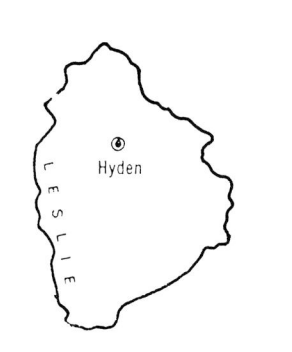

Leslie County, 117th in order of formation, was named for Governor Preston H. Leslie. Hyden was established as the county seat.

The first Leslie County courthouse was built in the early 1880s and is of the standard type designed by H. P. McDonald & Brothers, architects of Louisville. The structure, a brick, two-story building of the Victorian period is an eclectic design.

The second and current Leslie County courthouse was built in 1953-54. The building is a glass and stone structure of modern design. Renovation in the 1970s closed in the front windows and added an addition to the front.

56. INDEPENDENCE in KENTON COUNTY

Year Formed: 1840

Formed From: Campbell County

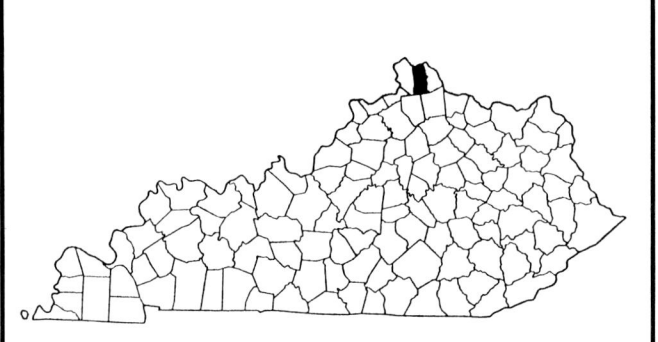

Kenton County, 90th in order of formation, was named for General Simon Kenton — a famous early Kentucky explorer. Independence was established as the first county seat in 1840 and named for Kenton County, gaining its independence from Campbell County. Kenton County is one of two counties in Kentucky that have two county seats, the other county being Campbell County (see pp. 4, 174). The other county seat in Kenton County is Covington (see p. 50).

The first Kenton County courthouse in Independence was built in 1840-43. Hiram Klette, Robert Perry, Lewis Collins, A. F. Fleming, and Reuben McDonald were appointed commissioners to supervise construction in May 1840. At the next meeting of the court, David Houston contracted to erect a brick, two-story, Greek Revival style courthouse.

The second and present Kenton County courthouse in Independence was built in 1911. The courthouse was a brick two-story structure of classical Beaux-Arts influenced design fronted by a Roman Ionic portico. The architects for the building were Robertson and Fahnstock and the Northcutt Brothers were the contractors.

57. INEZ in MARTIN COUNTY

Year Formed: 1870

Formed From: Floyd, Johnson, Lawrence, and Pike Counties

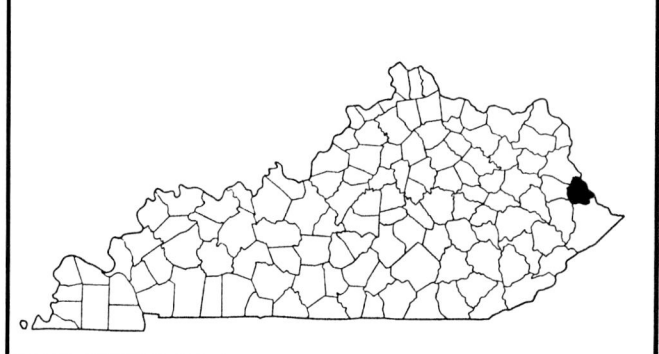

Martin County, 116th in order of formation, was named for Colonel John P. Martin of Floyd County — Kentucky congressman and legislator. Warfield was originally established as the county seat in 1870, but in 1871 Inez became the county seat.

The first Martin County courthouse was built about 1873. The log courthouse was used until 1881.

The second Martin County courthouse was built in 1882. The courthouse was a frame structure that burned in 1892.

The third Martin County courthouse was built in 1892-93. This building served until 1933.

The fourth and present Martin County courthouse was built in 1936. The courthouse was built under a grant provided by the Public Works Administration of the New Deal. The two-story building is of unique design combining a rough texture with flattened out classical details incorporated in the design. The stone was quarried from nearby mountains using local labor. Construction started on August 10, 1938 and the building was finished on April 23, 1941, the whole costing $ 108,217.

Third Courthouse, 1892 — in the 1930's *(Kentucky Department of Archives and Records, WPA Martin County File)*

Fourth Courthouse, 1938 *(Goodman-Paxton Collection, University of Kentucky Special Collections)*.

58. IRVINE in ESTILL COUNTY

Year Formed: 1808

Formed From: Clark and Madison Counties

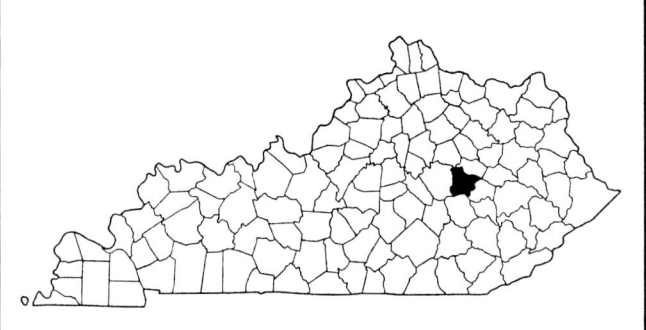

Estill County, 50th in order of formation, was named for Captain James Estill — an early Kentucky explorer who established Estill's Station in Madison County. Estill was killed by marauding Wyandotte Indians in a battle near Mt. Sterling in March 1782. Irvine was established as the county seat in 1808 and named for Colonel William Irvine — also an early settler who built "Irvine's Station" in Madison County with his brother Christopher.

The first Estill County courthouse was ordered built on the land of Benjamin Holliday on May 1808. Built of white oak logs, the courthouse measured 24 feet square. The building survived a raid of Confederate guerrillas, who burned the jail in October 1864, only to collapse a year later. Fortunately the collapse occurred on a Sunday afternoon and there were no injuries.

The second Estill County courthouse replaced the first structure in 1867. The brick, two-story courthouse was a front gabled building of the Greek Revival style, even though the style was out of date by this time. An interesting feature is the inset front portico with a small square above. The building was dismantled in 1939 to make way for a new structure.

The third and current Estill County courthouse was started January 25, 1939 and completed on May 19, 1941 under a grant provided by the Public Works Administration. H. A. Churchill & Associates of Lexington designed the courthouse, built of native Estill County stone. The building cost $118,510, of which $84,765 was paid by the P. W. A.

Second Courthouse, 1867 *(C. Frank Dunn Collection, The Kentucky Historical Society)*.

59. JACKSON in BREATHITT COUNTY

Year Formed: 1839

Formed From: Clay, Perry, and Estill Counties

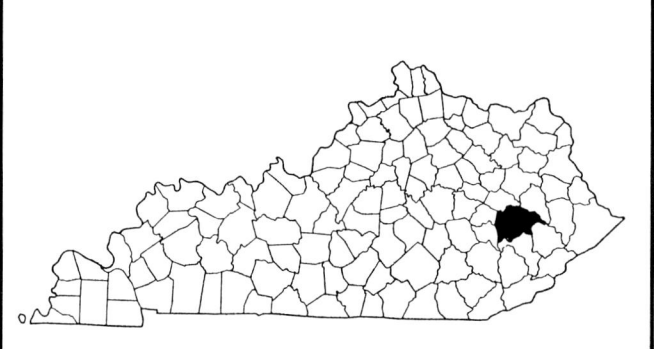

Breathitt County, 84th in order of formation, was named for Governor John Breathitt elected in 1832. Jackson, originally called Breathitt Town, was established as the county seat in 1845 and named for Andrew Jackson.

The first Breathitt County courthouse was a log structure built in about 1840. This structure was partially damaged by Confederate troops during the Civil War.

The second Breathitt County courthouse was a two-story, brick structure built in 1866. The first floor contained the courtroom and the second floor, three jury rooms. The building burned in 1873 under questionable circumstances.

The third Breathitt County courthouse was constructed in 1876-77. The two-story, brick building of Victorian period, eclectic design was remodeled in 1899 and again in 1912, when the clock tower was added. The building was condemned in January, 1958, for being in poor condition, and was dismantled.

The fourth and present Breathitt County courthouse was constructed in 1965. The Lexington architectural firm of Bayless, Clotfelter and Johnson designed the modern structure.

Third Courthouse, 1876-77, under construction *(University of Kentucky)*.

Third Courthouse, 1876-77 *(Collection of John W. Carpenter)*.

60. JAMESTOWN in RUSSELL COUNTY

Year Formed: 1825

Formed From: Adair, Cumberland, and Wayne Counties

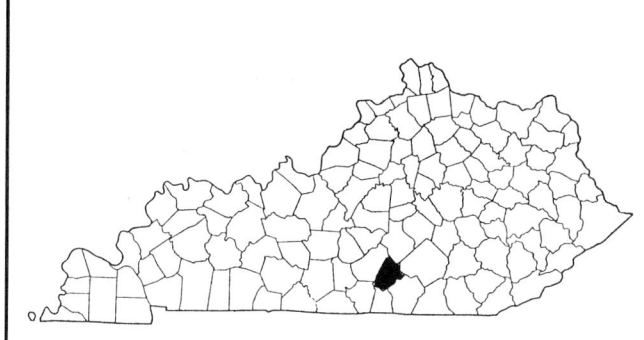
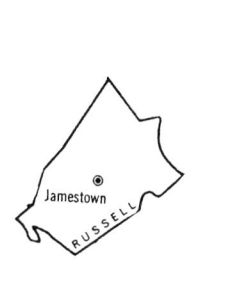

Russell County, 81st in order of formation, was named in honor of Colonel William Russell of Fayette County, a veteran of the Battles of Tippcanoe and Fallen Timbers, after which he replaced General Harrison as commander. Jamestown was established as the county seat and named for James Woolridge who, with his brother William, was the original owner of the town site.

The first Russell County courthouse was built in 1826. No description has been located of the courthouse, although it remained standing several years after its successor was completed.

The second Russell County courthouse was built in 1877-78. The courthouse was designed by Thomas T. Milburn and is identical to the Wayne County courthouse of his design. On May 21, 1877, the contract for construction was awarded to J.B. Patten of Nashville for $10,943. The finished courthouse was accepted by the court on November 1, 1878. The courthouse is a brick, two-story structure of the Italianate style. Alterations included covering the cupola with metal shingles around the turn of the century and addition of a portico in the 1960s. A fire on June 8, 1976 damaged the courthouse to the extent that it was replaced by the current structure.

The third and present Russell County courthouse was built in 1977-78. The courthouse is a two-story, brick structure of modern colonial styling, fronted by a doric order portico.

Second Courthouse, 1877.

Second Courthouse, 1877 — after remodeling

61. LaGRANGE in OLDHAM COUNTY

Year Formed: 1823

Formed From: Henry, Jefferson, and Shelby Counties

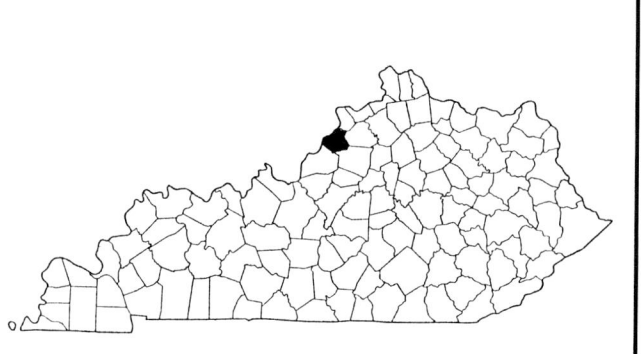

Oldham County, 74th in order of formation, was named for Colonel William Oldham of Virginia — killed during St. Clair's defeat of 1794. LaGrange was established as the county seat, but temporarily moved to Westport from 1828 until 1838, then returned. LaGrange is named for the French city of Lafayette's origin.

The first Oldham County courthouse was built in 1827-28. The courthouse was a square, two-story, brick building of the foursquare form covered by a hip roof topped by a large square cupola. Fire destroyed this courthouse in 1873.

The second Oldham County courthouse was built in 1875. Monroe Q. Wilson, architect of Louisville, designed the courthouse in the classical style at a cost of $15,780.80. The west wing of the courthouse was built shortly after completion, and the east in the 1920s.

First Courthouse, 1827 (*Oldham Era Bicentennial Edition,* July 18, 1974).

Second Courthouse, 1875 *(Collection of William Turner)*.

62. LANCASTER in GARRARD COUNTY

Year Formed: 1796

Formed From: Lincoln, Madison, and Mercer Counties

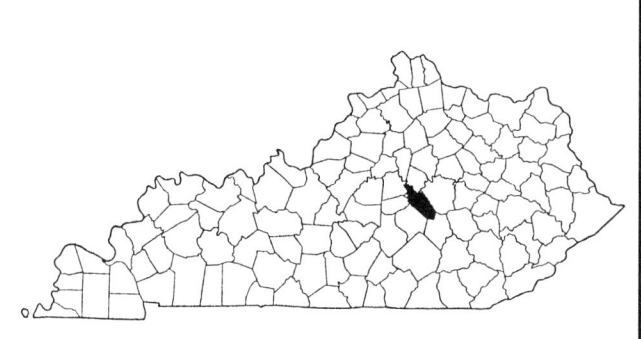

Garrard County, 25th in order of formation, was named in honor of Governor James Garrard of Bourbon County — two term Governor of Kentucky. Lancaster was established as the county seat in 1797 and named for the Pennsylvania city of the same name.

The first Garrard County courthouse was built in 1797-99. Samuel Gill, William Jennings, Alexander Carns, and Will Bryant were appointed commissioners for construction at a meeting of the court on July 4, 1797. Stephen Giles Letcher and his son Benjamin contracted for construction of a brick courthouse on February 2, 1798. Jesse Gooch provided the woodwork. The work was to be completed by February 1799. Eventually the court outgrew the building and it was sold to help pay for the a new courthouse.

The building of the second Garrard County courthouse commenced in 1811. William Jennings, Ben Letcher, Augustine Jennings, A. Wright, A. Ballinger, and Thomas Buford were appointed commissioners for construction in December 1811. The first session was held in the new courthouse on July 19, 1813. During the Civil War Union troops occupied and badly damaged the courthouse. The Federal government compensated the county for the damage about 1903. The courthouse outgrew the needs of the court and was dismantled in 1866.

The third and current Garrard County courthouse was completed on August 20, 1868. The court authorized $35,000 in bonds to be sold for the construction of the new courthouse at its meeting of November 28, 1865. The building committee consisted of W.H. Kinnaird, John Y. Leavell, and John W. Walker, appointed at the same meeting. Prolific Frankfort builder, John Haly, constructed the c.1866 courthouse. An Irish immigrant, he is also responsible numerous Frankfort buildings and the 1858 Anderson County Courthouse.

The original cupola was a tall observation tower used by the geological survey. This cupola was replaced in 1914-18 using yellow brick left over from construction of the Lancaster High School. The Garrard County courthouse was listed on the National Register of Historic Places in 1984 as a contributing property of a historic district.

Third Courthouse, 1866-68.

63. LAWRENCEBURG in ANDERSON COUNTY

Year Formed: 1827

Formed From: Franklin, Mercer, and Washington Counties

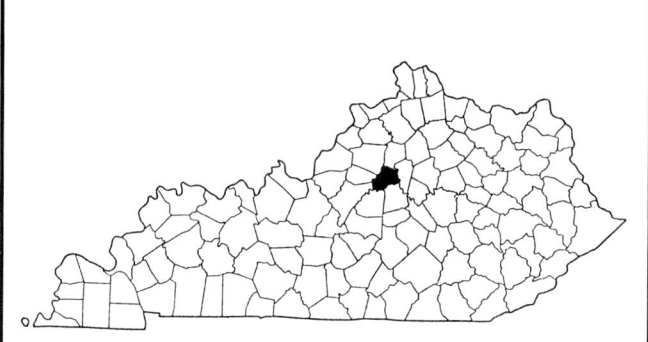

Anderson County, 82nd in order of formation, was named for Richard Clough Anderson, Jr. who was elected to the United States Congress in 1817, member of the Kentucky Legislature, served as foreign minister to Columbia under President Monroe, and was minister to Panama under President Adams. Lawrenceburg, established as the county seat in 1820, was named after Captain James Lawrence. Lawrence, commander of the United States Naval ship the Chesapeake, is credited with coining the phrase, "Don't Give Up the Ship," as his ship sank.

Construction for the first Anderson County Courthouse, although planned as early as 1827, did not commence until 1828. The committee to superintend construction, William Lawrence, David White, John F. Hudgins, and Ephraim Lillard let the contract for construction to Robert Logan. The building was readied for use by late 1829 and completed on July 12, 1830. Described as a brick, two-storied structure with a cupola at the front, it cost just over $3,000. The first floor contained the clerk's office and court room; the second floor had jury rooms which were also used by the local Masonic Lodge. The courthouse burned on the night of October 26, 1859.

The building of the second Anderson County courthouse was immediately addressed by the court and at its meeting of December 12, 1859. The court considered two designs, one by Cincinnatus Shryock, younger brother of Gideon and Lexington architect, and the second by Dennis Haly of Frankfort. Haly's design was chosen and his brother John's low bid of $14,000 for the construction was accepted on January 10, 1860. John Haly, an Irish immigrant, is noted for his stone construction including numerous structures in Franklin County and the Garrard County Courthouse of 1866. J.D. Parker was supervisor of construction and the building was completed in one year. Remodeling in 1905 by C.E. Bond included moving the front wall forward, reducing the size of the cupola, and numerous other minor alterations. Fire almost totally destroyed the building on the night of April 13, 1915, only the outside stone walls survived.

On April 24th, 1915, plans by the Louisville architectural firm of Joseph and Joseph were accepted to rebuild the courthouse. Retaining the original walls, Joseph and Joseph imposed a very dramatic, classically domed, Beaux-Arts design. The current structure was constructed by A. J. Stair of Knoxville, Tennessee for $34,722 under the architect's supervision. The entire project cost $39,146.

Left: Second Courthouse, 1959 *(Collection of Wyatt Shelby)*.
Right: Third Courthouse, 1915 *(Joseph & Joseph Brochure of 1925)*.

64. LEBANON in MARION COUNTY

Year Formed: 1834

Formed From: Washington County

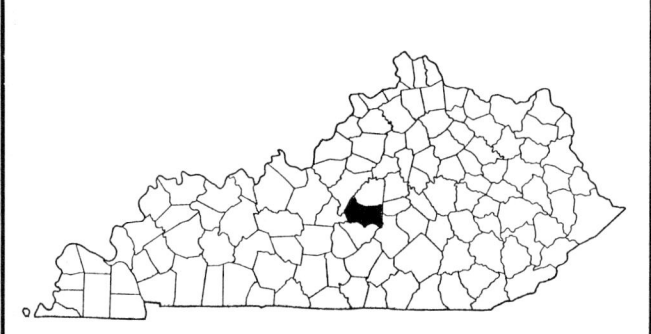

Marion County, 84th in order of formation, was named in honor of General Francis Marion — hero of the American Revolution. Lebanon was established as the county seat and named for the growth of "Cedars of Lebanon" in the area.

The first Marion County courthouse was built in 1835. The Washington County courthouse, 1814-16, served as a model for the courthouse. The contractor for the courthouse was Foster Ray, who hired Joseph Wimsatt as chief bricklayer and William Bean and Ambrose Smith as chief carpenters. The courthouse was of the foursquare form and was built at a cost of $5,000. In 1838, a County Clerk's office was built behind the courthouse to house the county records. After the Battle of Lebanon, on July 5, 1863, this building was burned by John Hunt Morgan in order to burn the indictments of treason filed there against Marion County soldiers in his command. The courthouse was condemned in January 1935 and Judge T. Scott Mayes convened court on the lawn to stress the poor condition of the courthouse.

The second Marion County courthouse was built in 1935. Thomas J. Nolan, architect of Louisville, designed the building. The courthouse was a three-story building of Belden red brick trimmed with stone, measuring 66' X 100'. The cost of the building was approximately $70,000.

First Courthouse, 1835 *(Collection of John Dahringer)*.

65. LEITCHFIELD in GRAYSON COUNTY

Year Formed: 1810

Formed From: Hardin and Ohio Counties

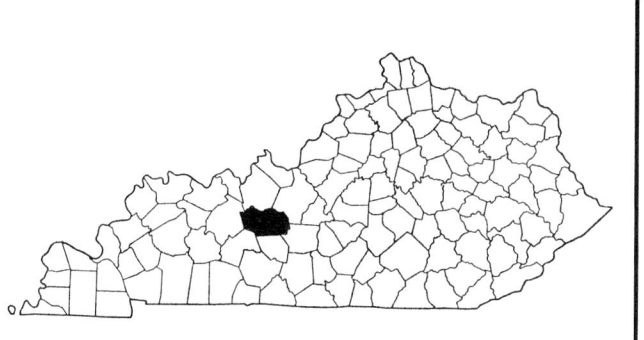

Grayson County, 54th in order of formation, was named in honor of Colonel William Grayson of Virginia — a United States Senator and Representative. Leitchfield was established as the county seat in 1810 and named for Major David Leitch of Campbell County — who originally owned the town site.

The first Grayson County courthouse was built shortly after 1810.. During Confederate General Hylan B. Lyon's march through western Kentucky his troops passed through Leitchfield and destroyed this courthouse on December 24, 1864.

The second Grayson County courthouse replaced the previous structure soon after it burned. Fire also destroyed this courthouse on June 16, 1896.

The third Grayson County courthouse was built during the late 1890s.

Fire destroyed this courthouse as well on April 3, 1936.

The fourth Grayson County courthouse was built under a grant provided by the Public Works Administration of the New Deal. Work began in 1937 and the first session was held here in January 1938. The courthouse is a two-story, brick structure of classical Beaux-Arts style highlighted by an elaborate Corinthian order portico. The Grayson County courthouse was listed on the National Register of Historic Places in 1988 as a contributing property of a historic district.

Third Courthouse, 1866 *(Pictorial Edition, 1903)*.

Fourth Courthouse, 1937 — in 1937 *(The Courier Journal)*.

66. LEXINGTON in FAYETTE COUNTY

Year Formed: 1780

Formed From: Kentucky

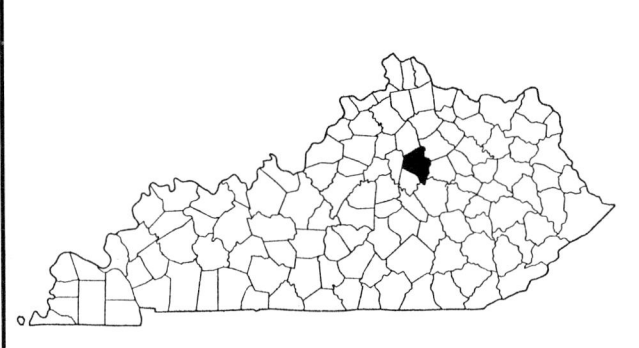

Fayette, Lincoln and Jefferson Counties were Kentucky's first three counties created by the Virginia legislature on November 1, 1780. Fayette County was named for the Revolutionary War general, the Marquis de Lafayette, the French nobleman who came to the aid of the American revolutionaries and later played a leading role in the politics of his native country. Lexington was established as the county seat on May 6, 1782.

The first Fayette County courthouse began shortly after establishment of Lexington in 1780. The two-story structure was "built of logs rived with a whip saw" and described as containing "two rooms on each floor, eighteen feet square, with fire places in each, and two good dry cellars, eighteen feet."

The second Fayette County courthouse was built in 1787-88, the first on current site. Captain John Cape contracted to build the new structure of native limestone, which was completed during the autumn of 1788. Each floor of the two-storied courthouse contained four rooms divided by a central hall. Fire destroyed the building in 1803.

The third Fayette County courthouse was designed in 1806 by amateur architect David Sutton. The contractors for the project were Hallett M. Winslow and Luther Stephens, leading builders of the period. The courthouse was three-story brick structure measuring 50 X 60 feet and constructed at a cost of $15,000. A cupola containing a bell tower and clock topped the hip roof, the whole being supported by four large, awkward columns rising through the center of the structure. During the 1840s, a pair of two-story brick flankers were added to the building. In 1872 a ten-year campaign to replace delapidated structure commenced.

The building of the fourth Fayette County courthouse commenced in October 1882 when the elaborate Renaissance-Eclectic design of Pittsburg architect Thomas Boyd was adopted. The contract for construction was awarded the next February to F. Bush & Sons. The construction supervisor was local architect Cincinnatus Shryock, younger brother Gideon Shryock, well known Kentucky architect. The cornerstone was laid on July 4th, 1883, and construction completed July 28, 1885 at a cost of $130,365. The building and statue were tragically destroyed by fire on May 14, 1897.

The building of the fifth and present Fayette County courthouse started on March 1, 1898 and completed in 1900. The Romanesque Revival design was by Lehman & Schmitt, a Cleveland firm responsible for several courthouses in Ohio, Indiana and Pennsylvania. The contractors were Albert Howard and George Clarke of Lexington, the construction costs amounting to $187,181. During the 1950s and 1960s, the building went through several renovations which destroyed the majority of the interior and replaced exterior doors and windows. The Fayette County courthouse was listed on the National Register of Historic Places in 1983 as a contributing property of a historic district.

Left: Third Courthouse, 1806 *(Lyle Collection)*. Center: Fourth Courthouse, 1882 *(Lexington Public Library)*. Right: Fifth Courthouse, 1898 — original interior *(Lexington Herald Leader, August 28, 1960)*.

67. LIBERTY in CASEY COUNTY

Year Formed: 1806

Formed From: Lincoln County

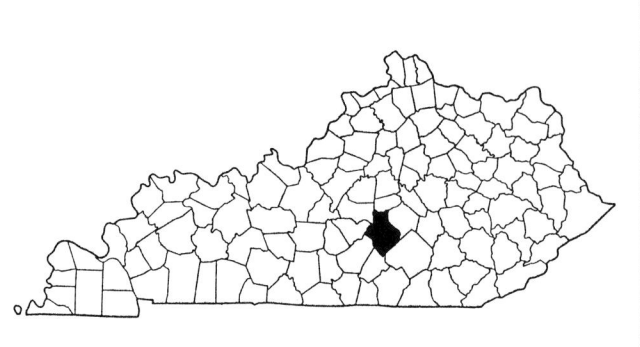
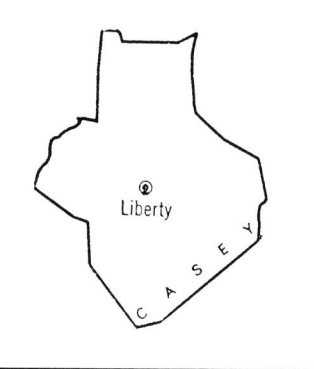

Casey County, 46th in order of formation, was named for Colonel William Casey of Adair County — an early settler and member of the second Constitutional Convention of Kentucky. Liberty was established as the county seat in 1808.

The first Casey County courthouse was constructed shortly after 1808. A log courthouse was built under the supervision of William Nash and William Goode who were appointed by the court.

The second Casey County courthouse was a brick structure started in 1837. Jesse Coffey, the builder, finished the project in 1844.

The third Casey County courthouse, an elaborate Victorian structure designed in 1887 by H.P. McDonald & Brothers of Louisville, reflects a departure from their standard courthouse design. The Richardsonian-Romanesque-influenced building was finished in 1889. McCoy and Milbern were the general contractors and Thomas D. Dunhauser was responsible for the stonework. The Casey County courthouse was listed on the National Register of Historic Places in 1977.

68. LONDON in LAUREL COUNTY

Year Formed: 1825

Formed From: Clay, Knox, Rockcastle, and Whitley Counties

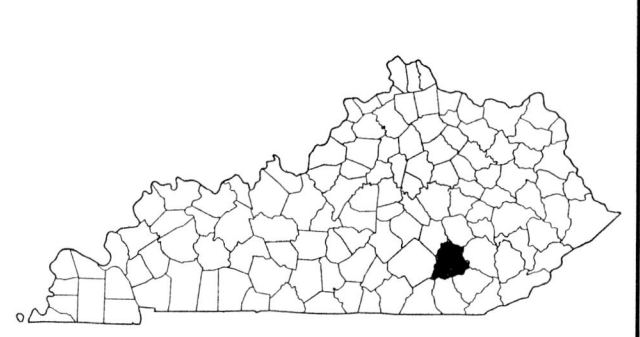

Laurel County, 80th in order of formation, was named for the Laurel River. London was established as the county seat.

The first Laurel County courthouse was built in 1826-27. The contract for the courthouse was let on May 1, 1826, specified to be a two-story, brick structure measuring 30 x 40 feet.. The land used for the site was given by the contractors John and Jarvis Jackson. Jarvis Jackson was also the contractor for the Knox County courthouse.

The second Laurel County courthouse was built in 1884-85. By 1881 the court realized the need for a new courthouse. Due to the burning of the jail, the project had to be postponed until 1884 when court appropriated funds. H.P. McDonald and Brothers, architects of Louisville, designed the courthouse in a manner similar to several others they designed in Kentucky. John W. Mullins was awarded the contract for construction in May 1885 for $16,350. Work started June 1 and was to be completed by May 15, 1886. Fred Hugi, a Swiss immigrant, supervised construction. Fred Born, another Swiss, was employed on the job. Fire destroyed the building on December 9, 1958.

The third and present Laurel County courthouse was finished in 1961. The colonial Georgian style structure was designed by Bayless, Coltfelter, & Johnson architects of Lexington.

Second Courthouse, 1884 *(The Filson Club)*.

69. LOUISA in

LAWRENCE COUNTY

Year Formed: 1821

Formed From: Floyd and Greenup Counties

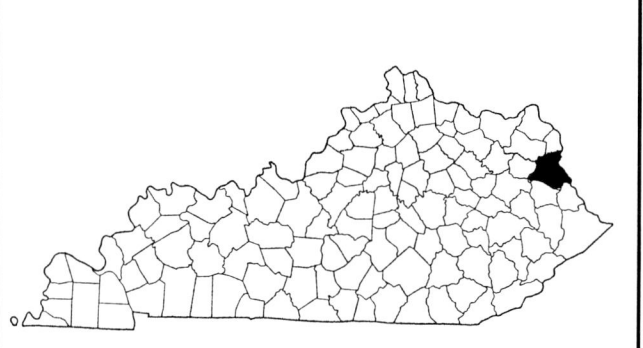

Lawrence County, 69th in order of formation, was named for Captain James Lawrence — a distinguished naval officer during the War of 1812. Louisa was established as the county seat.

The first Lawrence County courthouse, described only as a wooden structure, was built in 1823.

The second Lawrence County courthouse was built during the 1870s. Judge J.J. Jordan lead efforts to obtain the new building. The courthouse was a two-story, brick structure of the Italianate style. An addition was made to the building in 1922.

The third and present Lawrence County courthouse was built in 1961-64. Judge J. J. Jordan guided the project, the above Judge of the same name was his great-great-uncle. The glass and stone courthouse of modern design was built at a cost of $390,000.

70. LOUISVILLE in JEFFERSON COUNTY

Year Formed: 1780

Formed From: Kentucky County

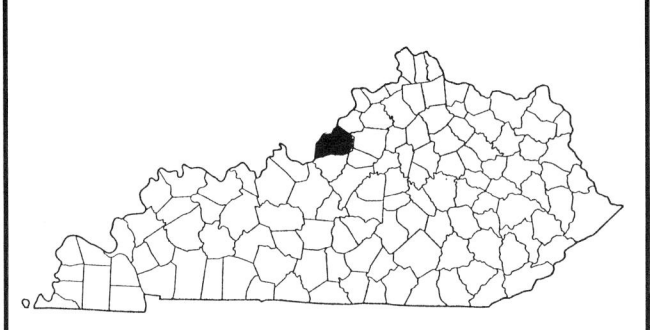

Jefferson, Fayette, and Lincoln Counties were Kentucky's first three counties created by the Virginia legislature in 1780. Jefferson County was named for Thomas Jefferson. Louisville was established as the county seat and named for Louis XVI — King of France.

The first Jefferson County courthouse was built in the summer of 1785. The courthouse, a log building measuring 16' X 20', was built by George Wilson for $310. Fire destroyed this courthouse.

The second Jefferson County courthouse was a temporary structure built in the summer of 1787. Richard Taylor (father of President Zachary Taylor) and Richard Eastin were appointed commissioners to supervise construction. This courthouse was also log, measuring 16' X 18'.

The third Jefferson County courthouse was built in 1788-90. Alexander Breckinridge, William Croghan, and Benjamin Johnston were appointed commissioners to supervise construction. The courthouse was a two-story, stone building measuring 48' X 36' with a hip roof topped by a small cupola. The designer and builder of the courthouse, Captain John Cape, also built the Nelson and Fayette County courthouses of similar descriptions.

The fourth Jefferson County courthouse was built in 1810-12. John Gwathmey, an amateur architect, is credited with the design. The courthouse was a two-story, brick structure of a classical design, fronted by a two-story, Doric portico. By 1835 the building was in poor condition and ordered replaced.

The fifth and present Jefferson County courthouse was designed in 1835 and finished in 1860. Designed by Gideon Shryock, Kentucky's first major architect, the courthouse represents one of the major Greek Revival structures in the United States. It was built as a city hall and courthouse by city and county governments. The cornerstone laying of the massive two-story structure took place on October 17, 1836 and the over budget project was opened in 1842. It would be 1860 before the building was completed under the supervision of Albert Fink and Charles Stancliff, local architects. The interior was reorganized by Fink, who suggested putting a dome on the building, similar to the United States Capitol.

On December 25, 1905 a fire destroyed the roof and damaged the interior. Brinton B. Davis, a local architect, supervised the repairs and renovation of the building. The Jefferson County courthouse was listed on the National Register of Historic Places in 1971. The courthouse was completely renovated and upgraded between 1977 and 1980.

Left: Fourth Courthouse, 1812.

Right: Fifth Courthouse, 1835-59 *(Collin's History of Kentucky)*.

71. MADISONVILLE in HOPKINS COUNTY

Year Formed: 1806

Formed From: Henderson County

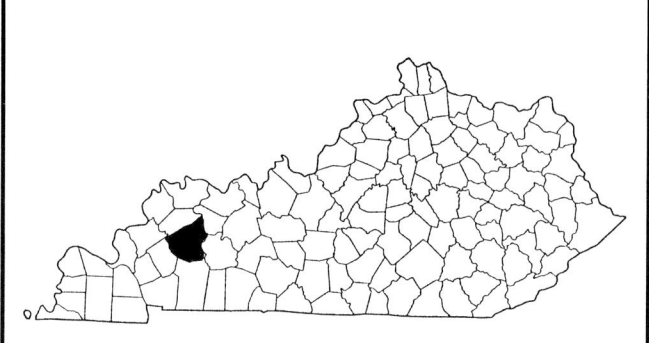

Hopkins County, 49th in order of formation, was named for General Samuel Hopkins — noted Revolutionary War veteran and Kentucky legislator. Madisonville was established as the county seat and named for President Madison.

The first Hopkins County courthouse was begun in July of 1807 and completed in exactly one year. The courthouse, of log construction measuring 18' X 20', was built by Solomon Silkwood for $329.

The second Hopkins County courthouse, a frame structure, was built in the 1820s.

The third Hopkins County courthouse was built in 1840s. The two-story, brick building was of the Greek Revival style in a temple form with a cupola above the entrance. In 1864, during Confederate General Hylan B. Lyon's march through western Kentucky, his troops passed through Madisonville. They burned this courthouse on December 17.

The fourth Hopkins County courthouse must have been built shortly after this, but no record of this courthouse has been located.

The fifth Hopkins County courthouse was built in 1892. Maury & Dodd of Louisville designed the building. The High Victorian structure is an eclectic design combining several historical styles and is highlighted by an enormous central bell tower. The courthouse was torn down in 1936.

The sixth and present Hopkins County courthouse was dedicated in March 1937. The courthouse is a three-story, brick structure fronted by a classical two-story, stone portico.

Fourth Courthouse, 1892 *(University of Kentucky Special Collection)*.

72. MANCHESTER in CLAY COUNTY

Year Formed: 1806

Formed From: Floyd, Knox, and Madison Counties

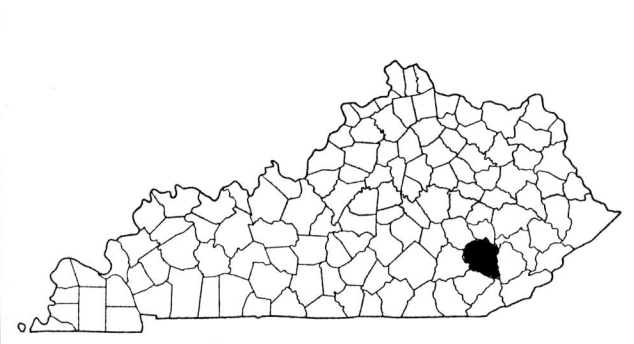

Clay County, 47th in order of formation, was named for General Green Clay of Madison County — an early Kentucky surveyor and statesman. Manchester, the county seat, was named for the great English manufacturing town.

No information is available on the first and second Clay County courthouses.

The third Clay County courthouse, an important structure in the history of Kentucky courthouses, is the earliest work of Bowling Green native architect, Frank Pierce Milburn, who was practicing in Columbia, South Carolina. The courthouse was a two-story, brick structure completed in 1889 and is reminiscent of an Italianate villa. Milburn's father, Thomas T. Milburn, was the contractor for the building. The building burned the night of January 20, 1936.

The fourth and present Clay County courthouse was built under a grant provided by the Public Works Administration of the New Deal. The classical style building was constructed of native stone. Construction began on February 17, 1936 and was finished on September 19, 1939. The building cost $95,587, $74,847 provided by the W.P.A.

Third Courthouse, 1889.

Fourth Courthouse, 1939 *(Goodman-Paxton Collection, University of Kentucky)*.

73. MARION in CRITTENDEN COUNTY

Year Formed: 1842

Formed From: Livingston County

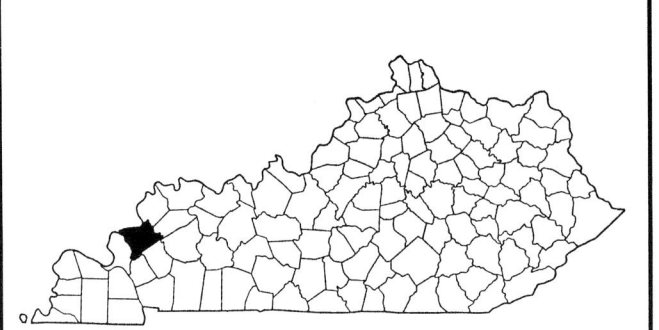

Crittenden County, 91st in order of formation, was named for John Jordan Crittenden of Franklin County — Henry Clay's successor in the United States Senate. Marion was established as the county seat, named in honor of General Francis Marion, Revolutionary War hero.

The first Crittenden County courthouse was built in 1842. The building is believed to have been of log construction. This courthouse was destroyed by fire.

The second Crittenden County courthouse was a small brick structure built in 1860. In January 1865, during Confederate General Hylan B. Lyon's march through western Kentucky, his troops passed through Marion. Lyon burned the courthouse destroying numerous records.

The third Crittenden County courthouse was built shortly after the Civil War. The new building utilized the remaining walls of the former structure. The new building was short-lived, as it was destroyed by fire in May 1870.

The fourth Crittenden County courthouse replaced this structure and was completed in October 1871. The brick, two-story building represents the transitional period between the Greek Revival and Italianate styles.

The fifth and present Crittenden County courthouse was dedicated on December 6, 1961, and reflects the utilitarian style of the time, possessing few ornamental features. The courthouse was built at a cost of $176,000.

Fourth Courthouse, 1871 (*The Courier-Journal*).

74. MAYFIELD in GRAVES COUNTY

Year Formed: 1821

Formed From: Hickman County

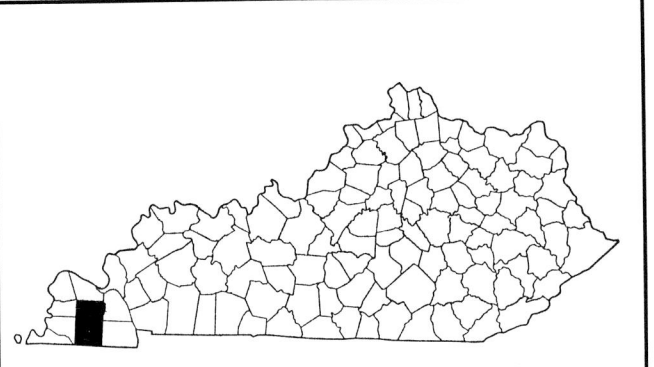

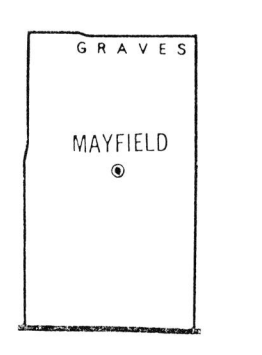

Graves County, 75th in order of formation, was named in honor of Captain Benjamin Graves of Fayette County — a Kentucky veteran of the War of 1812, killed at the Battle of River Raisin. Mayfield was established as the county seat in 1824.

The first Graves County courthouse was completed in November 1824. The log courthouse was built under the supervision of William Berklow and John Cunningham at a cost of $139.

The second Graves County courthouse was built in 1834. R.L. Mayes, Stephen M. Jenkins, John Anderson, and Jesse Wells were appointed commissioners to obtain plans in 1832, but satisfactory plans were not obtained until late 1833. A two-story, brick courthouse of the foursquare form measuring 40 feet square was built by Michael Eaker and Benjamin McGee for $5,400. Union troops occupied the building during the Civil War, leading to the building's destruction in 1864. The Federal Government eventually paid $1,500 for the building in 1910.

The third Graves County courthouse was completed in 1866. John Eaker, Joshua Boaz, T. J. Puryear, L .B. Holifield, J. S. Thomas, C. T. Greer, and A. Williams were appointed commissioners to supervise construction in April 1865. The two-story, brick courthouse was designed by J. K. Frick, architect of Cairo, Illinois, at a cost of $32,000. Frick also designed the Christian County courthouse during the same period. Fire destroyed this courthouse, with most of the county records, on December 18, 1887.

The fourth and current Graves County courthouse was begun in December of 1888 and was finished in 1889. H. P. McDonald Brothers of Louisville designed the elaborate Victorian courthouse in early 1887, by this time deviating from their standard courthouse design like the Adair County courthouse. The cost of the courthouse including the surrounding iron fence, cost $40,000.

Second Courthouse, 1834 (*Davis, Story of Mayfield Through a Century*).

75. MAYSVILLE in MASON COUNTY

Year Formed: 1788

Formed From: Bourbon County

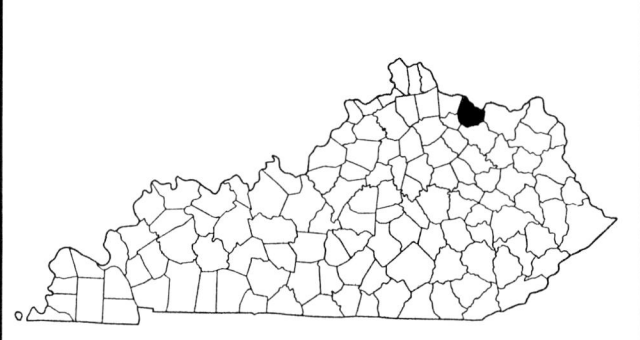
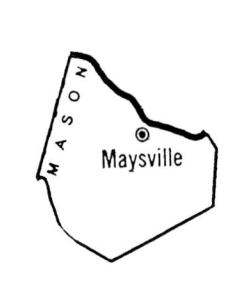

Mason County, 8th in order of formation, was named for George Mason of Virginia. Washington was established as the first county seat but Maysville, known for many years as Limestone, became the county seat effective January 22, 1848.

No description could be found of the first Mason County courthouse, built in 1790. The only reference being — in 1790 "the first Mason county court held in the Court House."

The second Mason County courthouse was built in 1794. Crowned by a 25' cupola, the two-story, stone courthouse with walls of native limestone two-feet thick, measured 50' X 23'. Over the front door the keystone was inscribed with "1794" and "L. C" for the builder--Lewis Craig, a stone mason and Baptist minister who in 1781 brought the "Traveling Church" from Virginia to Kentucky. After the county seat moved to Maysville in 1848, this building was used as a school until fire destroyed the building on August 13, 1909.

The third and present Mason County courthouse was built in 1844-46. Originally built as the Maysville city hall, the building was constructed with anticipation of the county seat being relocated and easily accommodated the county offices. A. M. January, General Richard Collins, F. T. Hord, and H. McCollough were appointed commissioners to supervise construction. Stanislaus and Ignatius Mitchell, two Washington carpenters, were responsible for the brickwork and Christopher Russell and Lenin Purnell, hired as the carpenters. A movement to build a city hall began on February 1, 1844, due in part to the city council meeting in the Market House. Construction of the elaborate Greek Revival style courthouse was supervised by A. M. January. The city hall was designated the Mason County courthouse on January 22, 1848, and the first session of the court was held in the building on May 8, 1848. The Mason County courthouse was listed on the National Register of Historic Places in 1982 as a contributing property of a historic district.

Second Courthouse, 1794.

76. McKEE in JACKSON COUNTY

Year Formed: 1858

Formed From: Clay, Estill, and Laurel Counties

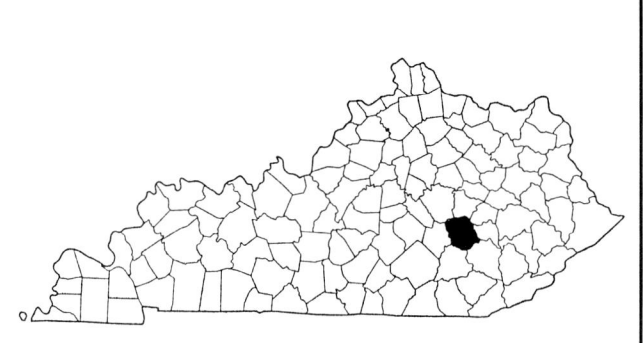
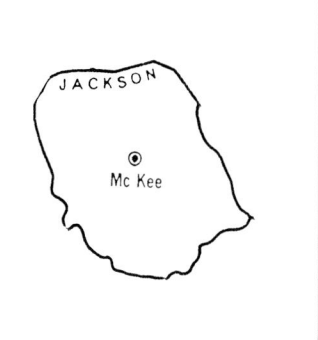

Jackson County, 104th in order of formation, was named for President Andrew Jackson of Tennessee. McKee was established as the county seat and named for Judge George R. McKee.

The first Jackson County courthouse, described as a double or dogtrot log structure, was built shortly after 1858.

The second Jackson County courthouse was built in 1872. The two-story courthouse was a large, frame, front-gable building.

The third Jackson County courthouse was built in 1923-24. The courthouse was a two-story brick structure, destroyed by fire in 1949.

The fourth and present Jackson County courthouse was built in 1950-51. The architect of the building was J. M. Ingram of Louisville and the contractors were McWhorter Brothers of McKee. The courthouse was built at a cost of $95,000.

A — First Courthouse, 1858
B — Second Courthouse, 1872
C — Third Courthouse, 1923
(*When They Hanged the Fiddler*).

Third Courthouse, 1923 (*The Kentucky Historical Society*).

77. MONTICELLO in WAYNE COUNTY

Year Formed: 1800

Formed From: Cumberland and Pulaski Counties

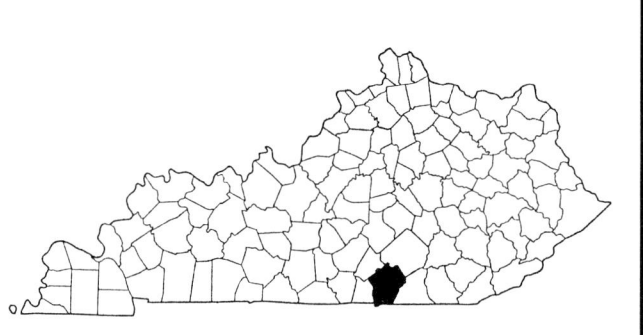
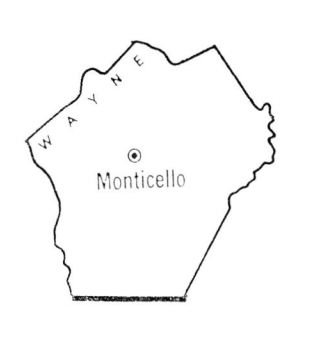

Wayne County, 43rd in order of formation, was named for General Anthony Wayne — Revolutionary War veteran and Indian fighter. Monticello was established as the county seat and named for the Virginia home of Thomas Jefferson.

The first Wayne County courthouse was built in 1801. The court ordered the construction of a two-story, log structure measuring 30 X 20 feet.

The second Wayne County courthouse was built about 1816. The courthouse was specified "of good stone, 25 X 35 feet, 1 chimney on the north side, two stories high." The building was removed to make way for the third courthouse in 1825.

The building of the third Wayne County courthouse commenced in 1825. The courthouse was a two-story, brick structure. In 1840 an addition was made to the rear of the building. The building was used until 1866, being torn down in July of that year.

The fourth Wayne County courthouse was completed in 1878. This was the first building to occupy the current courthouse site on North Main Street. On May 24, 1875, the court ordered the building of a new courthouse and a committee went to Mount Vernon to see the Rockcastle County courthouse designed by Thomas Thurmond Milburn. The plan was approved and Milburn designed a similar two-story, brick courthouse in the Italianate style. His son, T. T. Milburn contracted to build the courthouse. This courthouse burned in March 1898.

The fifth Wayne County courthouse was built in 1898-99. The courthouse was designed by Milburn's son Frank Pierce Milburn. The courthouse is a brick, two-story structure, Milburn's standard courthouse design of the period. The courthouse was torn down in 1949.

The sixth and present Wayne County courthouse was built in 1950. The courthouse is a concrete, brick, and steel structure of modern construction with slightly colonial references in the concrete pilasters around the building.

Fifth Courthouse, 1898 *(John W. Carpenter Collection)*.

78. MOREHEAD in ROWAN COUNTY

Year Formed: 1856

Formed From: Fleming and Morgan Counties

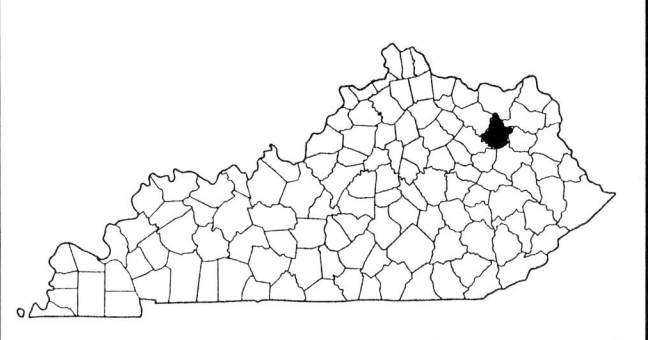

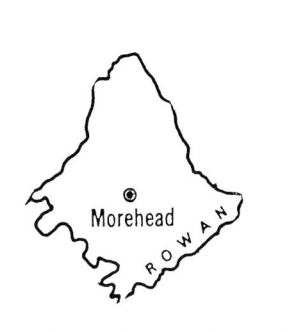

Rowan County, 104th in order of formation, was named in honor of Judge John Rowan of Nelson County — noted attorney owner of Federal Hill in Bardstown, known as "My Old Kentucky Home." Morehead was established as the county seat and named for Governor James Morehead.

The first Rowan County courthouse was built shortly after formation of the county in 1856. No description exists of this courthouse. On March 21, 1864, Confederate guerillas burned this building. This was the easternmost destruction done in the state during the Civil War.

The second Rowan County courthouse was built shortly after the Civil War ended in 1865. The building is simply described as a large frame structure. This courthouse burned the 1890s, destroying all prior county records preventing accurate knowledge of the courthouses.

The third Rowan County courthouse was built in 1899. The courthouse was a brick, three-story structure of Victorian styling with rough stone work typical of the Romanesque style. The building was highlighted by a four-story clock tower. By 1959 the building was in such bad condition the court moved into other facilities. Shortly after, the building was renovated including the removal of the tower. Further renovations occurred in 1977 and 1987. Despite these efforts, a new courthouse was built in 1980-81, although the old courthouse was retained. The Rowan County courthouse was listed on the National Register of Historic Places in 1983.

The fourth and present Rowan County courthouse was started in 1980 and completed in the spring of 1981.

Left: Second Courthouse, 1865 — about 1890 *(Collection of Norma Powers)*. Center: Third Courthouse, 1899 *(University of Kentucky Special Collection)*. Right: Third Courthouse, 1899 — after tower was removed *(University of Kentucky Special Collection)*.

79. MORGANFIELD in UNION COUNTY

Year Formed: 1811

Formed From: Henderson County

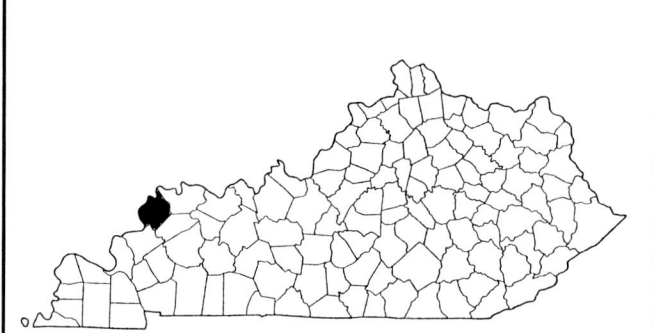

Union County was 55th in order of formation. Morganfield was established as the county seat in 1812 and "named after Gen. Morgan, of the revolutionary army."

The first Union County courthouse was built in 1811-12. A suitable plan chosen, at the courts meeting of July 23, 1811, Daniel McKenney, Joseph Owen, John Blue, and Samuel Givens were appointed commissioners to let a the contract for construction by August 1. The courthouse was described as a rough log, one-and-a-half-story structure measuring 26 X 20 feet of only one room. The courthouse was finished in July 1812.

The second Union County courthouse was built in 1819-20. James Townsend, Daniel McKenney, Josiah Williams, and Samuel Casey were appointed commissioners to draw a suitable plan in May 1818. A contract was let to build the courthouse in July 1818 and the brick building was completed in 1820 at cost of $3,800.

The third and current Union County courthouse was built in 1871-72. The court adopted plans by J.K. Frick, of Boyd & Frick — architects of Evansville, Indiana, at their meeting of August 14, 1871. The contractors for the courthouse were A.B. Weaver, G.E. Bell, G.W. Falloon, and William Brown, who completed the building in September 1872 at a cost of $58,067.77. The courthouse more than doubled in size under a grant provided by the Public Works Administration of the New Deal and allowed a large addition to be built in a similar style at the rear of the original building. Construction began on April 26, 1938, and was finished on June 9, 1940, the whole costing $138,393. The Union County courthouse was listed on the National Register of Historic Places in 1978.

Top: Third Courthouse, 1871 *(History of Union County — 1886 - c. 1890)*. Lower left: Third Courthouse, 1871 — 1890 *(The Kentucky Historical Society)*. Lower right: Third Courthouse, after P. W. A. renovation, 1939-40 *(Goodman-Paxton Collection, University of Kentucky Special Collection)*.

80. MORGANTOWN in BUTLER COUNTY

Year Formed: 1810

Formed From: Logan and Ohio Counties

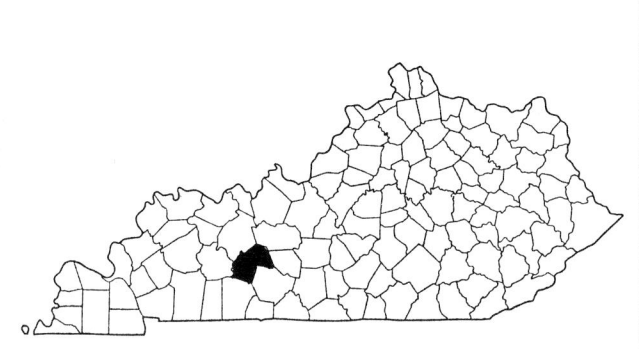

Butler County, 53rd in order of formation, was named for General Richard Butler of Pennsylvania — a distinguished soldier of the Revolutionary War. Morgantown was established as the county seat in 1810.

The first Butler County courthouse was authorized by the court in June of 1811. The brick courthouse measured 26 X 33 feet. The Hardin County courthouse of 1806 served as a model for the building. The public building also doubled as the local house of worship. Fire destroyed the building in 1872.

The building of the second Butler County courthouse commenced in 1873 under the administration of Judge Thomas C. Carson. The Italianate style building was a two-story, brick structure with a hexagonal cupola. James A. Shirley of Glasgow, the contractor for the construction, also built the Edmonson County courthouse of the same period.

The third and present courthouse was dedicated on October 4, 1975. The courthouse is a colonial style building built under the administration of Judge Robert Lamastus.

Second Courthouse, 1873, in 1974 *(The Courier-Journal)*.

81. MOUNT OLIVET in ROBERTSON COUNTY

Year Formed: 1867

Formed From: Bracken, Harrison, Mason, and Nicholas Counties

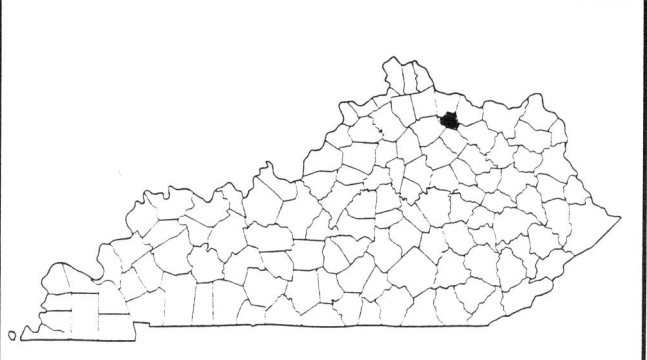

Robertson County, 111th in order of formation, was named in honor of George Robertson — Chief Justice of the Kentucky Court of Appeals. Mount Olivet was established as the county seat.

The first and present Robertson County courthouse was built in 1872. A committee, headed by Judge O.S. Deming and including George H.B. Thompson and John D. Gough, was appointed commissioners to obtain a suitable plan. On February 12, 1872, G.M. Williams, a local builder, was awarded the contract to build the courthouse, which he is also credited with designing. When half built, the county found it lacked the funds to complete the building. The F. & A.M. Masons Blue Lodge Chapter donated $1,500 towards construction of the second story which was reserved for their use. The two-story courthouse is of Italianate design and when built is said to have been the only brick structure in the county. The building was first used in January 1873. The additions flanking the structure were added in the 1960s. The Robertson County courthouse was listed on the National Register of Historic Places in 1978.

First Courthouse, 1872.

82. MOUNT STERLING in MONTGOMERY COUNTY

Year Formed: 1796

Formed From: Clark County

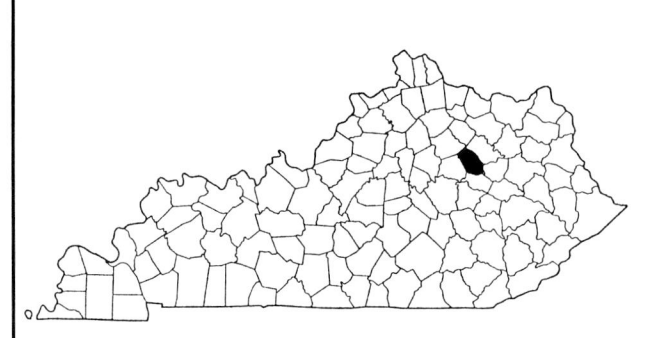

Montgomery County, 22nd in order of formation, was named for General Richard Montgomery, early Indian fighter and Revolutionary War veteran. Mount Sterling was established as the county seat and named for Sterling, the original owner of the land.

The first Montgomery County courthouse, built in 1797-98, was located on the site of the current city building. The one-and-one-half story courthouse, the earliest brick structure in the city was topped by a "tall steeple." Nathan Divine is said to be the builder. In 1835 the court let contracts for "recovering the courthouse" to Robert Evans. This courthouse burned in 1851 - "Tuesday night, March 4, about 7."

The second Montgomery County courthouse was built in 1851-53. John McMurtry, prominent Lexington builder, built the courthouse and probably designed it as well. The courthouse was finished by November of 1853, but the roof proved to cause McMurtry great problems. By April 1856 the roof was in such bad condition that the court ordered the cupola be taken down and rebuilt. The brick, two-story courthouse with the new final cupola formed an outstanding example of the Greek Revival style. During the Civil War the courthouse served as Federal garrison. The Confederate cavalry under Captain Peter Everett destroyed the building on December 2, 1863.

The third Montgomery County courthouse was built in 1868-71. The Civil War, which ended in 1865, delayed construction of this courthouse. O.S. Tenny and Thomas Hoffman contracted to build the courthouse for $25,000, but added expenses brought the cost to $27,190.

The fourth Montgomery County courthouse was built in 1890-91. The brick, stone, and terra cotta courthouse exemplifies the Romanesque Revival, popular during this period. B. J. Bartlett of Nashville was the architect and J.H. Walker, the contractor. In March of 1955 the court declared this courthouse structurally unsafe and condemned.

The fifth and present Montgomery County courthouse was built in 1958-60. Meriwether, Marye, and Associates, architects of Lexington, were hired in 1955 to design the two-story, brick courthouse of modern colonial design, fronted by a four column doric portico. The contract to build was let to the Alderman Company in July of 1958 and the courthouse dedicated on September 19, 1960. The Montgomery County courthouse was listed on the National Register of Historic Places in 1980 as a contributing property of a historic district.

Left: Second Courthouse, 1851.
Center: Third Courthouse, 1868 *(Collection of Edwin R. Lockridge)*.
Right: Fourth Courthouse, 1890 *(Collection of John W. Carpenter)*.

83. MOUNT VERNON in ROCKCASTLE COUNTY

Year Formed: 1810

Formed From: Knox, Lincoln, Madison, and Pulaski Counties

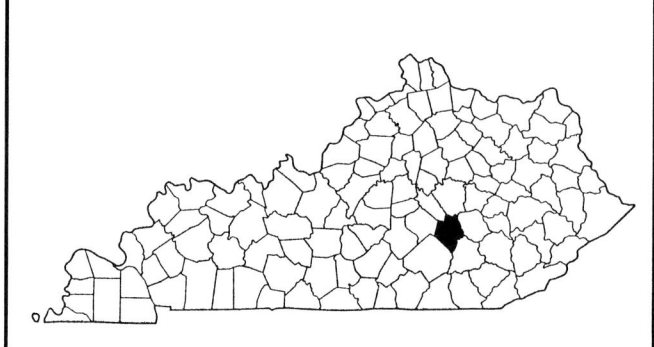

Rockcastle County, 52nd in order of formation, was named for Rockcastle River. Mount Vernon was established as the county seat.

The first Rockcastle County courthouse was built in 1811.

The courthouse was a log, two-story building measuring 40 X 20 feet. The materials were donated by local citizens. This building burned in 1871, attributed to arson in order to destroy the court records and to remove evidence of land claims in question.

The second Rockcastle County courthouse was built immediately after the fire in 1871 and completed in 1873. The new courthouse was a two-story, brick building of Italianate design with typical details of the style, including brackets supporting a wide roof overhang and an elaborate hexagonal cupola. The bricks were hauled ten miles from Mullins Station. This building was torn down in February 1964 to make way for the current building.

The third Rockcastle County courthouse was built in 1964-65. The courthouse is a three-story building of modern design with a modern sculpture flanking the entrance. The distinguishing feature of this structure is its almost complete lack of windows.

Second Courthouse, 1871 (*Renfro Valley Bugle,* February, 1964).

84. MUNFORDVILLE in HART COUNTY

Year Formed: 1819

Formed From: Green and Hardin Counties

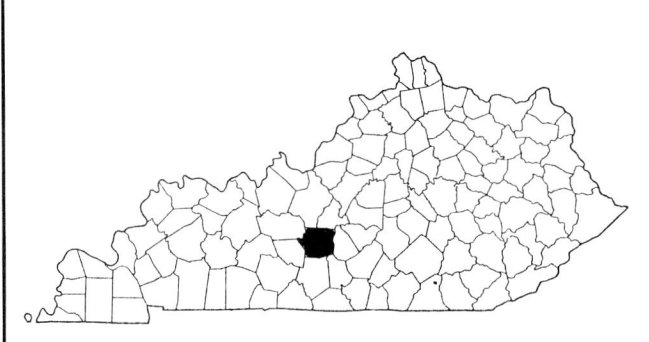

Hart County, 61st in order of formation, was named for Captain Nathaniel G.T. Hart of Fayette County — a veteran of the War of 1812, killed by Indians shortly after the Battle of River Raisin. Munfordville was established as the county seat in 1819 and is named for Richard T. Munford who originally owned the town site.

The first Hart County courthouse was built in 1819-21. Dudley Roundtree, Thomas B. Holt, George T. Wood, John Harris, and Isham Hardy were appointed commissioners for construction in September 1819. The courthouse was specified to be a brick, two-story building measuring 40 by 30 feet. The courthouse was accepted by the court at the September 1821 session.

The second Hart County courthouse was built in 1893. The brick, two-story courthouse was designed in the Second Empire style with a mansard roof and large hexagonal cupola. This courthouse burned on January 3, 1928.

The third and present Hart County courthouse was built in 1928. The courthouse is a three-story, brick structure of classical Beaux-Arts influence. Louisville architect Clarence J. Stinson designed the courthouse and Jenkins & Essex Lumber Company of Elizabethtown contracted to build the $45,000 courthouse. The Hart County courthouse was listed on the National Register of Historic Places in 1980.

Left: Second Courthouse, 1893 *(Western Kentucky University)*.
Right: Third Courthouse, 1928 — about 1935 *(Caufield & Shook Collection, University of Louisville Photographic Archives)*.

85. MURRAY in CALLOWAY COUNTY

Year Formed: 1821

Formed From: Hickman County

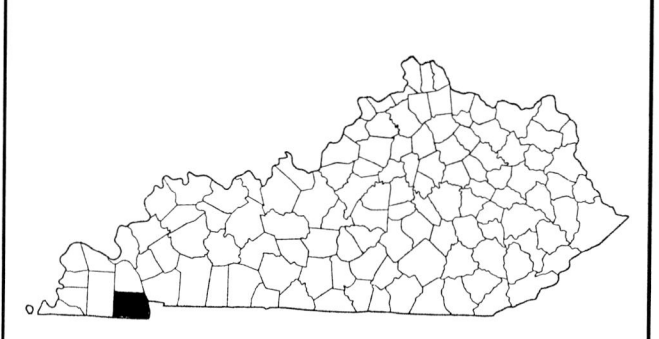
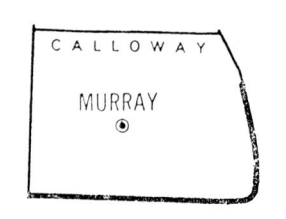

Calloway County, 72nd in order of formation, was named for Colonel Richard Calloway who came to Kentucky in 1776 as a trustee of Boonsborough. Calloway and John Todd were elected the first burgesses to the general assembly of Virginia. Wadesboro was established as the county seat shortly after formation. When the northern part of the county cut off to form Marshall County in 1842, Murray became the county seat, named in honor of Thomas L. Murray — lawyer and founder of Murray State University.

The first Calloway County courthouse was the first order of business at the second meeting of the court on January 17, 1823. Commissioners of the court, William Jones and Eli Cochran, prepared plans for the building, described as a one-and-a-half-story, log structure of a single room measuring 20 feet square. Reuban E. Rowland built the structure in Wadesboro for $100. In 1964 the courthouse was moved to the campus of Murray State University, where it remains today.

The second Calloway County courthouse was ordered built in 1830 under supervision of commissioners John Irvin, David Smith, George Denny, William Curd, and Thomas H. Grubbs. The two-story, brick structure of the foursquare form measuring 36 feet square was finished the next year. The courthouse built at Wadesboro was used until 1842 when the county seat moved. The building also served as the local religious structure.

The third Calloway County courthouse was ordered in 1843, shortly after relocation of the county seat to Murray. The two-story, brick courthouse of the foursquare form measured 50 feet square. Commissioners were Jesse P. Stephens, B. G. Imes, G. D. McDonald, and D. C. Lynch. The first floor contained the courtroom and the second floor, four rooms for court offices. The third courthouse was used until 1906 when fire destroyed the building.

The fourth and present Calloway County courthouse was a classical Beaux-Arts influenced design built in 1913. The first two attempts for passage of a bond issue for construction failed. The next attempt to pass the bond issue was made on the first Tuesday in November of 1912. The results counted the night of the election failed to reveal the two-thirds vote necessary for passage. That night the tally sheets were altered resulting in the announcement by the county clerk that he had made a gross error in counting, thus allowing passage of the bond. The Falls Construction Company of Louisville, the successful bidders for the job at $49,679, finished the building in 200 days. The Calloway County courthouse was listed on the National Register of Historic Places in 1986.

Left: First Courthouse, 1823 — as residence (*The Murray Ledger & Times* — April 7, 1975)
Center: First Courthouse, 1823 — as restored (*History of Marshall County*).
Right: Fourth Courthouse, 1913 (*The Kentucky Historical Society*).

86. NEW CASTLE in HENRY COUNTY

Year Formed: 1798

Formed From: Shelby County

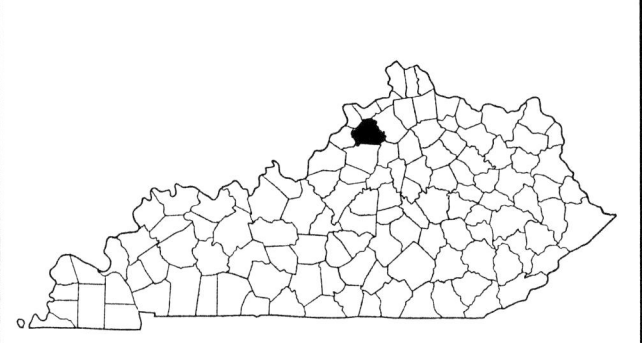
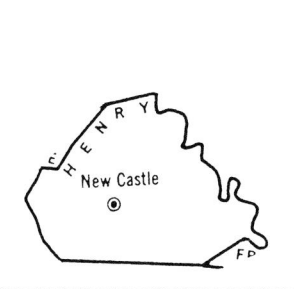

Henry County, 31st in order of formation, was named in honor of Patrick Henry — patriot and Governor of Virginia. New Castle was established as the county seat.

The first Henry County courthouse was built in 1799. The courthouse is believed to have been log, but no accurate accounts exist.

The second Henry County courthouse was built in 1804. No description of the structure survives other than Lewis Collins stating it was "an excellent courthouse." John H. Bullock & Company were the contractors.

The third and present Henry County courthouse was built in about 1875. The courthouse is a two-story, brick building of Italianate design with Romanesque double windows on the second floor. The cupola is of a classical Beaux-Arts influenced design, probably added about 1910. The Henry County courthouse was listed on the National Register of Historic Places in 1977.

Third Courthouse, 1875 — in 1957 (*Collection of Avery Holland*).

87. NEWPORT in CAMPBELL COUNTY

Year Formed: 1794

Formed From: Harrison, Mason, and Scott Counties

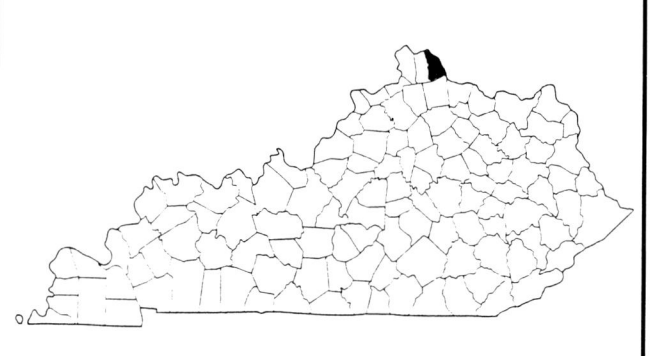

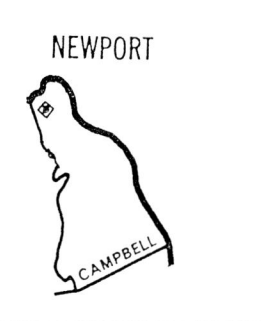

Campbell County, 19th in order of formation, was named in honor of Colonel John Campbell — Jefferson County's representative at Kentucky's first Constitutional Convention. Campbell County has had several county seats, the first was Wilmington, but it changed almost immediately to Newport.

Little is known of Campbell County's first and second courthouses in Newport. Both were apparently of log construction, the first constructed about 1795 and the second in 1805 on a lot donated by James Taylor, the city's founder.

The third Campbell County courthouse was built in 1814-15 due to the efforts of commissioners John Brown Lindsay (later first mayor of Newport), William Caldwell, and Jonathan Huling. The two-story, flemish-bond brick building of the foursquare form measured 40 feet square. Joel Hills and Elijah Pierce were the brick masons, John Eversull and Samuel Perry, the carpenters and roofers.

During the year 1827 the town of Visalia was county seat due to its proximity to the proposed railroad. The county government later moved back to Newport and in 1840 moved again to Alexandria - deemed the center of the county.

Frustration at being the county's largest city but not the county seat, prompted the citizens of Newport in 1883 to raise money through private subscription and build a courthouse. Completed in 1884, the Second Empire style courthouse is a wonderful example of Victorian eclectic architecture. None-the-less, the county seat remained at Alexandria. This Campbell County courthouse was listed on the National Register of Historic Places in 1988.

Third Courthouse, Newport, 1815.

Fifth Courthouse, Newport, 1883 *(Collection of John W. Carpenter)*.

88. NICHOLASVILLE in JESSAMINE COUNTY

Year Formed: 1798

Formed From: Fayette County

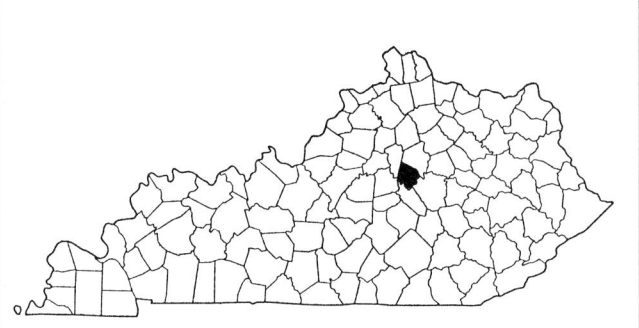

Jessamine County, 36th in order of formation, was named for the nearby creek named by James Douglass for his daughter, Jessamine. Nicholasville was established as the county seat and named for George Nicholas of Fayette County — a well known lawyer of the period.

The first Jessamine County courthouse was built in 1823. The red-brick courthouse was simply described as "uncomfortable and inconvenient." Thompson Howard, who later moved to Missouri, built the courthouse which served until 1878, when the new courthouse was started.

The second and present Jessamine County courthouse was built in 1878. E. J. Young, J. S. Bronaugh, Dudley Portwood, and William H. Phillips were appointed commissioners to supervise construction. Thomas Boyd, a Pittsburgh architect, designed the Victorian period courthouse in an eclectic style, combining several styles such as the classical portico and French mansard roof of the Second Empire. Boyd would later design the Scott and Fayette County courthouses. On April 19, 1878, F. Bush and Son of Lexington were awarded the contract for the building which eventually cost $38,385. Bush later constructed Boyd's Fayette County courthouse. The building was renovated by Standafer Construction Company of Lexington in 1965 at a cost of $345,000. The architect for the renovation was Donald B. Shelton of Lexington.

The Jessamine County courthouse was listed on the National Register of Historic Places in 1984 as a contributing property of a historic district.

89. OWENSBORO in DAVIESS COUNTY

Year Formed: 1815

Formed From: Ohio County

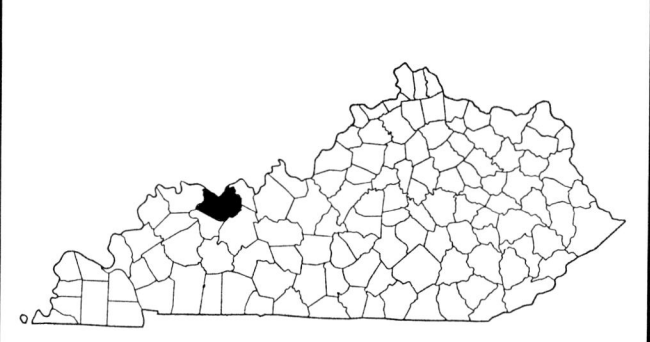

Daviess County, 58th in order of formation, was named for Major Joseph Hamilton Daviess — most noted as Aaron Burr's prosecutor for treason. Owensboro, originally Owensborough, was established as the county seat.

Little is known of the first Daviess County courthouse. Court records show that proceedings of the court from 1816-19 met in a courthouse.

The second Daviess County courthouse was built in 1819. The courthouse was small brick building. The court eventually outgrew the building, which in September 1853 was dismantled to make way for a new structure.

The third Daviess County courthouse was commenced on October 30, 1854, the cornerstone laid in July 1855 and the building completed in 1858. Barnett Trible designed and constructed the courthouse. The Greek Revival style two-story brick building measured 60 X 80 feet and cost $17,500. Both Union and Confederate troops used the courthouse during the Civil War, heavily damaging the structure. Finally on January 4, 1865, the building was burned by the troops of Confederate Captain William Davidson, as retribution for black Union soldiers occupying the building as barracks.

The fourth Daviess County courthouse was begun soon after the War and completed in 1868. This courthouse, built on the foundations of the previous structure, had the same dimensions. Barnett Trible and W. McLoyd contracted for the building which eventually cost $63,000. The three-story, brick courthouse was designed in the Italianate style with a extremely tall cupola in the center. Many interesting legends surround the building, the most interesting in 1889 when it was reported haunted, a story that persisted for a year. The building was extensively remodeled in 1887, the cupola was condemned and removed in 1927, and the building needed to be replaced by 1938.

Efforts to pass a financing proposal for the fifth Daviess County courthouse were unsuccessful from 1938 to 1963. In 1963, however, the Federal government provided a grant for one-half of the $750,000 building cost.

The fifth and current Daviess County courthouse was started in April 1963 and dedicated on September 5, 1964. The architect of the new building was Max W. Bisson & Associates. Clark Construction Company built the Indiana Limestone courthouse.

Left: Third Courthouse, 1858. Center: Fourth Courthouse, 1868 *(Caufield & Shook Collection, University of Louisville)*. Right: Fourth Courthouse, 1868 — post-1927 *(University of Kentucky Special Collection)*.

90. OWENTON in OWEN COUNTY

Year Formed: 1819

Formed From: Franklin, Gallatin, and Scott Counties

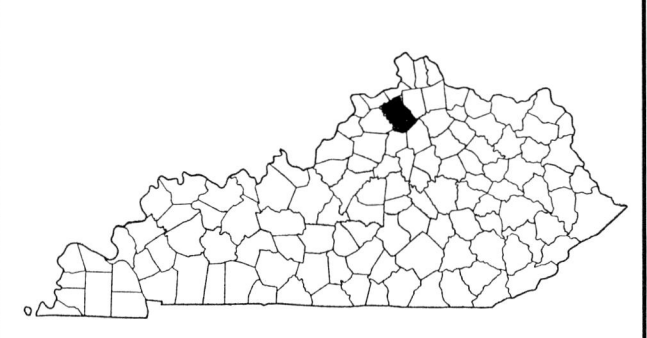

Owen County, 62nd in order of formation, was named for Colonel Abraham Owen of Shelby County — early member of the state Senate and Legislature, killed in the Battle of Tippecanoe. Owenton was established as the county seat in 1822, the court previously met at the home of Jacob Hesler at Heslerville.

The first Owen County courthouse was built in 1823. The courthouse was a log structure. Unfortunately no further information is known.

The second Owen County courthouse was built in 1857-58. The courthouse is a brick, two-story structure of the Greek Revival style, fronted by a Doric order portico. Nathaniel C. Cook, architect and builder of Frankfort, designed the building. Cook also acted as the contractor for the sum of $15,909.59. James A. Rice and Steve Wess, a black man, assisted in the building's construction. During the Civil War Confederate troops, under Humphrey Marshall of Franklin County, occupied the courthouse. Union troops occupied the courthouse as barracks after October 1862. The one-story wings on each side of the main body were part of the original plan; but were not built until 1868 after the conclusion of the war. The courthouse was renovated in the 1930's under a grant provided by the Public Works Administration of the New Deal, with funds matched by the county and the Junior Chamber of Commerce. The doors and windows of the building were replaced in the mid-1970's. The Owen County courthouse was listed on the National Register of Historic Places in 1977.

Second Courthouse, 1857 — original plan by N. C. Cook *(Collection of William B. Scott, Jr)*.

91. OWINGSVILLE in BATH COUNTY

Year Formed: 1811

Formed From: Montgomery County

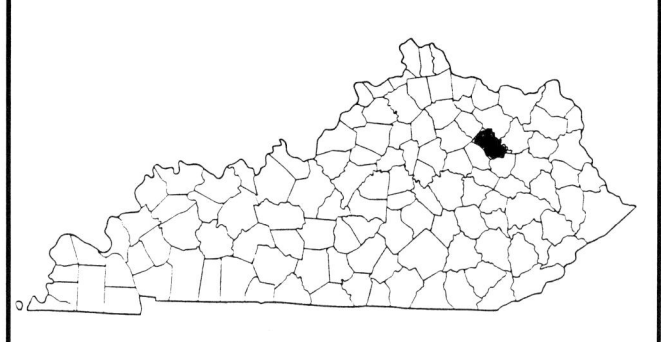

Bath County, 56th in order of formation, was named for the numerous springs in the region. Owingsville was established as the county seat in 1811 and named for Colonel Thomas Dye Owings — a veteran of the War of 1812 and proprietor of well-known Olympia Springs only 8 miles southeast.

The first Bath County courthouse was completed by May 3, 1813, when the first session of court was held there. The brick, two-story building, constructed by Jacob and Issac Warner, measured 30 X 40 feet and was located in the center of what is now Main Street.

The second Bath County courthouse replaced the previous courthouse in 1831. Union troops occupied the brick, two-story courthouse as barracks during the Civil War. On March 21, 1864, Confederate troops drove them from the building and an overheated stove left by the federal troops started a fire, burning the building. The Federal government later compensated the county for the building.

The building of the third and present Bath County courthouse commenced in 1866 and was finished two years later at a cost of $34,000. Frederick Visscher was the contractor of the transitional Italianate style building. During an 1903-04 remodeling interior changes were made including replacement of the building's original cupola, forward extension facade with a new Beaux-Arts entrance and creation of wings at the sides of the building. These changes were made by Bud Colliver and Oscar Palmer. The Bath County courthouse was listed on the National Register of Historic Places in 1978 as a contributing property of a historic district.

92. PADUCAH in Mc CRACKEN COUNTY

Year Formed: 1821

Formed From: Hickman County

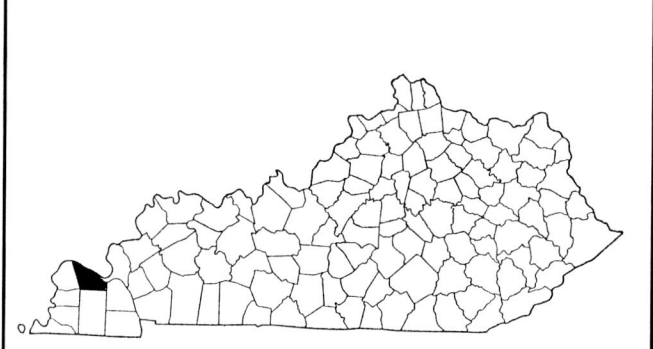
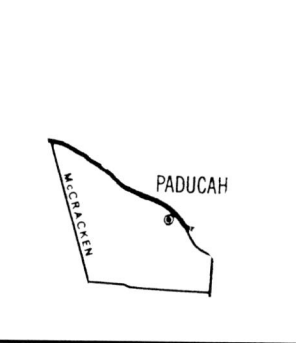

McCracken County, 78th in order of formation, was named for Captain Virgil McCracken of Woodford County — a veteran of the War of 1812, killed at the Battle of River Raisin. Wilmington was established as the first county seat in 1825, but in 1831 the county seat moved to Paducah.

The first McCracken County courthouse at Wilmington was built in 1829-30. On October 12, 1829, a plan was approved for the courthouse. Frederick Harper, the builder, finished the building by May 10, 1830.

The second McCracken County courthouse in Paducah was built in 1832. G. A. Flournoy, Milton Perry, and Braxton Small were appointed commissioners to draft a plan at the March 12, 1832, meeting of the court. The courthouse was specified as a two-story, brick building of the foursquare form not to exceed 36 feet square. The contract for construction was let on June 11 to Jesse Yondel for $3,049. The building served until 1857, when replaced.

The third McCracken County courthouse was built in 1857-61. L. D. Husbands, J. C. Calhoun, and John H. Terrell were appointed commissioners to supervise construction. On July 30, 1857, it was announced that the design of Stancliff & Vodges, architects of Louisville, had been accepted by the court. On September 15, 1857, the site was purchased of Braxton Small for $6,000, and John F. Hendren of Louisville was contracted to build the courthouse for $27,830. The cornerstone was laid in June 1858 by Braxton Small.

The fourth and present McCracken County courthouse was built in 1941-42. The courthouse was built under a grant provided by the Public Works Administration of the New Deal at a cost of $344,919. The concrete and brick, two-story structure is of colonial styling fronted by a Doric order portico.

Third Courthouse, 1857 *(Harper's Weekly — October 26, 1861)*.

Fourth Courthouse, 1941-42 — architect's original perspective *(Goodman-Paxton Collection, University of Kentucky)*.

93. PAINTSVILLE in JOHNSON COUNTY

Year Formed: 1843

Formed From: Floyd, Lawrence, and Morgan Counties

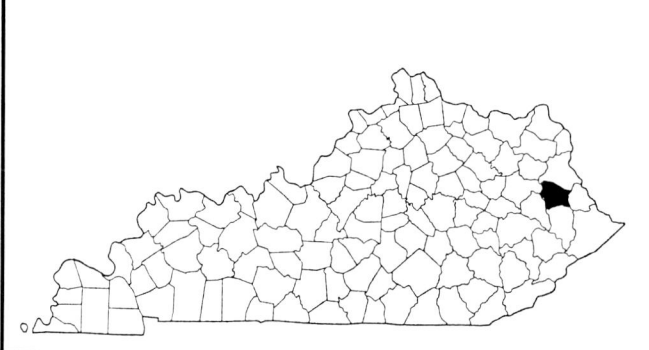

Johnson County, 97th in order of formation, was named for Colonel Richard M. Johnson of Scott County — elected Vice President of the United States in 1836. Paintsville was established as the county seat and named for nearby Paint's Creek.

The first Johnson County courthouse was begun in 1844 and completed in November 1846. The courthouse, a brick building, was ready for occupation by March 3, 1845. John B. and Henry C. Harris were the builders.

The second Johnson County courthouse was built in 1890-92. Frank P. Milburn of Kenova, West Virginia, designed the courthouse in a Richardsonian Romanesque style. Stone and brick for the building came from local quarries and was kilned on the site.

The third and present Johnson County courthouse was built in 1957-58. The modern brick, concrete, and glass courthouse was designed by James Allen Clark of Winchester. The structure cost just over $300,000.

Second Courthouse, 1890 — in March, 1928 *(The Courier-Journal)*.

94. PARIS in BOURBON COUNTY

Year Formed: 1785

Formed From: Fayette County

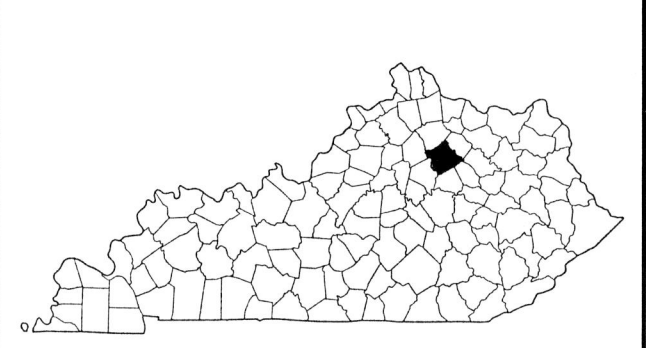

Bourbon County, 5th in order of formation, was named in recognition of the royal house of Bourbon of France — who aided the American colonials during the Revolutionary War. Hopewell, established as the county seat in 1789, changed its name to Bourbonton, and by 1790 was finally named Paris.

The first Bourbon County courthouse was ordered during the November 1786 meeting of the court. Three members were appointed to purchase two acres for a public square and let a contract to the lowest bidder for construction. The courthouse was specified as "a frame [building], thirty-two by twenty feet" and covered with a wooden shingle roof. The building was ready for occupation by the October 16, 1787, meeting of the court.

The second Bourbon County courthouse was ordered by the court in February 1797. The motivating factor was "to rival the great stone temple of justice in Lexington" by Captain John Cape. Upon Cape's death in 1794, the Metcalfe brothers, John and Thomas, became the leading builders in central Kentucky. The Bourbon court contracted with the Metcalfes for the stonework and a Mr. McCord for carpentry of the new courthouse which was finished in 1799. Originally the building had a small box cupola, which was replaced in 1816 by a tall spire cupola made by Aquilla Talbott, similar to those on the 1806 Lexington courthouse and new Bardstown Cathedral. This building burned on May 8, 1872.

The building of the third Bourbon County courthouse commenced in 1873 and was finished in October 1874 at a cost of $125,000. Albert C. Nash, a leading Cincinnati architect, designed the three-story, Second Empire style building. Numerous contractors worked under the court appointed committee consisting of Joseph Mitchell, William Shaw, and George C. White. Fire destroyed this courthouse in 1901.

The fourth and current Bourbon County courthouse was constructed between 1902 and 1905. Frank P. Milburn of Washington, D.C., designer of several Kentucky courthouses, provided the Beaux-Arts design. The first story is South Carolina granite and the upper floors are Bedford stone. Gibson & Crawford of Logansport, Indiana, were the contractors at a cost of $170,000. The Bourbon County courthouse was listed on the National Register of Historic Places in 1974.

Left: Second Courthouse, 1797.

Right: Third Courthouse, 1873 *(Ward Collection, University of Kentucky Special Collection)*.

95. PIKEVILLE in PIKE COUNTY

Year Formed: 1821

Formed From: Floyd County

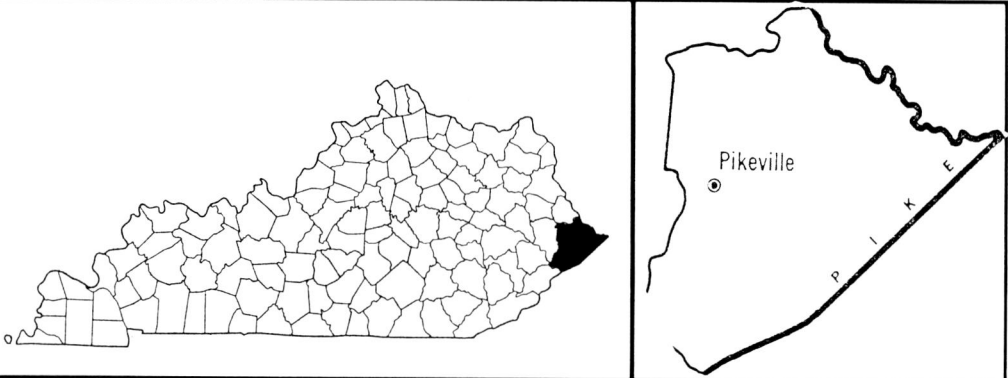

Pike County, 70th in order of formation, was named in honor of General Zebulon Montgomery Pike of New Jersey — famous explorer of the Mississippi River and Louisiana Territory, killed during the War of 1812 leading the attack against the Canadian capital of York. Liberty was established as the county seat in 1822, but the court became dissatisfied with this location and moved making Pikeville the county seat in 1824.

The first Pike County courthouse was built in 1824. John Bevins, Thomas May, and William Ferguson were appointed commissioners to supervise construction. The court ordered the building be 24 feet square, of chinked log construction. John Honaker apparently voluntarily built the courthouse which served the county until about 1888, when the current courthouse was built. This is a remarkable tribute to its construction.

The second and present Pike County courthouse was built in 1888-89. This courthouse was a standard design provided by H. P. McDonald & Brothers, architects of Louisville. The building is a brick, two-story structure of an eclectic design typical of the Victorian period. In 1932-33 the courthouse underwent a radical redesign and alteration, greatly enlarging the building. This work was done under a grant provided by the Public Works Administration of the New Deal paying part of the $110,000 cost. An elevator shaft has been added to the front of the building in recent years. The Pike County courthouse was listed on the National Register of Historic Places in 1976.

Second Courthouse, 1888 — Pikeville in the 1930's.

96. PINEVILLE in BELL COUNTY

Year Formed: 1867

Formed From: Harlan and Knox Counties

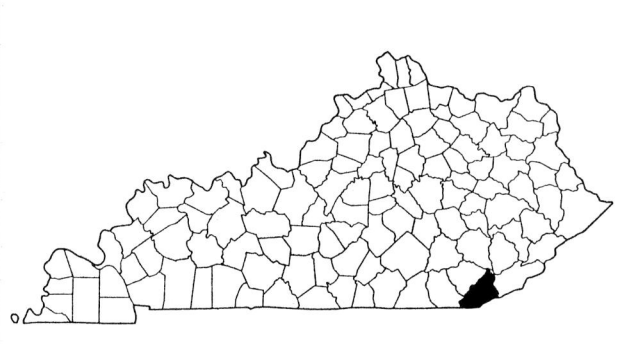

Bell County, 112th in order of formation, was named for Joshua Frye Bell — a Danville lawyer who served in the Kentucky legislature. Upon the formation of Bell County there were no towns yet established in the unsettled region. "Old Pineville," originally Cumberland Ford, was laid off by order of the court of October 15, 1867, and designated as the county seat. Pineville was named in reference to its location, where the Cumberland River breaks through Pine Mountain.

The first attempt to construct a Bell County courthouse was made in 1869 on property given by J. J. Gibson in January of that year. The proposed courthouse was described as a large frame building but was not accepted by the court on account of its poor construction.

The first Bell County courthouse was built in 1870-71. In March 1870, W. H. Baughman, Jr. signed a contract to built the courthouse which was finished in one year. No description of this courthouse is known.

The second Bell County courthouse was begun in 1888. H.P. McDonald & Brothers of Louisville, responsible for numerous Kentucky courthouses, designed the $30,000 courthouse. Built in the center of town, this courthouse burned about 1914.

The third Bell County courthouse was built in 1914. The two-story, brick courthouse of late-Victorian style burned on June 14, 1918.

The present and fourth courthouse was built between 1919 and 1920. The three-story, brick building is a classical Beaux-Arts influenced design by John W. Gaddis, architect of Vincennes, Indiana, who specialized in courthouse design. Fire gutted the building on March 4, 1944, which was renovated immediately afterwards.

Third Courthouse, 1914, just completed *(The Filson Club)*.

97. PRESTONSBURG in FLOYD COUNTY

Year Formed: 1799

Formed From: Fleming, Mason, and Montgomery Counties

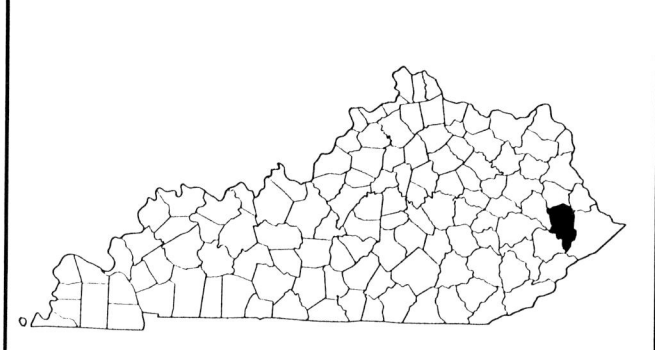

Floyd County, 40th in order of formation, was named in honor of Colonel John Floyd — one of Kentucky's earliest explorers and surveyors. Prestonsburg, originally "Preston's Station," was established as the county seat in 1799 and named for Colonel John Preston who originally owned the area.

The first Floyd County courthouse was contracted for at the March 1806 session of the court. Thomas Evans was to build the log structure covered with weatherboard. Nearly completed, the structure burned on April 16, 1808.

The second Floyd County courthouse was started immediately with Thomas Evans again acting as contractor. At the October 25, 1808, session of the court the new building was specified: "The house is to be 24 feet by 18 feet, of good sound logs, one-and-a-half-stories high, cracks chinked with stone and lime outside and covered with good shingles, two good floors and jury room above the stairs and the lower room entirely for the Court with a Justice's seat, a Clerk's table and Lawyers bar with the necessary doors, window sashes and glass." Evans was given one year to complete the structure. In fact the court met in the building for the first time on October 23, 1809, however the building was not accepted by the court until May 1815.

The third Floyd County courthouse commenced in 1818 and completed in September 1821. William J. Mayo, Henry B. Mayo and Richard Lee were appointed commissioners to supervise construction. The two-story brick courthouse was of foursquare form measuring 30 feet. Samuel May, Evan's brother-in-law constructed the building. The building was altered in 1867 and 1884.

The fourth Floyd County courthouse was commenced in 1888 when relocated to the current site and completed the next year. The lot was acquired from James M. Lackey. A brick building was completed in 1891. During the 1930s an annex was added to the building but even with this addition the building became inadequate and was demolished in 1963.

The fifth and present Floyd County courthouse was completed in 1964. The structure is a three-story building of modern concrete construction. George Lee Shannon was the architect and Ervin & Allen Akers Construction of Dana, Kentucky, the contractors. The building cost about $600,000.

Fourth Courthouse, 1888-91 — just completed *(The Filson Club)*.

98. PRINCETON in CALDWELL COUNTY

Year Formed: 1809

Formed From: Livingston County

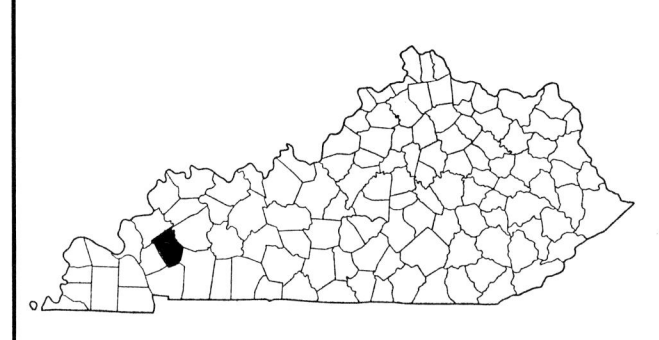
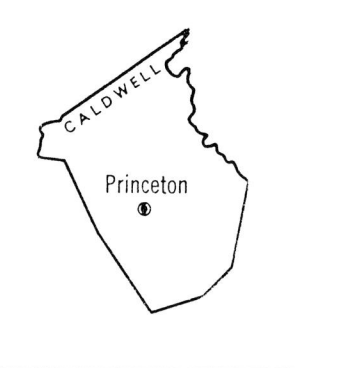

Caldwell County, 51st in order of formation, was named for General John Caldwell of Nelson County — a state legislator elected Lt. Governor in 1804. Princeton was established as the county seat in 1809.

The first Caldwell County courthouse was ordered built in the year 1817-20. Dr. William Carroll Hayden built the two-story log structure measuring 16 X 20 feet. The first floor was finished in 1818 and the second in 1820.

A second Caldwell County courthouse was constructed in 1838-40. The plans were drafted by S. Lindsay, which he modeled on the Christain County courthouse by Hugh Roland. The Greek Revival style courthouse was built at a cost of $3000. On December 15, 1864, during Confederate General Hylan B. Lyon's march through western Kentucky his troops passed through Princeton, burning this courthouse.

The third Caldwell County courthouse, started at the end of the Civil War in 1865 and completed the following year. The courthouse was of an advanced Italianate design, as were most of the period. The building was razed in September, 1938 to permit construction of the present building.

The fourth and present Caldwell County courthouse was begun on September 6, 1938 and was completed on February 15, 1941. The building was constructed with a grant and under the direction of the Works Progress Administration. The W.P.A. was represented by C. W. Thomason, Assistant District Supervisor in charge of buildings; A. B. Cates, Area Engineer; and Russell Petrie, field engineer-Portland Cement Association. Lawrence Casner, architect of Madisonville, designed the structure to be the most modern of any in western Kentucky. The building was constructed of poured concrete which utilized maximum manpower, a main objective of New Deal projects. Princeton Attorney R.W. Lisanby acted a the chief proponent of the project, the final cost of which was $178,997.

Third Courthouse, 1865-66, in 1937 (*The Courier Journal*).

Third Courthouse, 1865-66.

99. RICHMOND in MADISON COUNTY

Year Formed: 1785

Formed From: Lincoln County

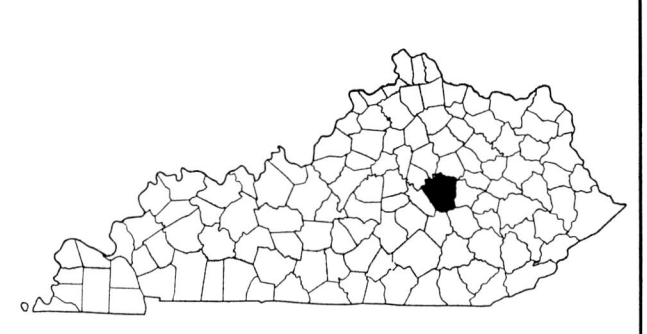

Madison County, 7th in order of formation, was named for President James Madison. Milford or Old Town was the first county seat. Richmond was established as the permanent county seat in 1798.

The first Madison County courthouse at Milford was built in 1786. Little is known of this courthouse, William Golden is believed to have built the courthouse. Green Clay states it was a two-story, log structure measuring 30' X 20' with a large stone chimney on the end.

The second Madison County courthouse at Richmond was built in 1799. John Miller, Robert Rodes, Green Clay, Robert Caldwell, and John Patrick were appointed commissioners to supervise construction. Tyre Rodes built the brick, two-story courthouse.

The third and present Madison County courthouse was built 1848-50. William Rodes, Joseph Turner, and J. M. Shackleford were appointed commissioners to procure a plan on April 3, 1848. At the meeting of the court on July 4, 1848, a plan by Major Thomas Lewinski, architect of Lexington, was adopted for which he received $260. Bowman & Thompson and Lewis & Bolt were the contractors, the entire work costing $35,000. The brick, two-story courthouse is of the Greek Revival style, a central temple form with wings. In an 1880 remodeling the porticos on the front of the wings were removed and replaced by windows. The interior was also remodeled, the court room receiving the major attention. A second major remodeling took place in 1964, consisting of the addition of a rear wing and major interior updating. The Madison County courthouse was listed on the National Register of Historic Places in 1975.

100. RUSSELLVILLE in LOGAN COUNTY

Year Formed: 1792

Formed From: Lincoln County

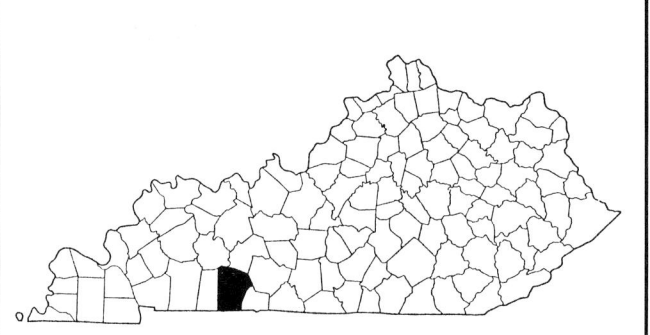

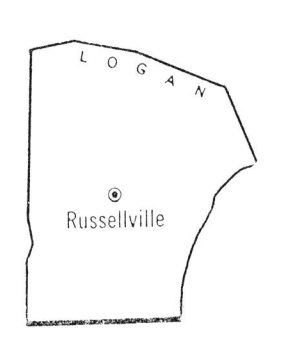

Logan County, 15th in order of formation, was named for General Benjamin Logan of Lincoln County — early settler who established St. Asaph's Station and member of the conventions which produced Kentucky's first Constitution in 1799. Russellville was established as the county seat and named for General William Russell of Virginia — original owner of the land.

The first Logan County courthouse was built in 1792-93. By January 22, 1793 the courthouse, located near Big Boiling Spring, was ready for occupancy. Built of cedar log, the building was known as the Cedar House.

The second Logan County courthouse was built in 1798-1822. At the March 1798 meeting of the court, it was order that a courthouse be constructed in Russellville. Reuben Ewing, William Reading, Robert Ewing, Samuel Caldwell, and Amos Balch were appointed commissioners to obtain a plan for the courthouse. The building, located at the corner of Fourth and Winter Streets, was two-story brick building of the foursquare form topped by a cupola. The building was not completed until 1822, due to the death of the contractor, Robert McReynolds. By 1900, the building was in poor condition and in need of replacement. In December of 1902, someone exploded a bomb in the courthouse making replacement imperative.

The third and present Logan County courthouse was built in 1903-04. Judge J. W. Clark, J. S. Flowers, J. Rice Gill, and Dr. S. S. McReynolds were appointed commissioners to supervise construction. The design of W. Chamberlin of Atlanta was chosen from several submitted to the court. The contractor, Robert Manley, also of Atlanta, was the low bidder for the project at $38,000. He proved unsatisfactory and was replaced by E. W. Furrey, who completed the work for $34,755.50. The courthouse was ready for occupancy on December 1, 1904. Lexington architectural firm Harrison, Hisle, and Associates supervised the renovation in 1972-73. Boogie Faulkner Contractors of Campbellsville performed the work. Numerous interior and exterior changes were made, including the addition of a new cupola with a clock. The Logan County courthouse was listed on the National Register of Historic Places in 1976 as a contributing property of a historic district.

Left: Second Courthouse, 1798 (*Collection of Mrs. Sara Clark & Mrs. Al Hunt*).

Right: Third Courthouse, 1903 (*Caufield & Shook Collection, University of Louisville Photographic Archives*).

101. SALYERSVILLE in MAGOFFIN COUNTY

Year Formed: 1860

Formed From: Floyd, Johnson, and Morgan Counties

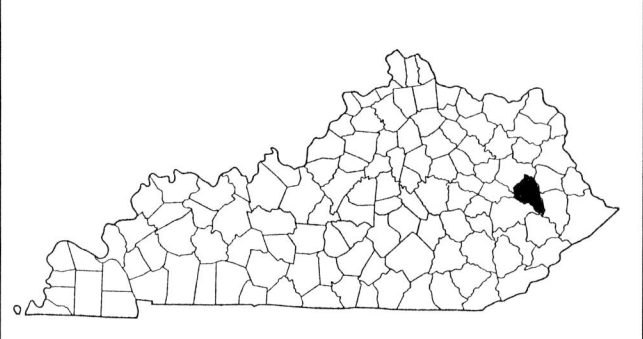

Magoffin County, 108th in order of formation, was named for Beriah Maggoffin — Governor of Kentucky when the county was formed. Salyersville, known as Adamsville until 1860, was established as the county seat. Salyersville was named for Samuel Salyer, the first representative in the Legislature from this county, who used his influence to get the county formed.

The first Magoffin County courthouse was built in 1861-62. The site of this and the future courthouses was donated to the county by William Adams. Sam May designed the courthouse. Sam Salyer, given the contract to build the courthouse, was unable to fulfill his obligation and Henry Hager completed the building. The courthouse was used until 1893.

The second Magoffin County courthouse was built in 1893. Frank P. Milburn, architect of Kenova, West Virginia, supplied a design based on his standard courthouse design. Only the Magoffin and Clay County courthouses are known collaborations of the father and son team, each known as a courthouse expert of his day. The stone trim of the courthouse was local sandstone. Fire destroyed the courthouse on February 22, 1957.

The third and present Magoffin County courthouse was built in 1959. The courthouse is a three-story, concrete, glass, and steel building of modern construction.

Second Courthouse, 1893.

102. SANDY HOOK in ELLIOTT COUNTY

Year Formed: 1869

Formed From: Carter, Lawrence, and Morgan Counties

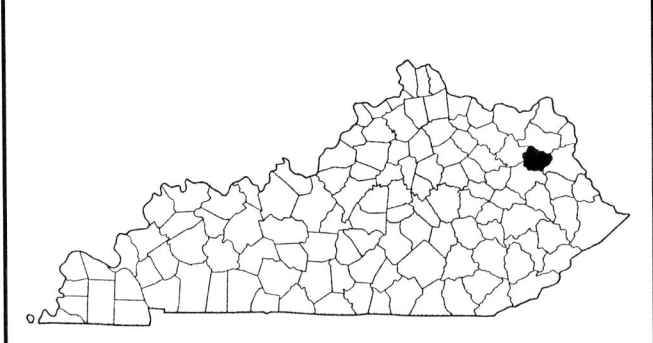

Elliott County, 114th in order of formation, was named for Judge John M. Elliott — a member of United States House of Representatives, Kentucky Representative, and Circuit Judge. Sandy Hook, once Martinsburg, was established as the county seat in 1869.

The first Elliott County courthouse is believed to have been built immediately upon formation of the county in 1869. The brick, two-story courthouse was a front-gabled building of the Greek Revival style, even though the style was out of date by this time.

The second Elliott County courthouse was built in 1937 under the supervision of the Works Progress Administration. The courthouse was a two-story stone building and featured an open first floor lobby covered by shutters. This courthouse burned on December 19, 1957, destroying some records dating from the formation of the county.

The third and current Elliott County courthouse is a modern-style structure dedicated in February 1968.

Left: First Courthouse, 1869 *(Historical Highlights of Elliott County)*.
Center: Second Courthouse, 1937 *(Historical Highlights of Elliott County)*.
Above: Second Courthouse, 1937 — after 1957 fire *(The Courier-Journal)*.

103. SCOTTSVILLE in ALLEN COUNTY

Year Formed: 1815

Formed From: Barren and Warren Counties

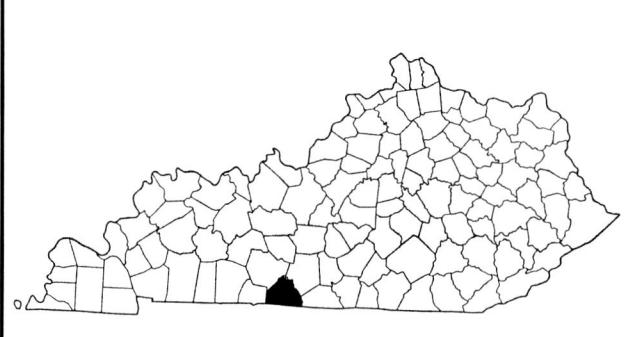

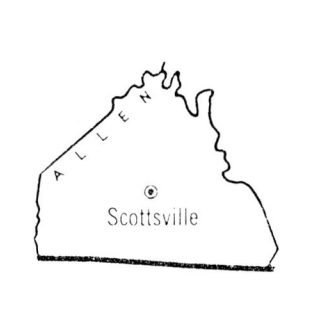

Allen County, 57th in order of formation, was named for Colonel John Allen of Mercer and Nelson Counties - an early settler and "Indian Fighter," killed at the Battle of River Raisin during the War of 1812. Scottsville was established as the county seat and named for General Winfield Scott of the United States Army.

The first Allen County courthouse was built in 1816, the same year Scottsville was laid out. The design of the brick, two-story, octagonal courthouse was a progressive form for public buildings of the period, not introduced in domestic architecture until the 1850s. John Bird was the contractor. The building was used by the court until it was replaced in 1900.

The second Allen County courthouse was built in 1903. Although constructed after the turn-of-the-century, the building retains an eclectic style typical to the Victorian period. The brick, two-story courthouse contains Italianate details such as the arched windows and brackets, topped by an enormous cupola. The building was demolished in May 1967 by order of the Kentucky Department of Transportation in order to speed the auto-traffic flow through the public square! County Judge Ernest C. Neil is credited with saving the bell from the structure which was placed atop the City-County Building.

The third Allen County courthouse was built in 1967-69. The two-story building is a modern design constructed of poured concrete and brick.

Left: First Courthouse, 1816 *(Collection of Mrs. Grace Hill, Scottsville)*.

Right: Second Courthouse, 1903, arrowing showing weathervane that disappeared *(The Courier-Journal)*.

104. SHELBYVILLE in SHELBY COUNTY

Year Formed: 1792

Formed From: Jefferson County

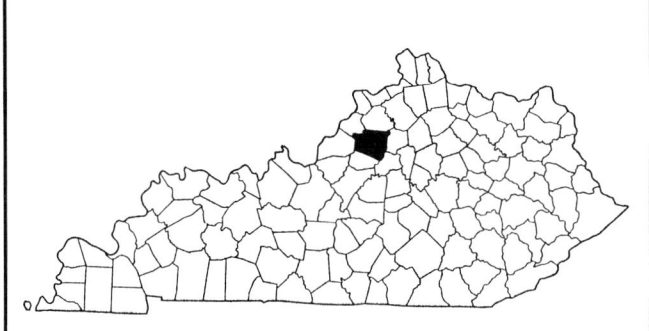

Shelby County, 12th in order of formation, was named in honor of Issac Shelby, first Governor of Kentucky, holding office at the time the county was formed. Shelbyville was established as the county seat and named for Shelby as well.

The first Shelby County courthouse was built in 1793. William Shannon was contracted to build the courthouse on January 15, 1793, for 15 pounds. The courthouse was built of log. Shannon also donated the land on which the courthouse was built.

The second Shelby County courthouse was built in 1796. John Allen, Benjamin Logan, Adam Steele, Martin Daniel, and Isham Talbot were appointed commissioners to obtain a plan and supervise construction. The plan chosen was by a Mr. Hunter and specified a two-story, brick structure measuring 36 X 42 feet. The building was to have a spire and pediment over the entrance. Josiah and Winfield Bullock were the low bidders for construction at 1076 pounds.

The third Shelby county courthouse was built in 1814. This was apparently a brick structure of the foursquare form covered by a hip roof with a cupola in the center. In 1841 this building was declared unsafe by the court and the offices moved to other quarters.

The fourth Shelby County courthouse was built in 1844-47. William Kinkade, George W. Johnson, Robert T. Robb, William S. Helm, and Samuel W. Moore were appointed commissioners to supervise construction in February 1844. Thomas B. Caldwell contracted in the same month to build the courthouse at a cost of $11,150.84. The cornerstone was laid on June 11, 1844. The courthouse was a square, three-story, brick structure fronted by a two-story, Doric order portico over which a spire rises above the roof. The courthouse was dismantled in 1911 the make way for the current structure.

The fifth and present Shelby County courthouse was built in 1912. The courthouse is a very elaborate classical Beaux-Arts influenced building designed by the Louisville architectural firm of Joseph & Joseph. The building is a two-story stone structure fronted by a Corinthian order portico. The Shelby County courthouse was listed on the National Register of Historic Places in 1978 as a contributing property of a historic district.

Left: Fourth Courthouse, 1844 *(University of Kentucky Special Collection, Postcard Collection)*.
Right: Fifth Courthouse, 1912 — shortly after completion *(Joseph & Joseph Brochure of 1925)*.

105. SHEPHERDSVILLE in BULLITT COUNTY

Year Formed: 1796

Formed From: Jefferson and Nelson Counties

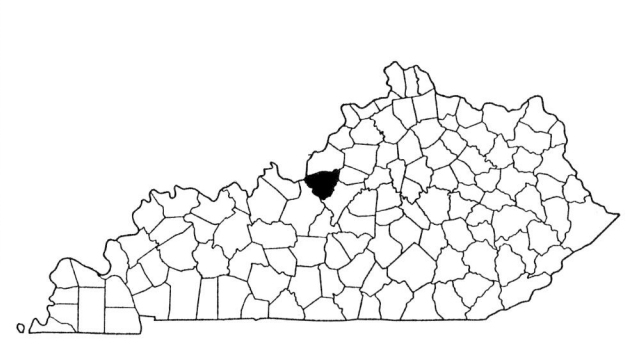

Bullitt County, 20th in order of formation, was named for Alexander Scott Bullitt of Jefferson County — a prominent statesman, elected lieutenant governor in 1800. Shepherdsville was established as the county seat contemporary with establishment of the county.

The first Bullitt County courthouse, conceived in 1801, remained only an idea until July 1803 when the court contracted with Henry Crist to build the two-story, brick structure which measured 28 X 46 feet. The building, completed in July 1804 at a cost of $3,150, was topped by a cupola containing a bell cast in Philadelphia.

The second and present Bullitt County courthouse was built in 1900-1901 at a cost of $11,500. The building is an early courthouse of classical Beaux-Arts influenced design. The contractors were Brashear and Johnson.

First Courthouse, 1804 *(The Filson Club)*.

Second Courthouse, 1900 *(The Kentucky Historical Society)*.

106. SMITHLAND in LIVINGSTON COUNTY

Year Formed: 1798

Formed From: Christian County

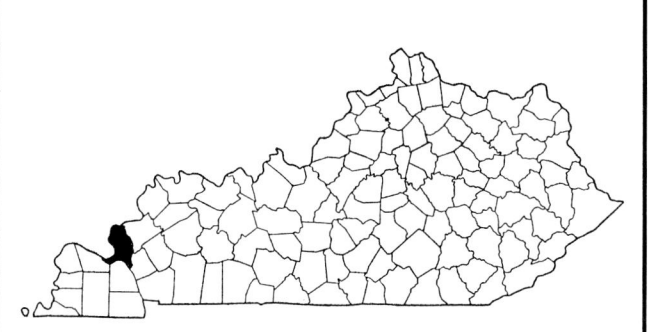

Livingston County, 29th in order of formation, was named for Robert R. Livingston of New York — signer of the Declaration of Independence. The first county seat was Eddyville in 1799, but moved to Centerville in 1804, then Salem in 1809. Smithland was established as the permanent county seat in 1841.

The first Livingston County courthouse at Eddyville was built in 1800-01. On March 25, 1800, the court ordered a public building be built not to exceed $500. The courthouse was completed and received by the court on December 7, 1801.

No courthouse is known to have been built in Centerville while it was the county seat from 1804 to 1809.

The second Livingston County courthouse at Salem was built shortly after 1809. The courthouse of hewn logs was built by William Rodgers who also donated the site. It served until 1841 when the county seat was moved to Smithland.

The third and present Livingston County courthouse at Smithland was built in 1844-45. At the July 1842 meeting of the court, the site for the courthouse was chosen to be on land donated by James Lillard. At the same meeting, Blount Hodge, R. W. Alcorn, Issac Shelby, David Fort, and William Garden were appointed commissioners to let the contract for the building. The contract was let to Preston Grace of Princeton, Kentucky on August 8, 1842. The courthouse was finished and accepted by the court on August 8, 1845, at a cost of $6,800. The two-story, brick building originally measured 50' X 40', and was of vernacular design. A front addition in the Italianate style appears to have been added in the 1870s. Several other additions have been made to the building over the years.

107. SOMERSET in PULASKI COUNTY

Year Formed: 1798

Formed From: Green and Lincoln Counties

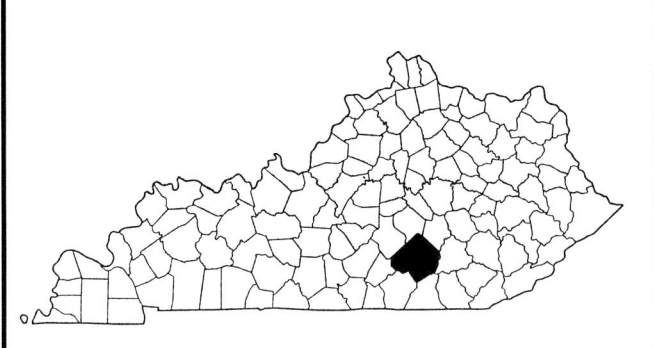

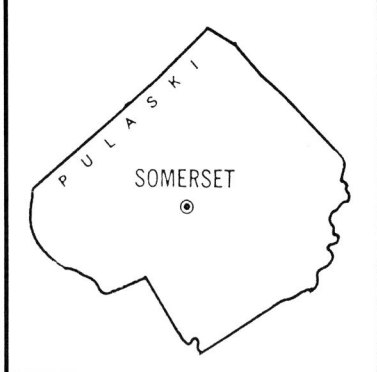

Pulaski County, 27th in order of formation, was named for Count Joseph Pulaski, a Polish native who fought for the colonies during the Revolutionary War, killed at the Battle of Savannah. Somerset was established as the county seat and named for Somerset County, New Jersey, the origin of a number of early settlers.

The first Pulaski County courthouse was built in 1801. On February 25, 1801, Samuel McKee, James Hardgrove, Edward Turner, James Prather, and Nicholas Jasper were appointed commissioners to supervise construction. Francis McGowan was hired to build the courthouse on June 24, 1801 for 23 dollars. The building, described as a log structure, was first used on September 22, 1801.

The second Pulaski County courthouse was built between 1804 and 1808. No good description of this courthouse exists other than its being built of brick. This courthouse burned in 1838.

The third Pulaski County courthouse was built in 1839-40. This was the first structure built on the present courthouse square. On December 7, 1871, fire destroyed the courthouse and quite a bit of the town.

The building of the fourth Pulaski County courthouse commenced in 1873 and was dedicated on February 23, 1874. The brick, two-story courthouse of the transitional Italianate style design, no doubt was designed by an architect. The estimated cost was $25,000. The rear addition was built under a grant provided by the Public Works Administration of the New Deal in 1939-40 at a cost of $85,999.

The fifth and present Pulaski County courthouse was completed in the summer of 1975. The new building is of a classical design being fronted by a well designed Doric order portico. The brick, two-story building reflects the pilasters from the previous structure. The 1939-40 addition built at the rear of the old courthouse was retained.

Fourth Courthouse, *1873 (Tuggle, George, Pulaski Revisited)*.

Fourth Courthouse, P. W. A. addition, 1939-40 *(Goodman-Paxton Collection, University of Kentucky Special Collection)*.

108. SPRINGFIELD in WASHINGTON COUNTY

Year Formed: 1792

Formed From: Nelson County

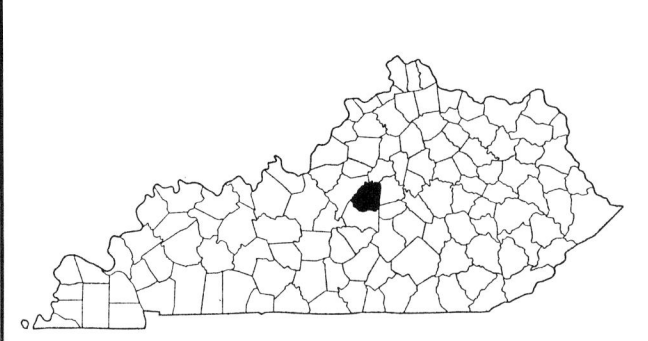

Washington County, 10th in order of formation, was named for President George Washington. Springfield was established as the county seat in 1793.

The building of the first Washington County courthouse began in 1793-94. Hugh McElroy contracted to build the log courthouse in February 1793 and he finished it the next January. Until that time the court met in his house, the first brick house on the "big trace" connecting Danville to Bardstown. This first courthouse burned just 11 months after completed.

The second Washington County courthouse was completed in July 1797. The courthouse was a side-gabled, brick building. John Dowdal erected the courthouse for 404 pounds, 20 shillings. Fire also consumed this courthouse in May of 1814.

The third Washington County courthouse was built in 1814-16. Robert Crouch, Paul Booker, John Reed, David Rodman, John Calhoon, Arthur Gibbins, and Jacob Seay were appointed commissioners to contract for a new courthouse. In May 1814, Thomas H. Letcher was awarded the contract to build the courthouse for $4,195. The two-story, brick courthouse is an approximately square building completed July 1816. The present cupola was added in 1840. In July 1918, a single-story, Doric order portico and new window sashes were added to the building under the direction of architect Frank Brewer. The two-story, stone structure at the rear was built in 1938-40 under a grant provided by the Public Works Administration of the New Deal. The Washington County courthouse was listed on the National Register of Historic Places in 1977.

Third Courthouse, 1814 *(Collection of Mrs. E. O. Kelly)*.

Third Courthouse, 1814 — about 1920.

109. STANFORD in LINCOLN COUNTY

Year Formed: 1780

Formed From: Kentucky

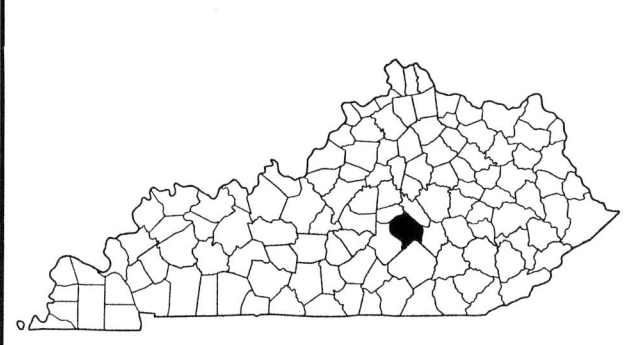
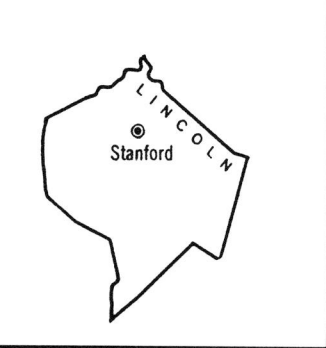

Lincoln, Fayette and Jefferson Counties were Kentucky's first three counties created by the Virginia legislature on November 1, 1780. Lincoln County is named in honor of General Benjamin Lincoln — a distinguished Revolutionary War veteran. The first courts held in Kentucky were in Lincoln County at the first county seat, Harrodsburg, but in 1785 with the formation of Mercer County, the courts moved to St. Asaph's, the fort built by General Benjamin Logan. Shortly afterward in May 1786, Stanford was established as the permanent county seat.

The first Lincoln County courthouse was built in 1785. The building is reported as a simple two room log courthouse built at St. Asaph's.

The second Lincoln County courthouse at Stanford was built in 1787. In February 1787, the court appointed four magistrates to "let the building of a courthouse, the body to be of good white ash or oak log well hewn and Dufftailed, 30 feet long, 20 feet wide, and 14 feet pitch, to be covered with lapt shingles; two jury rooms of the same kind of logs and roof, one on each side of the house, ... the whole building shall form a T ...". The new building was first used by the court in April, 1787, with Issac Shelby (later first the Governor) presiding.

The third Lincoln County courthouse was built in 1832. Little is known concerning the construction of this courthouse other than its being a brick structure. From an existing photograph of the building it appears to have originally been a two-story brick structure of the foursquare form. The courthouse had several remodelings since construction including the addition of two wings, a classical portico and elaborate cupola. The building served until 1909 when the new courthouse was built.

The fourth and present Lincoln County courthouse was built in 1909. F. Kruger and Sons of Mount Vernon were the contractors for the courthouse. J. R. Powell was the supervisor of construction. Frank P. Milburn, who designed several Kentucky courthouses, designed the building through his Washington, D. C. office, Milburn, Heister & Company. The three-story brick building is a classical Beaux-Arts influenced design with an Ionic order portico fronting the courthouse, incorporating unique brick-rounded columns. In 1940-41, an annex was added to the building built under a grant provided by the Public Works Administration of the New Deal at a cost of $ 65,538. The Lincoln County courthouse was listed on the National Register of Historic Places in 1976.

Third Courthouse, 1832 — after 1909 wings added *(Collection of Judge Leonard Boone)*.

110. STANTON in POWELL COUNTY

Year Formed: 1852

Formed From: Clark, Estill, and Montgomery Counties

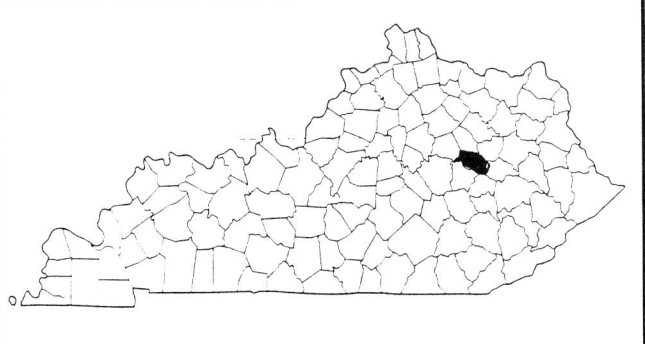

Powell County, 101st in order of formation, was named in honor of Lazarus W. Powell — Governor of Kentucky when the county was formed. Stanton, originally called Beaver Pond, was established as the county seat and named for Richard H. Stanton of Maysville - member of the U.S. House of Representatives and Circuit Judge.

The first Powell County courthouse was probably built shortly after the county was formed in 1852. No description of this courthouse or a predecessor is known. During the Civil War Confederate guerillas burned the courthouse in the summer of 1863. The jail burned on June 1, 1864 destroying all county records.

The second Powell County courthouse, built after the Civil War, served until the third courthouse was built in 1890.

The third Powell County courthouse was built about 1890. This is the second courthouse in the state designed by Bowling Green native Frank Pierce Milburn. The building was possibly built by Thomas T. Milburn, the father of Frank, a noted courthouse architect and builder himself. The courthouse is a brick, two-story structure which combines elements of the outgoing Victorian period and the classical features which were rising in popularity. Originally the cupola was a tall spire, but it had to be removed in 1955 due to deterioration. A two-room addition was made on the west side of the building in the 1960s. In 1977 the courthouse was demolished to make way for the present building.

The fourth and present Powell County courthouse was built in 1977-78. The building possibly reflects one of the most sensitive modern designs, making reference to traditional motifs such as the clock tower and fountain. The building is a single-story, brick structure designed by the Lexington architectural firm of Chrisman, Miller and Wallace.

Third Courthouse, 1890 *(Kentucky Heritage Council)*.

Third Courthouse, 1890 *(Kentucky Heritage Council)*.

111. TAYLORSVILLE in SPENCER COUNTY

Year Formed: 1824

Formed From: Bullitt, Nelson, and Shelby Counties

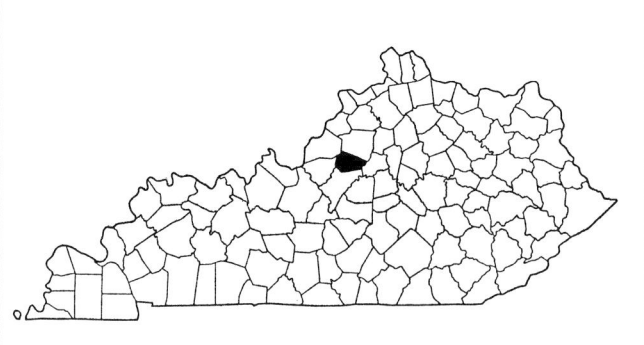

Spencer County, 77th in order of formation, was named for Captain Spear Spencer — killed at the battle of Tippecanoe. Taylorsville, originally Spencerville, was established as the county seat and named for Richard Taylor, original owner of the town site.

The first Spencer County courthouse was established in an existing structure on April 11, 1825. George Bourne, Raphael Lancaster, and Thomas Barker were appointed commissioners to submit a plan and let to the lowest bidder a contract for remodeling a house purchased from Taylor Boyse for use as the courthouse.

The second Spencer County courthouse was built in 1828. The courthouse is only described as a brick building. Confederate guerrillas burned this courthouse in January 1865; fortunately, the records were saved. Federal troops caught the culprits in Mount Eden, killing one and capturing and executing the other.

The third Spencer County courthouse was built in 1866. The building was a brick, two-story structure of Italianate design. This courthouse burned as well in 1914.

The fourth and present Spencer County courthouse was built in 1914-15. The courthouse is a brick, two-story structure of classical Beaux-Arts influenced design. The raised basement building is fronted by a Roman Ionic order portico.

112. TOMPKINSVILLE in MONROE COUNTY

Year Formed: 1820

Formed From: Barren and Cumberland Counties

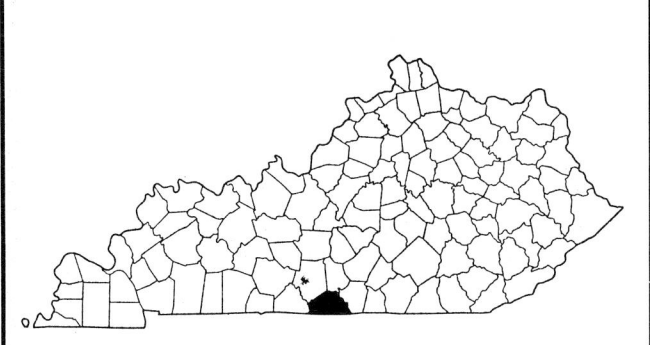
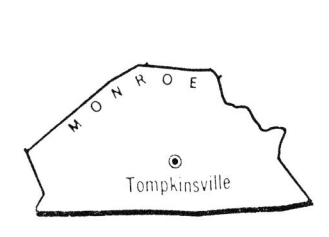

Monroe County, 65th in order of formation, was named for President James Monroe. Tompkinsville was established as the county seat.

The first Monroe County courthouse was built in 1822-23. The courthouse, the first brick structure in the county, was supported by a stone foundation. Confederate guerillas under Colonel Ollie Hamilton burned the courthouse on April 22, 1863. This was done in reprisal for the burning of the Celina, Tennessee courthouse by Federal troops.

The second Monroe County courthouse, built in 1864-65, was to follow similar lines of the previous building, utilizing its foundations. Fire consumed this courthouse in 1877.

The third Monroe County courthouse, a brick, two-story building of the Italianate style, was built in 1887-89. Decorative features included the semi-circular, arched windows and doors, brackets supporting the extended eave of the roof, and a small circular cupola. This courthouse was dismantled in 1975.

The fourth and present Monroe County courthouse was built in 1976. The brick, two-story building is of a modern Georgian design. The entrance is emphasized by a two-story, semi-circular arch, reflecting the previous building.

Third Courthouse, 1887 *(Caufield & Shook Collection, Univeristy of Louisville Photographic Archives)*.

113. VANCEBURG in LEWIS COUNTY

Year Formed: 1806

Formed From: Mason County

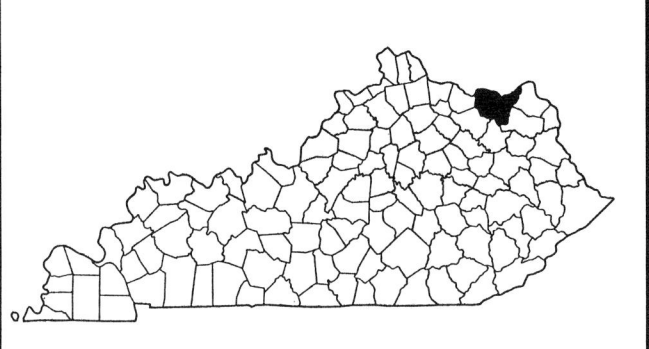
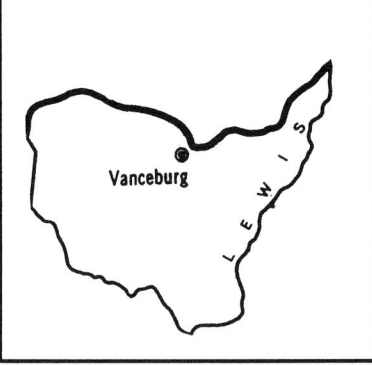

Lewis County, 48th in order of formation, was named for Captain Meriwether Lewis — the famed explorer of the western United States. Poplar Flat was the first county seat, Clarksburg the second in 1809, and Vanceburg the third county seat, established in 1863.

The first Lewis County courthouse at Poplar Flat was built in 1806.

The second Lewis County courthouse at Clarksburg was built in 1809-10. Aaron Stratton, J.G. McDaniel, and Winslow Parker were appointed commissioners to decide on both the site and the plan for the new courthouse. The courthouse was described as a two-story, log structure measuring 24' X 30'.

The third Lewis County courthouse at Vanceburg was built in 1864-65. John Ingrim, Fred M. Carr, and John Thomas Parker were appointed commissioners to let the contract for the new courthouse. A Mr. Flora of Bracken County built the courthouse at a cost of $25,000. The building was used until 1939 when the current courthouse was built.

The fourth and current Lewis County courthouse was built in 1938-40. The building was modeled on Independence Hall in Philadelphia and built under a grant provided by the Public Works Administration of the New Deal. The stone for the three-story courthouse was quarried four miles from Vanceburg. The entire cost was $ 98,277.

Third Courthouse, 1864 *(The Lewis Herald,* February 28, 1974)

Fourth Courthouse, 1939 — as finished in 1940
(Goodman-Paxton Collection, University of Kentucky).

114. VERSAILLES in WOODFORD COUNTY

Year Formed: 1788

Formed From: Fayette County

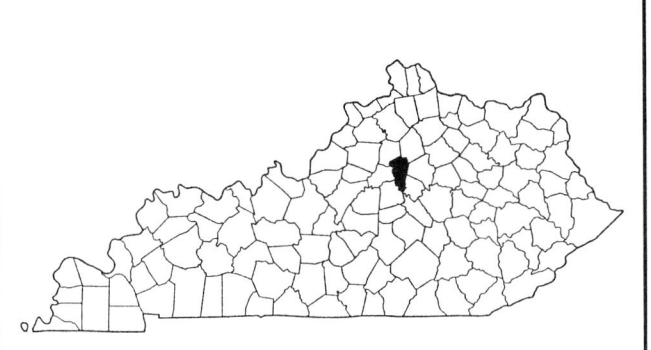
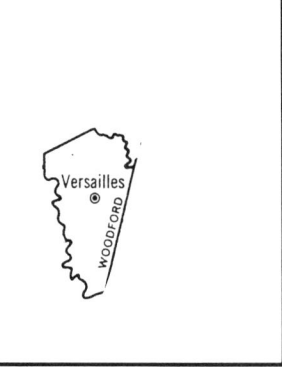

Woodford County, 9th in order of formation, was named for General William Woodford of Virginia — a veteran of the Revolutionary War captured at the Battle of Charleston and imprisoned in New York where he died in 1780. Versailles was established as the county seat in 1790 and named for the French city of the same title.

The first Woodford County courthouse was built in 1790. The courthouse was described as constructed of "buckeye logs with a platform for the judge, a place for the bar and some benches." Jesse Graddy built the courthouse at a cost of apparently only $22.50.

The second Woodford County courthouse was built in 1793. The courthouse was a two-story, stone structure located near Big Spring. James and Henry Tompkins built the courthouse for 330 pounds.

The third Woodford County courthouse was built in 1809. The courthouse was a brick structure of unknown dimensions. In 1845 a cupola containing a clock was added to the building. The building underwent a $22,300 alteration in 1880-83 under the direction of Lexington architect Phelix Lundin. A large addition was made to the front of the building including a columned portico flanked by mansard-roofed towers and a new cupola, of the Second Empire style. These additions were partially removed in a 1927 remodeling. In 1940 a two-room addition was made to the building. On October 11, 1965, the building burned.

The fourth and present Woodford County courthouse was built in 1968-70. The courthouse is a three-story, brick structure of modern Georgian design. Gault Brothers Construction Company of Lexington began construction in October 1968. The $1,100,000 building was dedicated on September 26, 1970.

Third Courthouse, 1880 *(University of Kentucky Special Collections)*.

115. WARSAW in GALLATIN COUNTY

Year Formed: 1798

Formed From: Franklin and Shelby Counties

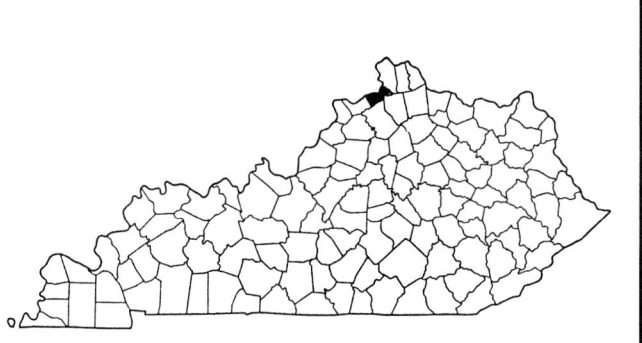

Gallatin County, 33rd in order of formation, was named for Albert Gallatin — Secretary of the Treasury under Thomas Jefferson. Carrollton, originally Port William, was established as the county seat of Gallatin County in 1798, but in 1836, with the formation of Carroll County it was separated from Gallatin County. Warsaw then became the county seat on January 1, 1838.

The first Gallatin County courthouse was built in Port William in 1799-1800. The courthouse was a log structure. This building was located on the bank of the Ohio River between 1st and 2nd Streets.

The second Gallatin County courthouse was built in 1810 at Port William on a new lot donated by Benjamin Craig in that year. The courthouse was built of brick. The courthouse was used until the county seat was moved to Warsaw.

The third and present Gallatin County courthouse was built shortly after the county seat was moved to Warsaw in 1838. The two-story, brick building is a Greek Revival style and originally fronted the river. In 1868, several additions were made to the building including a dome-topped cupola. During the New Deal, the courthouse was remodeled and had two wings added. The work was started on June 15, 1938 and was completed on January 30, 1940. The total cost was $ 47,770. The remodeling included the removal of the cupola and the addition of the portico and entablature, which reoriented the building toward US 42. The Gallatin County courthouse was listed on the National Register of Historic Places in 1982 as a contributing property of a historic district.

116. WEST LIBERTY in MORGAN COUNTY

Year Formed: 1822

Formed From: Bath and Floyd Counties

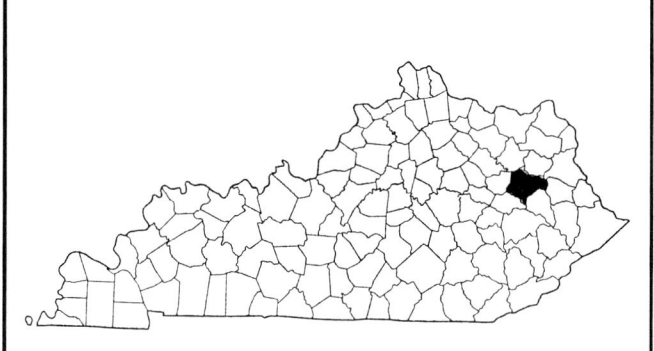

Morgan County, 73rd in order of formation, was named for General David Morgan — a veteran of the Revolutionary War. West Liberty was established as the county seat in 1824.

The first Morgan County courthouse was built in 1826. Commissioners were appointed to let a contract to build the courthouse at the October 1825 session of the court. In January 1826 Edmund Wells contracted to build the two-story, log structure measuring 24 X 26 feet. The building is reported to have been painted bright red.

The second Morgan County courthouse was probably built in the 1840s, but no exact date is known. The building, described as a two-story, brick structure measuring 40 X 44 feet was used during the Civil War as barracks by Union soldiers. The soldiers moved straw into the building to use as beds. On October 1862, one such bed caught on fire, not only burning the courthouse but 28 other downtown structures.

Built shortly after the Civil War, no specific date and no description is known of the third Morgan County courthouse.

The fourth and present Morgan County courthouse was built in 1907. The building follows the popular Beaux-Arts style. The classical two-and-a-half-story, brick structure is basically square with octagonal pavilions projecting at each corner. During 1936 the Public Works Administration of the New Deal provided a grant to stucco the exterior. The courthouse was again altered in the 1970s, enlarging the front entrance. The Morgan County courthouse was listed on the National Register of Historic Places in 1976.

Fourth Courthouse, 1907 — about 1930 *(National Archives)*.

117. WHITESBURG in LETCHER COUNTY

Year Formed: 1842

Formed From: Perry and Harlan Counties

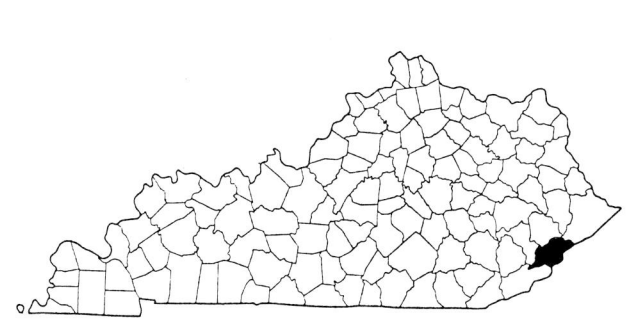

Letcher County, 95th in order of formation, was named for Governor Robert P. Letcher of Kentucky. Whitesburg was established as the county seat.

The first Letcher County courthouse was built in 1843-44. The building is described as being built from logs and planks. Ephraim Hammonds was the builder who started the building, and Rev. John A. Caudill finished the building early 1844. This building was torn down in 1897.

The second Letcher County courthouse was built in 1899. The architect was Frank P. Milburn and the contractor was Lewis R. Perry, whose initials appeared on the keystone over the front door. The courthouse was a brick, two-story, building with a large cupola. On November 29, 1935, an addition to the rear of the courthouse was started under a grant provided by the Public Works Administration of the New Deal. The addition was completed on October 13, 1937 at a cost of $34,062. This courthouse was torn down to make way for a new courthouse in 1963.

The third and present Letcher County courthouse was built in 1963-65. William Banton Moore, architect of Louisville, designed the courthouse, which was constructed by Ramsey and Clubb Construction of Shelbyville. The new modern glass and steel courthouse was dedicated on April 3, 1965.

First Courthouse, 1844 *(Alice Lloyd College)*.

Second Courthouse *(Collection of John W. Carpenter)*.

Second Courthouse, P. W. A. addition of 1937 *(Goodman-Paxton Collection, University of Kentucky)*.

118. WHITLEY CITY in McCREARY COUNTY

Year Formed: 1912

Formed From: Pulaski, Wayne, and Whitley Counties

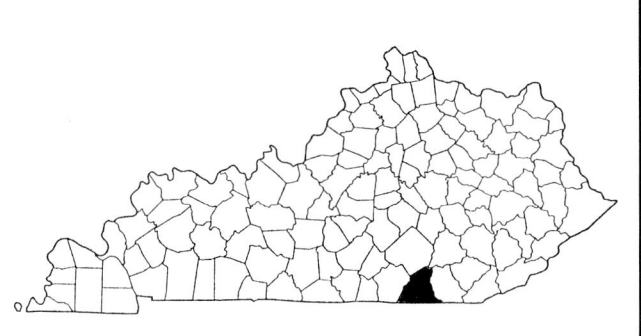

McCreary County, 120th in order of formation, was named for Governor James B. McCreary — in office when the County was formed. Whitley City was established as the county seat.

The first McCreary County courthouse was built in 1914. The building was a two-story "baloon frame" structure covered with a hip roof. The circuit court room and jury room were located on the second floor. On June 16, 1927, this building burned, taking several other buildings with it.

The second McCreary county courthouse was completed in 1929. Considered the county's handsomest building, it was of the Colonial Revival style. The whole cost $ 40,000. This building burned on November 19, 1951.

The third McCreary County courthouse was built from the ruins of the previous building. The rebuilt courthouse cost $118,000, and was occupied in May, 1953. A wing was added to the building in 1975.

First Courthouse, 1914 *(McCreary Conquest)*.

Second Courthouse, 1928 *(McCreary Conquest)*.

119. WICKLIFFE in BALLARD COUNTY

Year Formed: 1842

Formed From: Hickman and McCracken Counties

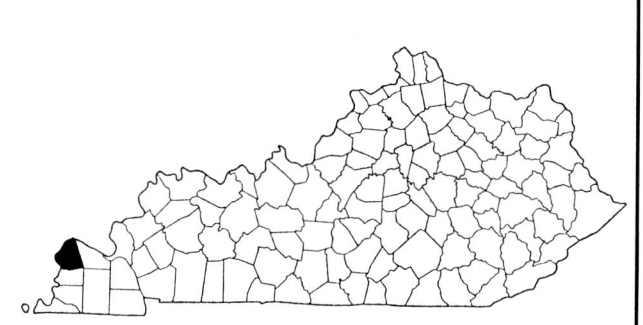
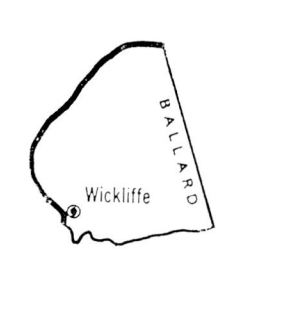

Ballard County, 93rd in order of formation, was named for Captain Bland Ballard — a veteran of the Revolutionary War, Indian Wars, and War of 1812. Blandville was established as the county seat in 1802 and named for Ballard as well.

The first Ballard County Courthouse was built on the public square in Blandville in 1842-44. The commissioners of the court awarded the contract for construction to a Mr. Coates in 1842. The building was completed in 1844 at a cost of $6000. A brick, two-story courthouse, the first story contained a courtroom and the second three jury rooms. The courthouse burned in 1880.

The second Ballard County courthouse was built in 1882-83 in Wickliffe. By 1882, the Ballard County court had been persuaded to relocated the county seat to Wickliffe, due to the efforts of Judge Samuel H. Jenkins who promised to privately raise funds for erection of a new courthouse. Jenkins personally donated the land for the site, which measured 100 yards square. The two-story, brick structure measured 40 X 60 feet. The first story contained three county offices and a grand jury room; the second, another court room and two jury rooms.

The building of the third and current Ballard County courthouse commenced shortly after 1900 and it was completed in 1905. The two-story, brick courthouse cost approximately $25,000. Jerome Bibb Legg, a prominent St. Louis architect, designed this classical structure in the popular Beaux-Arts style of the period, similar to numerous Missouri courthouses which he designed. The Ballard County courthouse was listed on the National Register of Historic Places in 1980.

Third Courthouse, 1905 *(Collection of Mrs. Hilda Kimsey)*.

120. WILLIAMSBURG in WHITLEY COUNTY

Year Formed: 1818

Formed From: Knox County

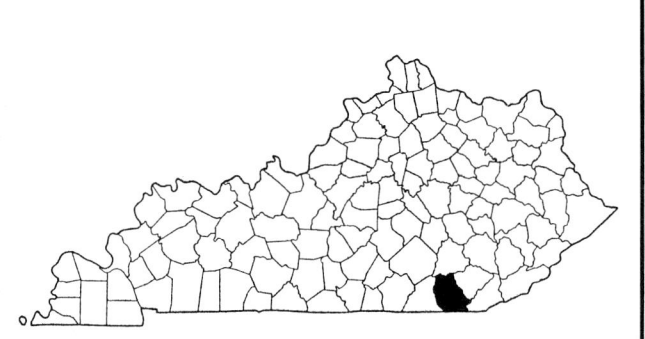

Whitley County, 59th in order of formation, was named for Colonel William Whitley — early Kentucky settler. Williamsburg, originally Whitley Court House, was established as the county seat and also named for Whitley.

The first Whitley County courthouse was built shortly after formation of the county in 1818. No description exists of this building. Combined with the jail, the structure cost $2,800. No mention is made of a courthouse in an 1847 description.

The second Whitley County courthouse was built in the mid-1880's. The courthouse was designed by H. P. McDonald and Brothers, architects of Louisville. The design is their standard design for courthouses that was built in numerous counties.

The third Whitley County courthouse was built in 1931. No description is known of this courthouse. The building was declared unsafe in 1969 and replaced in the mid-1970s.

The fourth and present Whitley County courthouse was built in the mid-1970s. The courthouse is of modern design of skeletal steel construction covered by a brick and cut stone face. A modern portico of four cut stone columns fronts the building.

Second Courthouse, 1880's *(The Filson Club)*.

121. WILLIAMSTOWN in GRANT COUNTY

Year Formed: 1820

Formed From: Pendleton County

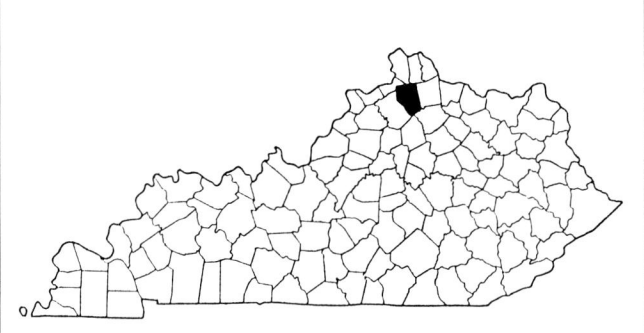

Grant County, 67th in order of formation, was named for Colonel John Grant — an early Kentucky settler on the Licking River. Williamstown, original Philadelphia, was established as the county seat in 1820 and named for William Arnold, the original owner of the town.

The first Grant County courthouse was built shortly after formation of the county in 1820-21. The courthouse was built by William Arnold for $2,199. The two-story, brick courthouse measured 30 X 34 feet, the first floor was twelve feet high and the second eight feet, to be similar to the courthouse at Falmouth. The structure was finished in December 1821 and served until 1856 when the second courthouse was built.

The second Grant County courthouse was built from 1852-1856. The brick, two-story courthouse is a front-gabled or temple-form structure in the Greek Revival style. Little information is recorded about this structure. The cupola appears to date from the turn-of-the-century.

The third and present Grant County courthouse was built between 1937-39 under a grant provided by the Public Works Administration. The Wren/Georgian Colonial Revival style building is a yellow brick, two-story courthouse measuring 98' X 60'. E. C. & G. T. Landberg were the architects, and Skinner Brothers of Lexington, the low bidders for construction. The courthouse was completed in January 1939 for $106,933. In 1976, the interior was remodeled under the supervision of Cincinnati architects McClorey & Savage, with TCS Contracting of Covington performing the work.

Second Courthouse, 1852 (*Williamstown Courier* — May 30, 1901).

Third Courthouse — 1937 (*Short and Stanley-Brown, Public Buildings*).

122. WINCHESTER in CLARK COUNTY

Year Formed: 1792

Formed From: Bourbon and Fayette Counties

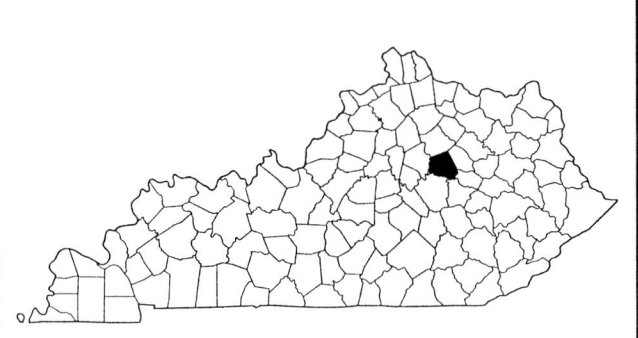

Clark County, 14th in order of formation, was named in honor of General George Rogers Clark — the famous Kentucky military leader. Winchester, immediately established as the county seat, was named for the Virginia town of the same name.

The first Clark County courthouse was considered immediately upon formation of the county. Hubbard Taylor, Original Young, Robert McKinney, and Dillard Collins were appointed on November 27, 1793, to procure a plan for the courthouse and other public buildings. Built by Robert Clark, the courthouse, a log structure measuring 20 X 30 feet with two rooms, was first used on July 22, 1794.

The second Clark County courthouse was built in 1796-97. A brick, two-story structure with a stone foundation, the building measured 30 X 42 feet. This building was demolished in early 1818.

A third Clark County courthouse was ordered by the court in 1819. The first meeting was held there on August 23, 1819, and the building finished in 1821. In April of 1852 the court decided this building must be replaced.

The fourth and current Clark County courthouse was built in 1852-55. A. H. Buckner, James Allen, John Catherwood, Phillip B. Winn, and James H. G. Bush were appointed commissioners to contract for and superintend construction of the new building. A plan by John McMurtry, a Lexington architect, was presented and accepted by the court in June 1852. McMurtry, also the contractor, finished the courthouse in the fall of 1855.

Several alterations have been made to the building. In 1889, the original cupola was replaced by one designed by architect E. N. Lamm. In 1938 the Works Progress Administration provided $29,624, with an additional $166,660 from the county, to remodel the courthouse. John T. Gillig, a Lexington architect, supervised construction of the alterations, including adding a wing on the rear which reflects the front of the building, and contains 20 new offices. The remodeling began in March 21, 1938, and concluded March 1, 1940. The Clark County courthouse was listed on the National Register of Historic Places in 1974.

Fourth Courthouse, 1852.

Fourth Courthouse, 1938 — P. W. A. addition, just after completion *(National Archives)*.

BIBLIOGRAPHY

GENERAL

Collins, Lewis. *Historical Sketches of Kentucky.* Lewis Collins, Maysville, Kentucky, 1847.

Garr, Elizabeth Headley. *The History of Kentucky Courthouses.* The National Society of the Colonial Dames of America, Resident in the State of Kentucky, 1972.

Sprague, Stuart. *A Pictorial History of Eastern Kentucky.* The Donning Company, Norfolk, Virginia, 1986.

ADAIR COUNY

Newspapers

August 3, 1966, Adair County News

September 7, 1966, Adair County News

Montgomery, Anna Mae, "Some changes have been made on original courthouse," Columbia Statesman, March 11, 1971.

Montgomery, Anna Mae, "Considering replacement," Columbia Statesman, March 15, 1973.

Public Documents

AD-C-1 Adair County Courthouse, Kentucky Historic Resource Inventory Form, Kentucky Heritage Council.

Kentucky Historical Highway Marker No. 1599

ALLEN COUNTY

Newspapers

"Joe Creason's Kentucky: Allen County moves into New Courthouse," Courier-Journal, November 20, 1965.

"Old Allen Courthouse To Be Torn Down," Courier-Journal, October 5, 1966.

"Flies Coop," Courier-Journal, December 2, 1966.

"Bell 'Rescued', Old Allen Courthouse, Built in 1903, Demolished," Courier-Journal, May 28, 1967.

ANDERSON COUNTY

Books

Joseph, Alfred S. & Joseph, Oscar G. Selections from the Work of Joseph & Joseph, Architects and Engineers, Louisville, Ky. Architectural Catalog Co., New York, 1929.

McKee, Lewis Witherspoon & Bond, Lydia K.. *A History of Anderson County, Begun in 1884, 1780-1936.* Roberts Printing Co., Frankfort, 1936.

Newspapers

Anderson News Supplement, 1906

"Typical of Kentucky Court Houses," Courier-Journal, May 23, 1937.

"Equality of Opportunity both Party Headquarters Anderson County Courthouse," Courier-Journal, October 12, 1952.

"Burned Courthouse," Anderson News, Centennial Edition, August 1, 1977.

Shely, Wyatt, "Our Heritage," Anderson News, n.d.

Public Documents

AN-L-22 Anderson County Courthouse, Kentucky Historic Resource Inventory Form, Kentucky Heritage Council.

Manuscript Collections

Frankfort Centennial Papers, The Kentucky Historical Society, John Haly to Col. John L. Scott, Sept. 27, 1886

BALLARD COUNTY

Books

Battle, J.H. *Histories and Bibliographies of Ballard, Calloway, Fulton, Graves, Hickman, McCracken and Marshall Counties,* Kentucky. Battey Publishing Co., Chicago, 1885.

James, Anthony O. *Survey of Historic Sites in Kentucky, Ballard County.* The Kentucky Heritage Commission, 1978.

Ohman, Marion. *Missouri's Counties, County Seats, and Courthouse Squares,* University of Missouri Press, 1983.

Public Documents

BA-1 Ballard County Courthouse, Kentucky Historic Resource Inventory Form, Kentucky Heritage Council.

Kentucky Historical Highway Marker No. 1374

BARREN COUNTY

Books

Gorin, Franklin. *The Times of Long Ago,* Barren County, Kentucky. J.P. Morton & Company, Louisville, 1929.

Goode, Cecil E. & Gardner, Woodford L., eds. *Barren County Heritage: A Pictorial History of Barren County, Kentucky.* Homestead Press, Bowling Green, Ky., 1980.

Newspapers

Smith, E.H. "A History of the Barren County Bar," The Green River Republican, February 27, 1941.

"Remodeling?," Courier-Journal, September 10, 1962.

"Barren Courthouse Referendum Fails by 5," Courier-Journal, November 7, 1962.

"Glasgow—New Courthouse Planned (Barren)," Courier-Journal, February 13, 1964.

"Governor Dedicates Barren County Courthouse," Courier-Journal, May 9, 1965.

"History of the Barren County Courthouses," The Glasgow Daily Times, May 9, 1965.

"New Barren County Courthouse—Traditional but Modern," Courier-Journal, June 6, 1965.

Public Documents

BN-G-1 Barren County Courthouse, Kentucky Historic Resource Inventory Form, Kentucky Heritage Council.

Unpublished Studies

Howard, Bess. "Early Settlement of Barren County," Presented to the Edmund Rogers Chapter, D.A.R., Glasow, Ky., 1931.

BATH COUNTY

Books

Bath County Sesquicentennial Committee. *Historical Scrapbook and Program of the Sesquicentennial Celebration of Bath County, 1811–1961.* Owingsville, Ky., 1961.

Richards, John Adair. *A History of Bath County, Kentucky.* Southwest Printers, Yuma, Ariz., 1961.

Young, Van B. *An Outline History of Bath County from January 15, 1811 to July 4th, 1876.* Transylvania Printing Co., Lexington, Ky., 1876.

Newspapers

"Joe Creason's Kentucky: Shape of Thing Bath County," Courier-Journal, November 10, 1965.

Metz, Gloria, "Remember When?," Bath County News Outlook, May 16, 1985.

Metz, Gloria, "Remember When?," Bath County News Outlook, June 30, 1983.

Metz, Gloria, "Remember When?," Bath County News Outlook, July 4, 1985.

Metz, Gloria, "Remember When?," Bath County News Outlook, November 28, 1985.

Public Documents

Kentucky Historical Highway Marker No. 592

BA-1 Bath County Courthouse, Kentucky Historic Resource Inventory Form, Kentucky Heritage Council.

BELL COUNTY

Books

Bell County Centennial Commission, Inc. *The Bell County Story,* 1867-1967, the unfoldin of a century. Sun Publishing Company, Pineville, Ky., 1967.

Fuson, Henry Harvey. *History of Bell County,* Kentucky, Volume I, 1947.

Articles and Essays

The Inland Architect, XIII, 1(Feb. 1889), 14. $30,000, under way. McDonald Brothers.

Newspapers

"Fire Sweeps Bell County Courthouse," Courier-Journal, March 5, 1944.

Public Documents

BL-P-1 Bell County Courthouse, Kentucky

Historic Resource Inventory Form, Kentucky Heritage Council.

BOONE COUNTY

Public Documents

BE-143 Boone County Courthouse, Kentucky Historic Resource Inventory Form, Kentucky Heritage Council.

BOURBON COUNTY

Books

Keller, G.D. & McCann. Sketches of Paris, Bourbon Co., Ky., 1876, Saturday Night. G.D. Keller, Paris, 1876.

Langsam, Walter E. & Johnson, William G.. Historic Architecture of Bourbon County, Kentucky. Historic Paris-Bourbon County, Inc., Paris, 1985.

Perrin, William H. History of Bourbon, Scott, Harrison and Nicholas Counties, Kentucky. O.L. Baskin & Co., Historical Publishers, 1882.

Articles and Essays

Bourbon County Historical Scrapbook, Vol. II, May, 1961.

Newspapers

Whitney, Edna T. article, Paris Daily Enterprise, July 17, 1959.

Thierman, Sue McClelland, "Bourbon Courthouse gets Fan Mail," Courier-Journal, April 24, 1960.

Stallons, Malcolm. "Bourbon County Offices Evacuated," Lexington Herald-Leader, March 10, 1977.

Perry, Doug, "Dome exile, Repairs force Bourbon officials from courthouse offices," Courier-Journal, March 10, 1977.

Public Documents

BB-P-149 Bourbon County Courthouse, Kentucky Historic Resource Inventory Form, Kentucky Heritage Council.

Unpublished Studies

Frye, Mary Kathryn, Frank Pierce Milburn, Architect, 1868-1926, Master's Thesis, University of South Carolina, 1978.

BOYD COUNTY

Newspapers

Kennedy, Robert, article, Ashland Daily Independent, no date.

"Boyd Courthouse robbed of $222," Courier-Journal, May 2, 1952.

"Ever Heard of Poage Settlement? ... It's Ashland," Tri-State Shopper's Guide, July

BOYLE COUNTY

Books

Coleman, J. Winston, Historic Kentucky, Henry Clay Press, Lexington, 1968.

Daviess, Maria. History of Mercer and Boyle Counties. Harrodsburg Hearld, 1924.

Daviess, Mrs. Maria T. History of Mercer and Boyle Counties. Harrodsburg Herald, Harrodsburg, 1924. First published in the early eighties.

Fackler, Calvin M. Historic Homes of Boyle County, Kentucky and the Three Courthouses, The Danville and Boyle County Historical Society, Danville, 1959.

Newspapers

"Boyle's Court House," Courier-Journal, September 4, 1935.

"Boyle County Court House Clock Still In Faithful Service After Seventy-three Years," Louisville Times, May 2, 1938.

Kiser, Walter H., "Neighboorhood Sketches-The Boyle County Courthouse, Danville, Ky.," Courier-Journal, June 27, 1939.

Rogers, Cheri, "Three Courthouses Have Been Constructed In Danville," Kentucky Advocate Magazine, February 7, 1971.

"Boyle's Loafers Need Hebensraum," Courier-Journal, March 12, 1940.

"Remodeling of Danville's Courthouse," Courier-Journal, November 28, 1971.

Public Documents

Kentucky Historical Highway Marker No. 49 & 756

BO-D-32 Boyle County Courthouse, Kentucky Historic Resource Inventory Form, Kentucky Heritage Council.

BRACKEN COUNTY

Books

Bracken County Homemakers, Heaverin, Mrs. Grayson, chair, Recollections: Yesterday, Today For Tommorrow, A History of Bracken County. The Bracken County Homemakers, 1969.

Newspapers

Moore, Ruth,"Old Homes and Buildings of Northern Kentucky," The Cincinnati Enquirer, n.d.(Liberty Hall)

BREATHITT COUNTY

Books

The Writers' Program of the W.P.A.. The Land of Breathitt, American Guide Service, 1941.

Newspapers

"Exit a Symbol of Violence, Breathitt County Courthouse," Courier-Journal, March 24, 1963.

Griffin, Gerald, "Assassination at Courthouse Claimed Life of Commissioner," Courier-Journal, n.d.

"Breathitt Fiscal Court Condemns Courthouse," Lexington Herald, January 22, 1958.

BRECKINRIDGE COUNTY

Newspapers

"Courthouse at Hardinsburg was Erected in 1869," Courier-Journal, April 11, 1937.

"Flames Raze Breckinridge Courthouse," Courier-Journal, February 8, 1958.

"Fire Razes Breckinridge Courthouse," Louisville Times, February 8, 1958.

Taylor, Lee, article, Breckinridge County Herald, February 14, 1958.

"Courthouse to Replace One Razed by Fire Hardinsburg (Breckinridge)," Courier-Journal, April 5, 1958.

"Construction is Progressing at Hardinsburg, Breckinrdge County Courthouse," Courier-Journal, November 8, 1959.

Public Documents

Kentucky Historical Highway Marker No. 584

BULLITT COUNTY

Books

Bullitt County News. Bullitt County, 1796-1912. Bullitt County News, Shepardsville, Ky., 1912.

Bullitt County—175th Aniversary, 1796-1971, 1971.

Garr, Elizabeth Headley. The History of Kentucky Courthouses. The National Society of the Colonial Dames of America, Resident in the State of Kentucky, 1972.

Gorin, Franklin. The Times of Long Ago, Bullitt County, Kentucky. J.P. Morton & Company, Louisville, 1929.

Newspapers

"Annex is Started for Courthouse at Shepardsville," Courier-Journal, March 27, 1947.

"Addition to Bullitt Courthouse Proposed," Courier-Journal, August 7, 1969.

Ryce, Judi,"Bullitt County may get federal aid for its courthouse," Louisville Times, August 17, 1976.

Public Documents

BU-1 Bullitt County Courthouse, Kentucky Historic Resource Inventory Form, Kentucky Heritage Council.

BUTLER COUNTY

Books

Bratcher, Bennett F. History of Butler County. Butler County sesqui-centennial, 1810-1960. Morgantown, Kentucky, 1960.

Dedication Program—Butler County Courthouse, October 4, 1975

Articles and Essays James, Hezekiah Adams, "History of Court and Bar of Butler County," 1898, Register of the Kentucky Historical Society, v. 42 (1944).

Newspapers

Bratcher, Bennett F. "The History of Butler County," The Green River Republican, October 1, 1975.

Public Documents

BT-M-25 Butler County Courthouse, Kentucky Historic Resource Inventory Form, Kentucky Heritage Council.

CALDWELL COUNTY

Local Sources

Mrs. Mary Grace Pettit

Books

Baker, Clauscine R., First History of Caldwell County, Kentucky, Commercial Printers, Madisonville, Ky., 1936.

Newspapers

Fowler, III Errle, "Political Divisions and Early Seats of Justice," n.p., n.d.

"First Courthouse in Caldwell County," Courier-Journal, October 31, 1937.

"Work On Court House Starts Soon," Courier-Journal, Sept. 1938.

"Work Starts On Caldwell Court House," Courier-Journal, January 10, 1939.

"New Courthouse To Be Completed By January 1st," Courier-Journal, August 22, 1940.

Public Documents

Kentucky Historical Highway Marker No. 579

CALLOWAY COUNTY

Books

Battle, J.H. Histories and Bibliographies of Ballard, Calloway, Fulton, Graves, Hickman, McCracken and Marshall Counties, Kentucky. Battey Publishing Co., Chicago, 1885.

McElrath, Hugh M.. Dr. McElrath's Murray. Self, Murray, 1964. (Calloway Co.)

Jennings, Dorothy and Kerby, The Story of Calloway County, 1822-1976, 1978.

Articles and Essays

Johnson, E.A., History of Calloway County, 1931.

Newspapers

"Calloway's First Court House Dedicated Sunday Afternoon," The Murray Ledger & Times, June 10, 1969.

"Move Underway To Save Cabin," The Murray Ledger & Times, August 10, 1964.

"Court To Aid In Saving Old Courthouse," The Murray Ledger & Times, August 11, 1964.

Hortin, L.J., "Fund Sought To Restore Old Calloway Courthouse," The Murray Ledger & Times, April 7, 1975.

Peterson, Nanci, "152-Year Old Court House to Be Restored," The Murray Ledger & Times, June 4, 1975.

Public Documents

CM-W-11 Calloway County Courthouse, Kentucky Historic Resource Inventory Form, Kentucky Heritage Council.

Kentucky Historical Highway Marker No. 1263

CAMPBELL COUNTY

Articles and Essays

Hartman, Margaret Strebel, "Campbell County History," n.d.

Lindsey, Helen Bradley, "Early Days in Campbell County, Kentucky, 1790-1850," Register of the Kentucky Historical Society, v. 26, (1928).

Newspapers

Matthews, Ralph, "Filming of All Campbell Records Aim of Judge," The Post and Times Star, January 11, 1966.

"Campbell County Tax for Courthouse Rejected," Courier-Journal, January 1, 1981.

Reis, Jim, "Spilt Decision—Campbell and Kenton counties ended up with two courthouses," The Kentucky Post, July 23, 1984.

Public Documents

CP-A-15 Campbell County Courthouse, Kentucky Historic Resource Inventory Form, Kentucky Heritage Council.

CP-N-142 Campbell County Courthouse, Kentucky Historic Resource Inventory Form, Kentucky Heritage Council.

CARLISLE COUNTY

Books

an. A History of Carlisle County for the Years 1820-1900: Celebrating America's Bicentennial 1776-1976. July, 1976.

Graves, Ran. History and Memories of Carlisle County. Advance-Yeoman, Wickliffe, Ky., 1958.

Newspapers

"Out Of The Past," Carlisle County News, December 3, 1970.

"Strings Attached, Grant gives Carlisle courthouse a lift, but not the one officials want," Courier-Journal, November 26, 1978.

"Arson is Suspected in courthouse blaze," Courier-Journal, October 23, 1980.

"Fire destroys Carlisle Courthouse; arson investigator says it was set," Courier-Journal, October 23, 1980.

"Carlisle Gets Grant to Rebuild Courthouse," Courier-Journal, October 26, 1980.

"Carlisle County's plan to build courthouse," Courier-Journal, September 7, 1981.

Public Documents

CE-B-8 Carlisle County Courthouse, Kentucky Historic Resource Inventory Form, Kentucky Heritage Council.

CARROLL COUNTY

Books

Gentry, Mary Ann. History of Carroll County, Kentucky. Coleman Printing Co., Madison, Ind, 1984.

Masterson, Mary. Historic Carroll County, Kentucky. Carroll County Chamber of Commerce, n.d.

Newspapers

"Bids For Construction Of New Courthouse Annex Due May 12," Carroll County News Democrat, April 23, 1964.

"New County Budget Adds Funds For Courthouse Repairs, Etc.," Carroll County News Democrat, June 3, 1965.

"Courthouse dedicated Saturday," Carroll County News Democrat, April 14, 1976.

Pardo, Mildred, "The Old Days In Carrollton," Carroll County News Democrat, December 13, 1953.

Public Documents

CL-C-41 Carroll County Courthouse, Kentucky Historic Resource Inventory Form, Kentucky Heritage Council.

CARTER COUNTY

Books

Carter County Bicentennial Committee, Grayson, Ky. Carter County History, 1838-1976. 1976.

Wolfford, George. Carter County, A Pictorial History. W.W.W. Co., Ashland, 1985.

Public Documents

CR-G-8 Carter County Courthouse, Kentucky Historic Resource Inventory Form, Kentucky Heritage Council.

CASEY COUNTY

Books

Watkins, Willie M. The Men, Women, Events, Institutions & Lore of Casey County, Kentucky. The standard printing co., Louisville, 1939.

Newspapers

"Casey's Courthouse—Court Advertises for Bids," Casey County News, February 13, 1975.

"Casey's Courthouse—Taxes Levied," Casey County News, February 27, 1975.

"Casey's Courthouse—Completed 1889," Casey County News, March 3, 1975.

"Casey's Courthouse—A Landmark?," Casey County News, March 6, 1975.

Public Documents

CSL-3 Casey County Courthouse—Kentucky Historic Resource Inventory Form

National Register of Historic Places Inventory — Nomination Form, 1976, Kentucky Heritage Council.

CHRISTIAN COUNTY

Books

Gibbs & Torma, Hopkinsville and Christian County Historic Sites, Kentucky Heritage Commission, Frankfort, Ky., 1982.

Meacham, Charles Mayfield. A History of Christian County, Kentucky from Oxcart to Airplane. Marshall & Bruce, Nashville, 1930.

Perrin, William Henry, ed. County of Christian, Kentucky. F.A. Battey Publishing Co., Chicago and Louisville, 1884.

Turner, William T. Gateway From the Past, Volume II, A Pictorial History of Hopkinsville and Christian County, Kentucky Since 1865, William T. Turner, 1981.

Public Documents

Kentucky Historical Highway Marker No. 577

CH-H-12 Christian County Courthouse, Kentucky Historic Resource Inventory Form, Kentucky Heritage Council.

CLARK COUNTY

Books

Bedford, A. Goff. Land of Our Fathers: A History of Clark County, Kentucky. A. Goff Bedford, Mt. Sterling, Ky., 1958.

Jillson, Willard Rouse. Early Clark County, Kentucky; A History, 1674-1824. Roberts Print. Co., Frankfort, Ky., 1966.

Newspapers

Winchester Daily, June 15, 1887.

"Clark County Chronicles," The Winchester Sun, February 8, 1923.

"Clark County Chronicles," The Winchester Sun, May 24, 1923.

Kiser, Walter H. "Neighborhood Sketches, The Clark County Court House, Winchester, Ky.," Louisville Times, June 18, 1940.

"Clark County's Third Court House, More Than Eighty Years Old, Undergoes Remodeling," Louisville Times, April 4, 1938.

"As Remodeled Courthouse Will Appear," Lexington Herald, February 19, 1938.

"Portraits To Be Hung In Clark," Lexington Herald, May 24, 1940.

"Clark Countians Proud Of Remodeled Court House," Courier-Journal, July 7, 1940.

Public Documents

CK-W-583 Clark County Courthouse, Kentucky Historic Resource Inventory Form, Kentucky Heritage Council.

Unpublished Studies

Doyle, George F., M.D., "Clark County Courthouse," n.d.

CLAY COUNTY

Newspapers

"Courthouse Burns In Clay County," Lincoln Republican News, January 1936.

"Clay County Courthouse," Courier-Journal, March 15, 1942.

Public Documents

CY-M-1 Clay County Courthouse, Kentucky Historic Resource Inventory Form, Kentucky Heritage Council.

Unpublished Studies

Frye, Mary Kathryn, Frank Pierce Milburn, Architect, 1868-1926, Master's Thesis, University of South Carolina, 1978.

CLINTON COUNTY

Newspapers

"Clinton County Courthouse built in 1895," Courier-Journal, September 2, 1959.

Article, Louisville Courier-Journal, October 10, 1969.

"Clinton County's Courthouse destroyed by fire," Courier-Journal, August 3, 1980.

"Clinton Courthouse burns a second time," The State Journal, August 3, 1980.

Public Documents

Kentucky Historical Highway Marker No. 597

CRITTENDEN COUNTY

Newspapers

"Crittenden County Court House in Marion, Ky.," Courier-Journal, December 24, 1939.

Kiser, Walter H. "Neighborhood Sketches, Crittenden County Court House, Marion, Ky.," Louisville Times, May 19, 1941.

"Crittenden Begins Planning 4th Courthouse on Same Site," Courier-Journal, November 30, 1959.

"Crittenden Courthouse Dedication of New $176,000 Courthouse," Courier-Journal, December 6, 1961.

Public Documents

Kentucky Historical Highway Marker No. 596

CUMBERLAND COUNTY

Books

Wells, Joseph William. History of Cumberland County. Standard Print Co., Louisville, 1934.

Newspapers

"The Burkesville Court House," Courier-Journal, January 5, 1934.

"Burkesville's New Court House," Courier-Journal, May 28, 1935.

"Courthouse Destroyed By Flood, Burned Twice," Cumberland County News, Sesqui-Centennial Edition, August 18, 1960.

"Favorite Photo — Cumberland County Courthouse," Glasgow Daily Times, January 1966.

Public Documents

CU-B-1 Cumberland County Courthouse, Kentucky Historic Resource Inventory Form, Kentucky Heritage Council.

Kentucky Historical Highway Marker No. 583

DAVIESS COUNTY

Books

an. History of Daviess County, Kentucky. Inter-state publishing co., Chicago, 1883.

Potter, Hugh O. Daviess County Sesquicentennial Historical Factbook. Daviess County Historical Society/WOMI, Owensboro, Ky., 1965.

Articles and Essays

Inland Architect, XXI 6 (July 1893) 78.

Newspapers

"Proposed New Daviess County, Kentucky, Courthouse," Courier-Journal, February 26, 1939.

"Seat of Daviess," Courier-Journal, January 14, 1940.

"Daviess voters Reject Bonds for Courthouse," Courier-Journal, November 11, 1955.

"Daviess Vote Set on Bonds For Courthouse," Courier-Journal, July 19, 1961.

"Daviess County Courthouse Ceiling Collapses," Courier-Journal, July 10, 1963.

"Joe Creason's Kentucky: Daviess County Courthouse," Courier-Journal, January 9, 1964.

"Courthouse within a Courthouse, Daviess County," Courier-Journal, January 12, 1964.

"Ceremony, Daviess Courthouse To Be Dedicated," Courier-Journal, August 3, 1964.

Courthouse Edition, The Owensboro Messenger and Enquirer, September 5, 1964.

"On Site of Old — New Courthouse at Daviess," Courier-Journal, September 20, 1964.

"History of Courthouses In Daviess County Covers Three Major Structures, 1858-1964," 1815-1965 Daviess County Sesquicentennial Edition, The Owensboro Messenger and Enquirer.

Public Documents

DA-OB-88 Daviess County Courthouse, Kentucky Historic Resource Inventory Form, Kentucky Heritage Council.

Kentucky Historical Highway Marker No. 590

Unpublished Studies

Bishop, Mrs. Elizabeth, "History of Burning of Owensboro Courthouse," Paper read before General John Breckinridge chapter, n.d.

Maps, Atlases, Gazeteers

D.J. Lake & Co., Atlas of Daviess County, Kentucky, 1876.

EDMONSON COUNTY

Books

Carroll, Ricky. 1825-1900 Edmonson County: The Past History and the People Who Made It. c. 1979.

ELLIOTT COUNTY

Books

Elliott County Centennial Commission. Historical High Lights of Elliott County, 1869-1969. Sandy Hook, Ky., 1969.

Newspapers

"Fire Destroys Courthouse in Elliott," Courier-Journal, December 20, 1957.

"Courthouse Fire Elliott County, Probe Ordered," Courier-Journal, May 9, 1958. Lexington Herald-Leader, February 1968.

ESTILL COUNTY

Books

Park, E.C. History of Irvine and Estill County, Kentucky.

Newspapers

"Modern Courthouse To Replace Old Irvine Building," Lexington Herald-Leader, February 19, 1939.

"Cornerstone Will Be Laid," Lexington Herald-Leader, November 23, 1939.

"Cornerstone Of New $104,000 Estill County Courthouse Will Be Laid By Masons Monday," Lexington Herald-Leader, December 3, 1939.

"New Estill County Courthouse Almost Ready," Courier-Journal, February 23, 1941.

Public Documents

ES-I-3 Estill County Courthouse, Kentucky Historic Resource Inventory Form, Kentucky Heritage Council.

FAYETTE COUNTY

Books

Coleman, Winston. The Courthouses of Lexington, 1937.

Perrin, William H., ed. History of Fayette County, Kentucky. F.A. Battey Publishing Co., Chicago and Louisville, 1884.

Newspapers

Kentucky Gazette, January 16, 1800

"Leader Reporters Vividly Told Courthouse Fire Story in 1897," Lexington Herald-Leader, May 19, 1963.

"Court House And Valuable Statue Were Lost In Biggest Local Fire of the Gay-Nineties," Lexington Leader, August 30, 1936.

Vaughn, Nell, "In The Good Old Days," Lexington Herald-Leader, April 17, 1954.

Pace, Norma, "Merry Laughter Of Beauteous Maidens' Marked Courthouse Opening," Lexington Herald-Leader, August 23, 1960.

"Courthouse Job Will Cost $11.90 Per Square Foot," Lexington Herald-Leader, July 7, 1960.

"Corporate Deal—Fayette Public Courthouse Corp.," Courier-Journal, July 21, 1960.

Chapman, Charles, "Courthouse Remodeling On Time; Return Move Slated For September," Lexington Herald-Leader, July 9, 1961.

Mastin, Bettye Lee, "Only One of Fayette's Five Courthouses Was Destroyed by Fire," Lexington Herald-Leader, July 15, 1980.

"Proposed Jail on Top of Court House," Lexington Herald-Leader, n.d.

Public Documents

FA-DT-110 Fayette County Courthouse, Kentucky Historic Resource Inventory Form, Kentucky Heritage Council.

Unpublished Studies

Lancaster, Clay, Antebellum Architecture in Kentucky, n.d.

Manuscript Collections

Draper Mss. 11CC164. John Shane interview with Ned Darnaby.

FLEMING COUNTY

Books

Coleman, J. Winston. Historic Kentucky, Henry Clay Press, Lexington, 1968.

Newspapers

"Old Courthouse (Fleming County)," Courier-Journal, August 16, 1936.

"Fleming Group Fights Court House Change—Changes New Entrance Would Mar Old Building's Beauty," Louisville Times, December 7, 1939.

Grannis, Harriet D., "A Court House Worth Protecting," Louisville Times, March 1, 1940.

Kiser, Walter H., "Neighborhood Sketches—Fleming County Court House, Flemingsburg, Ky.," Louisville Times, May 14, 1941.

"A Tempest in a Courthouse—Flemingsburg," Courier-Journal, October 1, 1950.

"Historic Fleming Courthouse Nearly Gone for New Edifice," Louisville Times, July 1, 1951.

Brewer, Melodye, "Old Flemming County Courthouse," Flemingsburg Times Bicentennial Edition, July 11, 1974.

Public Documents

FL-F-90 Fleming County Courthouse, Kentucky Historic Resource Inventory Form, Kentucky Heritage Council.

FLOYD COUNTY

Books

Wells, Charles C. Annals of Floyd County, Kentucky, 1800-1826. Gateway Press, Inc., Baltimore, Md., 1983.

Articles and Essays

Scalf, Henry P. The East Kentuckian Journal, June, 1966.

Newspapers

"Floyd County Can't Use Funds for Courthouse," Courier-Journal, February 27, 1954.

Floyd County Times, September 10, 1964.

Public Documents

Floyd County Order Book No. 1

FRANKLIN COUNTY

Books

Johnson, L.F. The History of Franklin County, Kentucky. The State Journal, Frankfort, 1912.

Glenn, Nettie Henry. Early Frankfort Kentucky, 1786-1861. Nettie Henry Glenn, Frankfort, 1986.

Newspapers

"Frankfort Will Trade," Louisville Times, April 2, 1940.

"Shryock's Other Work—Franklin Courthouse," Courier-Journal, November 30, 1957.

Kiser, Walter H., "Franklin County Court House, Frankfort, Ky.," Courier-Journal, July 9, 1940.

Public Documents

Franklin County Clerk—Sheriff's Settlement Book, 1826-1855, Kentucky Libraries and Archives.

Franklin County Circuit Court, Order Book K, 1834-1839, Franklin County Courthouse.

FR-FC-29 Franklin County Courthouse, Kentucky Historic Resource Inventory Form, Kentucky Heritage Council.

Unpublished Studies

Van Liew, Anne Barnard, "Franklin County Court House, Frankfort, Ky., 1835-1966," 1966.

FULTON COUNTY

Books

Battle, J.H. Histories and Bibliographies of Ballard, Calloway, Fulton, Graves, Hickman, McCracken and Marshall Counties, Kentucky. Battey Publishing Co., Chicago, 1885.

Jewell, Ouida. Backward Glance (Fulton

Co.). Fulton Publishing Co., Fulton, Ky., 1973.

Newspapers

Mueller, Angela, The Hickman Courier, January 14, 1971, p.4.

"Our Courthouse clock is an operating museum piece," The Hickman Courier, January 23, 1975.

Public Documents

Fulton County Court Order Book No. 1

FU-H-13 Fulton County Courthouse, Kentucky Historic Resource Inventory Form

National Register of Historic Places Inventory Nomination Form, 1971, Kentucky Heritage Council.

Unpublished Studies

Frye, Mary Kathryn, Frank Pierce Milburn, Architect, 1868-1926, Master's Thesis, University of South Carolina, 1978.

GALLATIN COUNTY

Books

Bogardus, Carl R. The Early History of Gallatin County. Warsaw, Ky., 1948.

Gray, Gypsy M. History of Gallatin County, Kentucky. Covington, 1968.

Public Documents

GA-W-13 Gallatin County Courthouse, Kentucky Historic Resource Inventory Form, Kentucky Heritage Council.

GARRARD COUNTY

Books

Calico, Forrest. History of Garrard County, Kentucky, and Its Churches. Hobson Book Press, New York, 1947.

Lancaster's Woman's Club. Patches of Garrard County: A History. Bluegrass Printing Co., Danville, 1974.

Articles and Essays

Kinnaird, J.B., "Looking Backward: Historical Sketches Of Lancaster And Garrard County From Authentic Sources And Tradition,"

Public Documents

GD-L-1 Garrard County Courthouse, Kentucky Historic Resource Inventory Form, Kentucky Heritage Council.

Manuscript Collections

Frankfort Centennial Papers, The Kentucky Historical Society, John Haly to Col. John L. Scott, Sept. 27, 1886

GRANT COUNTY

Books

Elliston, Robert H., The History of Grant County, Kentucky. Sentinel Office, Williamstown, Ky., 1876.

Newspapers

Williamstown Courier, May 30, 1901.

Powell, Bill, Lexington Herald-Leader, May 17, 1970.

Souder, Charles, "Dimensions Of Grant County's 1st Courthouse," The Williamstown Courier, Bicentennial Edition, 1976.

Public Documents

GR-W-1 Grant County Courthouse, Kentucky Historic Resource Inventory Form, Kentucky Heritage Council.

GRAVES COUNTY

Books

Davis, D. Trabue. Story of Mayfield Through a Century, 1823-1923. Billings Printing Co., Paducah, 1923.

Battle, J.H. Histories and Bibliographies of Ballard, Calloway, Fulton, Graves, Hickman, McCracken and Marshall Counties, Kentucky. Battey Publishing Co., Chicago, 1885.

Articles and Essays

Inland Architect, Volume X, 9(February 1887)14

Inland Architect, Volume XIII, 1(February 1889)104

Newspapers

"Joe Creason's Kentucky: Graves County Courthouse—Retirement of Lee Mason," Courier-Journal, August 7, 1965.

Public Documents

GV-M-6 Graves County Courthouse, Kentucky Historic Resource Inventory Form, Kentucky Heritage Council.

GRAYSON COUNTY

Newspapers

Pictorical Edition in the 20th Century, November 1903.

"Grayson County has new Court House," Courier-Journal, November 28, 1937.

Public Documents

GY-L-35 Grayson County Courthouse, Kentucky Historic Resource Inventory Form, Kentucky Heritage Council.

Kentucky Historical Highway Marker No. 589

GREEN COUNTY

Books

Lowe & Scott. Green County Historical Factbook. Greensburg Printing, Greensburg, Ky., 1970.

Newspapers

"Fight to Save Oldest Courthouse in Kentucky is Won," Courier-Journal, April 13, 1928.

"Fight to Save Green County Courthouse," Courier-Journal, April 22, 1928.

"Green County Boasts Oldest Courthouse," Courier-Journal, December 11, 1938.

"Green County Landmark," Courier-Journal, February 12, 1958.

Coleman, J. Winson, "Historic Kentucky—Old Stone Courthouse, Green County," Lexington Herald-Leader, December 11, 1960.

Creason, Joe, Courier-Journal, March 19, 1966.

Public Documents

GN-G-15 Green County Courthouse, Kentucky Historic Resource Inventory Form, Kentucky Heritage Council.

Kentucky Historical Highway Marker No. 165

Green County Order Book Numbers 2, 3, 4, 7, and 8.

Unpublished Studies

Vaughn, Randall, The Old Courthouses, Greensburg, Kentucky, The University of Kentucky, 1982.

GREENUP COUNTY

Books

Biggs, Nina M. & Mackoy, Mabel Lee. History of Greenup County. Franklin Press, Louisville, 1951.

Biggs, Nina Mitchell. A Supplementary Edition of a History of Greenup County, 1962. Vantage Press, New York, 1962.

Articles and Essays

Griffith, Dorothy Kendall,"The Courthouses Of Greenup County," Kentucky Ancestors, Vol. 19, No. 4, April 1984.

Newspapers

"Greenup to Start Work Dec. 18 On New Court House," Courier-Journal, December 2, 1937.

"Greenup Seeks Way to Keep Old Court Bell Ringing," Courier-Journal, December 29, 1937.

HANCOCK COUNTY

Books

Powell, Robert A., ed. Hancock, 29, Pictorial Heritage of Hancock County, Kentucky. Kentucky Images, Lexington, 1978.

Newspapers

Kiser, Walter H., "Neighborhood Sketches: Hancock County Court House, Hawesville, Ky.," Louisville Times, February 21, 1941.

"Fallin discovers valuable documents," The Hancock Clarion, December 27, 1979, Sesqui-Centennial Edition.

Cleaver, Leota, "Hawesville Began As Homesteads In 1820's," The Hancock Clarion, Special 75th Anniversary Edition.

Public Documents

HAH-1 Hancock County Courthouse, Kentucky Historic Resource Inventory Form, Kentucky Heritage Council.

HARDIN COUNTY

Books

Haycraft, Samuel. A History of Elizabethtown, Kentucky and Its Surroundings. Hardin County Historical Society, 1960.

Haycraft, Samuel. A History of Elizabethtown, Kentucky and Its Surroundings, 1869. The Woman's Club of Elizabethtown, Elizabethtown, Ky., 1921.

Winstead, Mrs. Thomas Durham. Chronicles of Hardin County, Kentucky, 1766-1974. Bicentennial ed., Citizens Bank of Elizabethtown, 1974.

Newspapers

"Party Office Ruled Legal in Courthouse in Hardin County," Courier-Journal, September 6, 1962.

"On Guard—Hardin County Judge Herbert Talbot, Courthouse Defense is On," Courier-Journal, February 9, 1964.

"December 6, 1932: the courthouse burned," Elizabethtown News Bicentennial Edition, Section E, May, 1974.

Unpublished Studies

Bowling, William W., "Hardin County," c.1955.

HARLAN COUNTY

Books

Condon, Mabel Amanda Green. A History of Harlan County. Parthenon Press, Nashville, Tn., 1962.

Newspapers

"Harlan will Sell Courthouse to Finish Buying Road Right of Way," Courier-Journal, April 13, 1953.

"Five Court Houses Used Here; First Burned During Civil War," Harlan Daily Enterprise, Sept. 23, 1962.

"Harlan's Heritage," Harlan Daily Enterprise, February 28, 1984.

Public Documents

HL-H-47 Harlan County Courthouse, Kentucky Historic Resource Inventory Form, Kentucky Heritage Council.

Kentucky Historical Highway Marker No. 588

Unpublished Studies

Green, Mabel, "Short History of Harlan County," n.d.

HARRISON COUNTY

Books

Perrin, William H. History of Bourbon, Scott, Harrison and Nicholas Counties, Kentucky. O.L. Baskin & Co., Historical Publishers, 1882.

Garr, Elizabeth Headley. The History of Kentucky Courthouses. The National Society of the Colonial Dames of America, Resident in the State of Kentucky, 1972.

Newspapers

"Courthouse Where Henry Clay Won Case Stands in Cynthiana," Lexington Herald-Leader, June 28, 1942.

Reis, Jim, "Harrison County," The Kentucky Post, October 12, 1966.

"Harrison County Courthouse Is Added To National Register," Lexington Herald-Leader, December 20, 1974.

Brock, Herb, "John Gillig has left his mark on Cythiana," The Cynthiana Democrat, May 19, 1977.

Public Documents

Harrison County Circuit Court Minute Book L, 1850-1852.

Harrison County Circuit Court Minute Book M, 1852-1854.

Kentucky Historical Highway Marker No. 1539

HR-C-31 Harrison County Courthouse, Kentucky Historic Resource Inventory Form, Kentucky Heritage Council.

HART COUNTY

Books

Catalogue of the Exhibition of the Architects of Louisville, J.B. Speed Museum, 1931.

Newspapers

"Hart County Courthouse," Courier-Journal, August 1, 1937.

Public Documents

HT-1 Hart County Courthouse, Kentucky Historic Resource Inventory Form, Kentucky Heritage Council.

Unpublished Studies

Cann, Roy A., "Early Mumfordville," paper read before the Mumfordville Ladies Club, March 5, 1953.

HENDERSON COUNTY

Books

Lake, D.J., & Co. The Atlas of Henderson and Union Counties, 1880.

American Guide Series, Henderson, A Guide to Audubon's Hometown in Kentucky. Bacon, Percy & Daggett, N.Y., 1941.

Starling, Edmund Lyne. History of Henderson, Kentucky. Henderson, Kentucky, 1887.

Merrill, Boynton, Jr., ed. Old Henderson Homes and Buildings. Historic Henderson Publishing Council/Henderson County Public Library, 1985.

Newspapers

"Henderson's Four Pillared Court House," Courier-Journal, April 14, 1940.

"Henderson County Court House, Henderson, Ky.," Louisville Times, September 16, 1940.

Bolster, Harry, "To Raze or Not To Raze—Henderson Courthouse Fight Grows," Courier-Journal, November 6, 1961.

"History Fights for Henderson," Courier-Journal, November 7, 1961.

"Henderson's Courthouse Gets Reprieve," Courier-Journal, November 14, 1961.

Bolster, Harry, "Old Courthouse at Henderson Still Doomed," Courier-Journal, November 28, 1961.

"Henderson to Replace Courthouse," Courier-Journal, December 5, 1961.

"Artist's View—Historic Henderson Inc. Fighting to Save Old Courthouse," Courier-Journal, March 21, 1962.

"Save-Courthouse Plan Shown," Courier-Journal, March 21, 1962.

"Henderson Court Votes New Courthouse," Courier-Journal, April 24, 1962.

"Joe Creason's Kentucky—Henderson Kentucky's New Courthouse," Courier-Journal, December 14, 1963.

"Injunction Lifted, Courthouse Going, Going ...," Courier-Journal, December 19, 1963.

"Old Courthouse Safe for the Moment, Henderson, Ky.," Courier-Journal, December 28, 1963.

"Razing is Resumed on Old Courthouse," Courier-Journal, December 29, 1963.

"Henderson Courthouse Tablets Saved," Courier-Journal, January 9, 1964.

"Courthouse suit is Settled in Henderson," Courier-Journal, February 1, 1964.

Public Documents

HEH-45 Henderson County Courthouse, Kentucky Historic Resource Inventory Form, Kentucky Heritage Council.

HENRY COUNTY

Books

Drane, Maude Johnston. History of Henry County, Kentucky. 1948.

Public Documents

HY-NC-24 Henry County Courthouse, Kentucky Historic Resource Inventory Form, Kentucky Heritage Council.

HICKMAN COUNTY

Books

Battle, J.H. Histories and Bibliographies of Ballard, Calloway, Fulton, Graves, Hickman, McCracken and Marshall Counties, Kentucky. Battey Publishing Co., Chicago, 1885.

Newspapers

"Court House," Hickman County Gazette, January 7, 1971.

"Historical Hickman County—Hall of Justice," Hickman County Gazette, May 13, 1971.

"Early Court Matter Required Long Horseback Trips," Hickman County Gazette, September 30, 1971.

"Hickman County Clock working Again," Courier-Journal, January 26, 1975.

"Courthouse in National Registry," Hickman County Gazette, September 25, 1975.

Jewell, Virginia, "County Courthouse was built a century ago," Hickman County Gazette, June 14, 1984.

Public Documents

HI-C-5 Hickman County Courthouse, Kentucky Historic Resource Inventory Form, Kentucky Heritage Council.

HOPKINS COUNTY

Books

Historical Society of Hopkins County. Original Atlas and Historical Data of Hopkins County, Kentucky. Historical Society of Hopkins County,

Pearce, Helen Baker. Early History of Hopkins County. Lexington, 1958.

Society of Hopkins County, Madisonville, Ky., 1974.

Gordon, Maurice K. Early History of Hopkins County. Lexington, 1958.

Maury & Dodd Brochure, The Standard Printing Company, Louisville, c. 1895.

Newspapers

"To Raze old Hopkins County Courthouse," Courier-Journal, February 16, 1936.

"Hopkins County's Courthouse Dedicated," Courier-Journal, July 4, 1937.

"Hopkins County Lacks Deed to Courthouse," Courier-Journal, June 15, 1967.

"Owning a Courthouse Can Be an Embarrassment (Hopkins Co.)," Courier-Journal, June 20, 1967.

"Clear Title Still Sought For Hopkins Courthouse," Courier-Journal, June 24, 1967.

Public Documents

Kentucky Historical Highway Marker No. 580

JACKSON COUNTY

Books

Jackson County Sesquicentennial Edition

When They Hanged The Fiddler

Articles and Essays

Second Jackson County Courthouse—Photo, Cooperative Spotlight Newsletter, March, 1980.

Newspapers

"Courthouse ruined by fire McKee," Courier-Journal, December 31, 1949.

"Jackson County Maps Plan to Rebuild it's Courthouse," Courier-Journal, January 18, 1950.

"One of the Finest Courthouses in Eastern Kentucky, Jackson County at McKee, Kentucky," Courier-Journal, June 29, 1951.

"New Jackson County Courthouse, at McKee, Kentucky," Courier-Journal, December 6, 1951.

JEFFERSON COUNTY

Books

Coleman, J. Winston, Historic Kentucky, Henry Clay Press, Lexington, 1968.

Thomas, Samuel W., Views Of Louisville, 1786-1920,

Newspapers

"Albert Fink, Courthouse Builder," Courier-Journal, December 11, 1949.

"Pencil Panorama of Pioneer Louisville," Courier-Journal, January 8, 1956.

"Joe Creason's Kentucky," Courier-Journal, September 23, 1965.

Public Documents

Kentucky Historical Highway Marker No. 1697

JF-CD-31 Jefferson County Courthouse, Kentucky Historic Resource Inventory Form, Kentucky Heritage Council.

JESSAMINE COUNTY

Books

Young, Bennett H. A History of Jessimine County, Kentucky, From Its Earliest Settlement to 1898. Courier-Journal Job Printing Co., Louisville, Ky., 1898.

Kentucky Heritage Commission and Jessamine County Historical Society. Survey of Historic Sites in Kentucky: Jessamine County. Jessamine County Historical Society, 1979.

Newspapers

Price, Anna K., "Jessamine Courthouse Has Remained Unchanged In Outward Appearance," Lexington Herald-Leader, January 14, 1962.

"Breathitt Will Dedicate New Jessamine Courthouse," Lexington Herald-Leader, April 4, 1965.

Hampton, Jim, "Jessimine County Dedicates Its Renovated Courthouse," Courier-Journal, April 22, 1965.

Public Documents

JS-N-47 Jessamine County Courthouse, Kentucky Historic Resource Inventory Form, Kentucky Heritage Council.

JOHNSON COUNTY

Books

Hall, Carl Mitchel. Johnson County, Kentucky; A History of the County, and Genealogy of Its People Up to the Year 1927. The Standard Press, Louisville, 1928.

Wells, J.K. A Short History of Paintsville and Johnson County. The Paintsville Herald, Paintsville, c.1962.

Newspapers

"Johnson County Will Accept Bids on new Courthouse," August 26, 1957.

KENTON COUNTY

Books

Ellerman, Charles B. Historic Covington, Proposed Subjects for Registration and Marking. 1973.

Sesquicentennial, City of Covington, Kentucky, 1815-1965, Souvenir Program.

Articles and Essays

"Covington's First City Hall," Kenton County Historical Society Quarterly Review, March 1979.

Public Documents

Kenton County Circuit Court Order Book No. 1, 1840

KEl-1 Kenton County Courthouse, Kentucky Historic Resource Inventory Form, Kentucky Heritage Council.

KNOTT COUNTY

Books

Time Was, A Bicentennial Album, The Knott County Bicentennial Committee, Inc. and Alice Lloyd College, 1976.

Newspapers

Griffin, Gerald, "Trouble On Troublesome As Knott County Founded," Courier-Journal, n.d.

Public Documents

KT-H-13 Knott County Courthouse, Kentucky Historic Resource Inventory Form, Kentucky Heritage Council.

KNOX COUNTY

Books

Warren, King Solomon. A History of Knox County, Kentucky. Daniel Boone Festival, Inc., 1976.

Newspapers

"$436,180 is Bid on Knox County Courthouse," Courier-Journal, December 20, 1963.

LARUE COUNTY

Newspapers

"Courthouse Contract Let—Hodgenville(Larue)," Courier-Journal, December 28, 1963.

"Bonds to Help Build LaRue Courthouse," Courier-Journal, January 17, 1964.

"$300,000 Courthouse Nearly Finished In LaRue," Courier-Journal, October 11, 1964.

"Women Try to Save Hodgensville(Larue) Courthouse," Courier-Journal, April 23, 1965.

"Joe Creason's Kentucky: Hodgenville Courthouse (Larue)," Courier-Journal, July 25, 1965.

Public Documents

Kentucky Historical Highway Marker No. 591

LAUREL COUNTY

Newspapers

"Courthouse at London(Laurel Co.) Hit By Fire," Courier-Journal, December 10, 1958.

"Office Site Sought in Wake of Blaze – London (Laurel Co.)," Courier-Journal, December 11, 1958.

"New Courthouse to be Dedicated Today at London (Laurel)," Courier-Journal, October 28, 1961.

"Laurel County Enjoys a New Courthouse," Courier-Journal, February 5, 1964.

Public Documents

LLL-6 Laurel County Courthouse, Kentucky Historic Resource Inventory Form, Kentucky Heritage Council.

LAWRENCE COUNTY

Books

Wolfford, George. Lawrence County: A Pictorial History. W W W Company, Ashland, 1972.

Newspapers

"Someting Old, Something New," Courier-Journal, July 21, 1964.

"Courthouse Is Dedicated," Lexington Herald-Leader, October 11, 1964.

"Perkins Dedicates New Courthouse," Lexington Herald-Leader, October 12, 1964.

LEE COUNTY

Books

Three Forks Investment Co. Prospectus of the Three Forks Investment Company, its Beattyville Town Site, with Maps, Plats, Illustrations, etc. Courier-Journal Printing Co., Louisville, 1889.

Public Documents

LE-B-14 Lee County Courthouse, Kentucky Historic Resource Inventory Form, Kentucky Heritage Council.

LESLIE COUNTY

Newspapers

"Leslie County Courthouse, Hyden, Kentucky," Courier-Journal, September 30, 1951.

"Leslie County's New Courthouse, Hyden," Courier-Journal, April 30, 1954.

LETCHER COUNTY

Books

Cornett, William T. Letcher County, Kentucky; A Brief History. State-wide Printing Company, Prestonsburg, Ky., 1967.

Newspapers

"Letcher County to Open Bids for Courthouse," Courier-Journal, September 1, 1963.

LEWIS COUNTY

Books

Ragan, O.G. History of Lewis County, Kentucky. Jennings & Graham Press, Cincinnati, Ohio, 1912.

Newspapers

"Independence Hall Recreated," Courier-Journal, September 25, 1940.

"The Old Court House," Lewis County Herald, February 28, 1974.

LINCOLN COUNTY

Books

Dunn, Mrs. M.H. Early Lincoln County History. c.196-.

Newspapers

"Courthouse at St. Asaph's," Courier-Journal, April 4, 1929.

"Lincoln County Courthouse," Courier-Journal, October 11, 1936.

"Thumb-nail sketch: A Long View of Lincoln County," Kentucky Advocate Sunday Magazine, March 8, 1970.

Public Documents

LIS-2 Lincoln County Courthouse, Kentucky Historic Resource Inventory Form, Kentucky Heritage Council.

LIVINGSTON COUNTY

Books

McDonald, Leslie. Echoes of Yesteryear. The Livingston Ledger, Smithland, Ky., 1972.

Newspapers

Kiser, Walter H., The Livingston County Court House, Smithland, Kentucky, Courier-Journal, n.d.

Public Documents

Kentucky Historical Highway Marker No. 1204

LVS-9 Livingston County Courthouse, Kentucky Historic Resource Inventory Form, Kentucky Heritage Council.

LOGAN COUNTY

Books

Coffman, Edward. The Story of Logan County. Russellville, Ky., 1962.

Turner, Jim. Memories and Milestone, 175th Anniversary Celebration Russellville, Kentucky, September 16-22, 1973.

Newspapers

"Joe Creason's Kentucky: Logan County Courthouse," Courier-Journal, January 14, 1964.

Vance, Kyle, "Courthouse in Logan In Danger of Collapse," Courier-Journal, February 18, 1970.

"Tempest revolves about Russellville Courthouse," Courier-Journal, February 20, 1971.

"One of our Courthouses sold for $215, Court moved to Armory," Logan County News Democrat, March 1, 1973.

"Old Russellville was getting New Courthouse–73 years ago," Logan County News Democrat, March 20, 1975.

Public Documents

LO-R-1 Logan County Courthouse, Kentucky Historic Resource Inventory Form, Kentucky Heritage Council.

Kentucky Historical Highway Marker No. 1071

McCRACKEN COUNTY

Books

Battle, J.H., Perrin, Wm., Kniffin, G.C. Histories and Bibliographies of Ballard, Calloway, Fulton, Graves, Hickman, McCracken and Marshall Counties, Kentucky. Battey Publishing Co., Chicago, 1885.

Wells, Camille. Architecture of Paducah and McCracken County. Society for the Preservation of Paducah, 1981.

Articles and Essays

Harper's Weekly, "Courthouse at Paducah, Kentucky," October 26, 1861.

Newspapers

"Fine Court House," Louisville Daily Journal, July 30, 1857.

"McCracken Has Only 2 Court Houses In 103 Years With Paducah As Seat," Courier-Journal, December 23, 1934.

Bolster, Harry S., Present Building Now 76 Years Old Still In Good Condition," Courier-Journal, December 23, 1934.

"Paducah's New Post Office and Courthouse," Courier-Journal, October 30, 1938.

"New Paducah Court House To Be Built," Courier-Journal, June 28, 1940.

"Razers of the old McCracken County Court House are looking for its cornerstone," Louisville Times, April 21, 1941.

Public Documents

MCN-P-81 McCracken County Courthouse, Kentucky Historic Resource Inventory Form, Kentucky Heritage Council.

Kentucky Historical Highway Marker No. 1027

McCREARY COUNTY

Newspapers

"McCreary Courthouse, Whitley City, destroyed by Fire—being Rebuilt," Courier-Journal, October 5, 1952.

"Fire Guts Courthouse in McCreary County," Courier-Journal, November 20, 1951.

"The McCreary County Courthouse at Whitley City," Courier-Journal, October 5, 1952.

"Courthouse Bond Issue Approved in McCreary County," Courier-Journal, November 7, 1952.

"Bomb damages Courthouse in McCreary," Courier-Journal, February 1, 1971.

McCLEAN COUNTY

Public Documents

MCL-2 McLean County Courthouse, Kentucky Historic Resource Inventory Form, Kentucky Heritage Council.

MADISON COUNTY

Books

Coleman, J. Winston, Historic Kentucky, Henry Clay Press, Lexington, 1968.

Dorris, Jonathan Truman. A Glimpse at Historic Madison County and Richmond, Ky. Richmond Daily Register Co., Richmond, Ky., 1934.

Ellis/Everman/Sears. Madison County: 200 Years in Retrospect. The Madison County Historical Society, Richmond, Ky., 1985.

Newspapers

"Historic Madison Court House Once Used As Prison," Courier-Journal, September 6, 1936.

Kiser, Walter H., "Neighborhood Sketches: Madison County Court House, Richmond, Kentucky," Louisville Times, May 3, 1939.

"Courthouse Renovation Groundbreaking Today," Lexington Herald-Leader, October 28, 1964.

"Joe Creason's Kentucky: Keeping the Old Madison County," Courier-Journal, October 24, 1965.

Public Documents

MA-R-65 Madison County Courthouse, Kentucky Historic Resource Inventory Form, Kentucky Heritage Council.

Madison County Circuit Court Order Book I, 1846-1850.

Combs, Mrs. Charles C., National Register of Historic Places Inventory—Nomination Form, 1971.

MAGOFFIN COUNTY

Books

Magoffin's First Century Committee. 1860-1960, Magoffin's First Century. Salyersville, Ky., 1960.

Newspapers

"Fire Destroys Magoffin Courthouse," Courier-Journal, February 23, 1957.

"Courthouse At Salyersville Burns; Damage May Total Quarter Million," Lexington Herald-Leader, February 23, 1957.

"Work Progressing Steadily on Magoffin County Courthouse," Courier-Journal, October 4, 1959.

MARION COUNTY

Newspapers

"Marion Court Held In Court House Yard," Courier-Journal, January 8, 1935.

"Marion County Courthouse Bonds Burned," Courier-Journal, November 20, 1947.

Public Documents

Kentucky Historical Highway Marker No. 585

MARSHALL COUNTY

Books

Battle, J.H. Histories and Bibliographies of Ballard, Calloway, Fulton, Graves, Hickman, McCracken and Marshall Counties, Kentucky. Battey Publishing Co., Chicago, 1885.

Freeman, Leon Lewis & Olds, Edward C.. The History of Marshall County, Kentucky. The Tribune-Democrat, Benton, Kentucky, 1933.

MASON COUNTY

Books

Best, Edna Hunter. The Historic Past of Washington, Mason County, Ky. The Hobson Book Press, Cynthiana, Ky., 1944.

Calvert & Klee. Maysville, Kentucky, From Past to Present in Pictures. Mason County Museum, 1983.

Clift, Garrett Glenn. History of Maysville and Mason County. Transylvania printing company, inc., Lexington, Ky., 1936.

Coleman, J. Winston, Historic Kentucky, Henry Clay Press, Lexington, 1968.

Gill, Alice Taylor. Glimpses of Kentucky & Early Maysville. 1964.

Maysville Centennial Exposition Commission, Maysville, Ky. As We Look Back, Maysville, 1883-1933. Daily Independent, Maysville, Ky., 1933.

Transylvania printing company, Lexington, Ky., 1936.

Newspapers

Kiser, Walter H., "Neighborhood Sketches: Court House and City Hall, Maysville, Kentucky," Louisville Times, October 7, 1940.

Public Documents

MS-M-48 Madison County Courthouse, Kentucky Historic Resource Inventory Form, Kentucky Heritage Council.

Kentucky Historic Resources Inventory Form, 1980

MEADE COUNTY

Books

Ridenour, George L. Early Times in Meade County, Ky. Western Recorder, Louisville, Ky., 1929.

Newspapers

"Meade Finances 'New' Courthouse by Saving Money," Courier-Journal, February 12, 1961.

Public Documents

Kentucky Historical Highway Marker No. 1652

MENIFEE COUNTY

Books

Menefee County Centennial Commission. Menefee County Centennial - Pictorial Review, 1869-1969.

MERCER COUNTY

Books

Daviess, Mrs. Maria T. History of Mercer and Boyle Counties. Harrodsburg Herald, Harrodsburg, 1924. First published in the early eighties.

Rue, A.B. Historical Sketch of Mercer County, Ky., for the Louisiana Purchase Exposition, St. Louis. Author, Harrodsburg, Ky., 1904.

Public Documents

ME-H-115 Mercer County Courthouse, Kentucky Historic Resource Inventory Form, Kentucky Heritage Council.

METCALFE COUNTY

Books

Martin, Judge Joseph. A Brief History of Metcalfe County, 1860-1970. Statesman Books, Edmonton, Ky., c.1971.

Metcalfe County, Kentucky Centennial Celebration. Metcalfe County Centennial Celebration, 1860-1960. Monroe County Press, Tompkinsville, Ky., c.1960.

Newspapers

"Contract is Let for Present Court House," Edmonton Herald-News, Special Bicentennial Edition, June 30, 1974.

"Civil War Guerrillas Burn Court House," Edmonton Herald-News, Special Bicentennial Edition, June 30, 1974.

Public Documents

MC-E-1 Metcalfe County Courthouse, Kentucky Historic Resource Inventory Form, Kentucky Heritage Council.

MONROE COUNTY

Books

Montell, William L. Monroe County History, 1820-1970. Tompkinsville Lions Club, Tompkinsville, 1970.

Public Documents

MR-T-17 Monroe County Courthouse, Kentucky Historic Resource Inventory Form, Kentucky Heritage Council.

Kentucky Historical Highway Marker No. 593

MONTGOMERY COUNTY

Books

Boyd & Boyd. A History of Mt. Sterling, Kentucky, 1792-1918. Carl B. Boyd, Jr., Mt. Sterling, Ky., 1984.

Reid, Richard. Historical Sketch of Montgomery County and History of Mt. Sterling. Democrat Job Rooms Prints, Mt. Sterling, 1882.

Articles and Essays

Massie, I.N., "Early History of the City of Winchester," n.d.

Newspapers

"New Courthouse Mount Sterling Plans," Courier-Journal, December 12, 1954.

"Abandonment Of Courthouse At Once Is Ordered By Mongomery Officials," Lexington Herald-Leader, March 17, 1955.

"Montgomery Courthouse to Be Abandoned," Courier-Journal, March 17, 1955.

"Montgomery to Vote on New Courthouse," Courier-Journal, September 8, 1955.

"Condemned Courthouse Stands Vacant, Useless Mt. Sterling," Courier-Journal, March 12, 1956.

"Montgomery Orders Courthouse Design," Courier-Journal, July 18, 1957.

"Montgomery Awards Courthouse Contract," Courier-Journal, July 24, 1958.

"Montgomery Courthouse Dedicated," Courier-Journal, September 25, 1960.

Public Documents

Kentucky Historical Highway Marker No. 586

MORGAN COUNTY

Books

Licking Valley Courier. Morgan County, Kentucky, Historical, Industrial, Past. Present, Future. A Historical Review of Morgan County, 1823 to 1923. Hovermale and Elam, West Liberty, 1923.

Newspapers

Stacy, Helen Price, "Old Courthouse At West Liberty May Be Razed For New Building," Lexington Leader, June 7, 1967.

Public Documents

MO-WL-1 Morgan County Courthouse, Kentucky Historic Resource Inventory Form, Kentucky Heritage Council.

MUHLENBURG COUNTY

Books

Camplin, Paul. A New History of Muhlenburg County, Kentucky. Williams Printing Co., Nashville, 1984.

Rothert, Otto A. A History of Muhlenburg County. J.P. Morton & Co., Louisville, Ky., 1913.

Newspapers

Carver, Gayle R., "Some Sketches Of The History Of Greenville And Muhlenburg County: Courthouses," The Greenville Leader, October 1, 1937.

Carver, Gayle R., "Some Sketches Of The History Of Greenville And Muhlenburg County: Courthouses," The Greenville Leader, October 8, 1937.

Carver, Gayle R., "Some Sketches Of The History Of Greenville And Muhlenburg County: Courthouses," The Greenville Leader, October 15, 1937.

Public Documents

MU-G-1 Muhlenburg County Courthouse, Kentucky Historic Resource Inventory Form, Kentucky Heritage Council.

NELSON COUNTY

Books

Smith, Sarah B. Historic Bardstown, Nelson County. Publishers Printing Co., Shepardsville, 1968.

Public Documents

NE-B-79 Nelson County Courthouse, Kentucky Historic Resource Inventory Form, Kentucky Heritage Council.

NICHOLAS COUNTY

Books

Perrin, William H. History of Bourbon, Scott, Harrison and Nicholas Counties, Kentucky. O.L. Baskin & Co., Historical Publishers, 1882.

Conley, Joan Weissinger, ed. History of Nicholas County. Nicholas County Historical Society, Carlisle, Ky., 1976.

Newspapers

Shannon, Roy, "A History of Nicholas County Courthouses," The Carlisle Mercury, June 29, 1972.

Public Documents

NI-C-33 Nicholas County Courthouse, Kentucky Historic Resource Inventory Form, Kentucky Heritage Council.

Kentucky Historical Highway Marker No. 660

OHIO COUNTY

Books

Fogle, McDowell Addington. A History of Ohio County, Kentucky. Ohio County Historical Society, 196-.

Taylor, Harrison D. Ohio County, Kentucky, in the Olden Days; A Series of Old Newspaper Sketches of Fragmentary History. Regional Publishing Co., Baltimore, 1969.

Newspapers

Ohio County Court House Edition, The Ohio County News, 1943.

Public Documents

OH-H-6 Ohio County Courthouse, Kentucky Historic Resource Inventory Form, Kentucky Heritage Council.

Kentucky Historical Highway Marker No. 581

OLDHAM COUNTY

Newspapers

"Courthouse at LaGrange," Lexington Herald, March 9, 1937.

The Oldham Era, Bicentennial Edition, July 18, 1974.

Public Documents

OL-1 Oldham County Courthouse, Kentucky Historic Resource Inventory Form, Kentucky Heritage Council.

OWEN COUNTY

Books

Houchens, Mariam Sidebottom. History of Owen County, Kentucky. Standard Printing Co., Louisville, 1976.

Owen County Almanac—1964-5.

Newspapers

Kiser, Walter H., "Neighborhood Sketches: Owen County Court House, Owenton, Kentucky," Louisville Times, April 11, 1939.

"Walls Reveal Past of Court House," Courier-Journal, January 19, 1941.

"Popular Improvement Target," Lexington Herald, June 25, 1968.

Public Documents

ON-O-47 Owen County Courthouse, Kentucky Historic Resource Inventory Form, Kentucky Heritage Council.

OWSLEY COUNTY

Newspapers

"Owsley Courthouse is Destroyed by Fire," Courier-Journal, January 6, 1967.

PENDLETON COUNTY

Newspapers

"New Courthouse for Falmouth

(Pendleton)," *Courier-Journal*, May 28, 1965.

Public Documents

PD-F-1 Pendleton County Courthouse, Kentucky Historic Resource Inventory Form, Kentucky Heritage Council.

PERRY COUNTY

Books

D.A.R.-Hazard Chapter, Kentucky. *History of Perry County, Kentucky*. D.A.R.-Hazard Chapter, Kentucky, 1953.

Johnson, Eunice Tolbert, ed. *History of Perry County, Kentucky*. Hazard Chapter of the Daughters of the American Revolution, Hazard, 1953.

Pilcher, Louis. *The Story of Hazard, Ky., the Pearl of the Mountains*. Citizens Printing Co., Lexington, Ky., 1913.

Newspapers

"Bids Will Be Opened Here June 20 at Perry Co., Ky.," *Courier-Journal*, June 7, 1962.

"New Perry Courthouse To Be Dedicated Today," *Lexington Herald-Leader*, September 17, 1966.

"Perry County's New Courthouse," *Courier-Journal*, January 28, 1967.

PIKE COUNTY

Books

Kelly, Claire, ed. *Pike County, Kentucky, 1822-1976, Its Sesquicentennial Issue, v.1*. Pike County Historical Society, Pikeville, 1976.

Roberts, Leonard & Forsyth, Frank & Kelly, Claire. *Pike County, Kentucky, 1822-1976, Their Historical Papers, v.2*. Pike County Historical Society, Pikeville, 1976.

Walter, Mrs. W.J., *Memories of Mrs. W.J. Walter*, n.d.

Newspapers

"Pikeville's Courthouse Dedicated by Speakers," *Louisville Times*, March 23, 1942.

Public Documents

PI-P-2 Pike County Courthouse, Kentucky Historic Resource Inventory Form, Kentucky Heritage Council.

POWELL COUNTY

Public Documents

PO-151 Powell County Courthouse, Kentucky Historic Resource Inventory Form, Kentucky Heritage Council. Kentucky Historical Highway Marker No. 587

PULASKI COUNTY

Books

Coleman, J. Winston, *Historic Kentucky*, Henry Clay Press, Lexington, 1968.

Tibbals, Alma Owens. *A History of Pulaski County, Kentucky*. G.O. Moore, Bagdad, Ky., 1952.

Tuggle & Kaurish. *Pulaski Revisited*. The Pulaski County Historical Society, Powell Printing, Lexington, Ky., 1982.

Newspapers

"Pulaski to Dedicate New Building," *Courier-Journal*, September 15, 1940.

"Pulaski Suit is Filed in Open and Shut Case," *Courier-Journal*, April 29, 1962.

Public Documents

PU-S-39 Pulaski County Courthouse, Kentucky Historic Resource Inventory Form, Kentucky Heritage Council.

ROBERTSON COUNTY

Books

Moore, T. Ross, ed. *Echoes From the Century, 1867-1967*. Mt. Olivet, Ky., 1967. (Robertson County)

Public Documents

RB-1 Robertson County Courthouse, Kentucky Historic Resource Inventory Form, Kentucky Heritage Council.

ROCKCASTLE COUNTY

Newspapers

"Bonds awarded for Courthouse at Mount Vernon, Rockcastle County," *Courier-Journal*, February 5, 1964.

ROWAN COUNTY

Newspapers

"Rowan is Losing it's Courthouse," *Courier-Journal*, July 12, 1959.

"Temporary Courthouse Set. (Morehead-Rowan Co.)," *Courier-Journal*, September 5, 1959.

"Rowan Arsonist Fails in Courthouse Burning," *Courier-Journal*, September 2, 1962.

"Rowan Courthouse Needs Repairs," *Courier-Journal*, July 5, 1977.

Public Documents

RW-M-5 Rowan County Courthouse, Kentucky Historic Resource Inventory Form, Kentucky Heritage Council.

Kentucky Historical Highway Marker No. 972

RUSSELL COUNTY

Articles and Essays

Sharp, Ben V., "Courthouse remains a landmark," *The Kentucky Historical Chronicle*, Vol. 2, No. 2, May 26, 1975.

Newspapers

"Courthouse Damaged," *The State Journal*, June 9, 1976.

Public Documents

RU-2 Russell County Courthouse, Kentucky Historic Resource Inventory Form, Kentucky Heritage Council.

SCOTT COUNTY

Books

Bevins, Ann Bolton. *A History of Scott County As Told By Selected Buildings*. Ann Bevins, Georgetown, Kentucky, 1981.

Garr, Elizabeth Headley. *The History of Kentucky Courthouses*. The National Society of the Colonial Dames of America, Resident in the State of Kentucky, 1972.

Perrin, William H. *History of Bourbon, Scott, Harrison and Nicholas Counties, Kentucky*. O.L. Baskin & Co., Historical Publishers, 1882.

Gaines, B.O. *History of Scott County*. B.O. Gaines Printery, Georgetown, Ky., 1905.

Newspapers

"Scott Circuit Judge Bemoans Condition Of Old Courthouse," *Lexington Herald*, October 20, 1970.

Powell, Bill, "New Courthouse For Scott County," *Lexington Herald-Leader*, November 22, 1970.

Bevins, Ann, "Blatant Yellow Justice Gets New Coat Of Subdued Gold," October 24, 1972.

"Rededication Of Renovated Courthouse Set Today In Scott," *Lexington Herald-Leader*, December 2, 1972.

Public Documents

SC-MC-19 Scott County Courthouse, Kentucky Historic Resource Inventory Form, Kentucky Heritage Council.

Kentucky Historical Highway Marker No. 1454

SHELBY COUNTY

Books

Shinnick, Edward D. *Some Old Time History of Shelbyville and Shelby County*. c. 1915

Willis, George L. *History of Shelby County, Kentucky*. C.T. Dearing Printing Co., Louisville, Ky., 1929.

Willis, George L. *History of Shelby County, Kentucky*. C.T. Dearing Printing, Inc., Louisville, Ky., 1929.

Newspapers

"Notice to Contractors," *The Frankfort Commonwealth*, February 24, 1844.

"Masonic Notice," *The Frankfort Commonwealth*, May 21, 1844.

Public Documents

SH-S-46 Shelby County Courthouse, Kentucky Historic Resource Inventory Form, Kentucky Heritage Council.

SIMPSON COUNTY

Newspapers

"New Courthouse," Courier-Journal, March 8, 1883.

Public Documents

SI-F-36 Simpson County Courthouse, Kentucky Historic Resource Inventory Form, Kentucky Heritage Council.

SPENCER COUNTY

Public Documents

SP-T-16 Spencer County Courthouse, Kentucky Historic Resource Inventory Form, Kentucky Heritage Council.

Kentucky Historical Highway Marker No. 594

TAYLOR COUNTY

Books

Graves, Garnett. Taylor County: Its Public Buildings, Officers and Principal Murder Trials. Taylor County Enquirer, Campbellsville, Ky., c.1975.

Nesbitt, Robert Lee. Early Taylor County History. The News-Journal, Campbellsville, 1941.

Newspapers

"New Courthouse for Taylor," Courier-Journal, April 24, 1965.

Public Documents
Kentucky Historical Highway Marker Nos. 582 & 1729

TODD COUNTY

Books

Williams, Frances Marion. The Story of Todd County, Kentucky, 1820-1970. The Parthenon Press, Nashville, 1972.

Newspapers

"Todd County Courthouse at Elkton," Courier-Journal, April 3, 1938.

Public Documents

TO-E-1 Todd County Courthouse, Kentucky Historic Resource Inventory Form, Kentucky Heritage Council.

TRIGG COUNTY

Public Documents

TR-C-25 Trigg County Courthouse, Kentucky Historic Resource Inventory Form, Kentucky Heritage Council.

Kentucky Historical Highway Marker No. 578

TRIMBLE COUNTY

Newspapers

"Fire Ruins Courthouse in Trimble, Bedford, Kentucky," Courier-Journal, March 6, 1952.

Barrett, Virginia, "Inside Old Walls," Louisville Times, October 14, 1952.

"Courthouse under Repair Trimble Court to hold Sessions in Church Building," Courier-Journal, January 11, 1953.

"New Trimble Courthouse To Be Dedicated Saturday," Courier-Journal, July 16, 1953.

"New $100,000 Courthouse is Dedicated in Trimble," Courier-Journal, July 19, 1953.

Strother, John C., "Trimble County Legacy," Trimble Banner, Bicentennial Edition, April 11, 1974.

Public Documents

TM-B-17 Trimble County Courthouse, Kentucky Historic Resource Inventory Form, Kentucky Heritage Council.

UNION COUNTY

Books

American Guide Series, Union County Past & Present. Schuhmann Printing Company, Louisville, 1941.

an. History of Union County, Kentucky. Courier Co., Evansville, Ind., 1886.

Newspapers

"Union County's 70-Year-Old Court House, Center of a Prosperous Square, to Be Remodeled," Louisville Times, May 10, 1938.

"Court House Dedication Planned In Union County," Courier-Journal, May 26, 1940.

Public Documents

UN-M-28 Union County Courthouse, Kentucky Historic Resource Inventory Form, Kentucky Heritage Council.

Maps, Atlases, Gazeteers

Lake, D.J., & Co. The Atlas of Henderson and Union Counties, 1880.

WARREN COUNTY

Books

Architecture of Warren County, Kentucky, 1790-1940. Landmark Association of Bowling Green and Warren County, Inc., Bowling Green, 1984.

Newspapers

"Rebuilt Courthouse Will Hold Open House – Bowling Green," Courier-Journal, September 25, 1958.

"Age is an Asset in Warren County," Courier-Journal, September 26, 1958.

Public Documents

WA-B-54 Warren County Courthouse, Kentucky Historic Resource Inventory Form, Kentucky Heritage Council.

WASHINGTON COUNTY

Books

Baylor, Orval Walker. Early Times in Washington County, Kentucky. The Hobson Press, Cynthiana, Ky., 1942.

Coleman, J. Winston, Historic Kentucky, Henry Clay Press, Lexington, 1968.

Newspapers

Kiser, Walter H., "Neighborhood Sketches: The Court House, Springfield, Kentucky," Louisville Times, June 8, 1936.

"Joe Creason's Kentucky: 150 Years in Use – Washington County Courthouse," Courier-Journal, April 21, 1966.

Baylor, Orval W., "Our Court House," The Springfield Sun, December 14, 1933.

Public Documents

WS-S-2 Washington County Courthouse, Kentucky Historic Resource Inventory Form, Kentucky Heritage Council.

WAYNE COUNTY

Books

Edwards, Bobby Gale. Glimpses of Historical Wayne County, Kentucky. Monticello, Ky., 1970.

Johnson, Augusta Phillips. A Century of Wayne County, Kentucky, 1800-1900. The Standard Printing Co., Louisville, 1939.

Walker, Garnet. Exploring Wayne County. 1966.

Newspapers

"High Court lets Wayne County Issue bonds for New Courthouse," Courier-Journal, June 8, 1949.

Public Documents

WN-M-37 Wayne County Courthouse, Kentucky Historic Resource Inventory Form, Kentucky Heritage Council.

WHITLEY COUNTY

Newspapers

"Whitney County Courthouse Closing Upheld," Courier-Journal, January 1, 1970.

WOLFE COUNTY

Newspapers

"The Wolfe Tells," Lexington Leader, June 11, 1970.

"In Syncopated Clock Keeper in the Wolfe County Courthouse," Courier-Journal, October 20, 1975.

Public Documents

WO-11 Wolfe County Courthouse, Kentucky Historic Resource Inventory Form, Kentucky Heritage Council.

WOODFORD COUNTY

Books

Railey, William E. History of Woodford County. Roberts Printing Co., Frankfort, Ky., 1928.

Newspapers

"Fire Destroys the Courthouse at Versailles (Woodford)," Courier-Journal, October 12, 1965.

"Joe Creason's Kentucky: Woodford Courthouse Decisions," Courier-Journal, March 10, 1966.

"Courthouse Takes Shape," <u>Lexington Herald</u>, August 20, 1969.

"Woodford Offices Being Moved Into New Building," <u>Lexington Herald</u>, June 19, 1970.

"Court In Woodford Dedicates New Courthouse In Versailles," <u>Lexington Herald-Leader</u>, September 27, 1970.

TECHNICAL DATA

CAMERA	Wisner 4 x 5 Convertable Classic with standard and bag bellows
TRIPOD	Topcon Surveyors Heavy Duty
HEAD	Gitzo V
LENSES	Schneider 90 mm f/5.6 Super Angulon Schneider 150 mm f/5.6 Symmar-S Schneider 210 mm f/5.6 Symmar-S Schneider 335 mm f/9 G-Claron
FILTERS	B + W 77 mm Medium Yellow B + W 77 mm KR 1.5 Sky Tiffen 77 mm # 25 Red
FILM	Kodak T-MAX 400 4 x 5 Sheets
DEVELOPER	Kodak HC110 — Dilution "B" (in trays)
STOP	Kodak Indicator Stop Bath
FIXER	Kodak Rapid Fixer with Hardener
PAPER	Kodak Elite 8 x 10 Grades 2, 3 & 4
DEVELOPER	Kodak Dekol. Working solution diluted 1/1
STOP	Kodak Indicator Stop Bath
FIXER	Kodak Rapid Fixer with Hardener. Working solution diluted 1/1
ENLARGER	Omega D 2 4 x 5 with Dichroic head
LENS	Schneider 150 mm f/5.6 Componon 4